Edexcel International GCSE Geography
Edexcel Certificate in Geography
Student Book

Michael Witherick and Steve Milner

LWAYS LEARNING

PEARSON

Published by Pearson Education Limited, a company incorporated in England and Wales, having its registered office at Edinburgh Gate, Harlow, Essex, CM20 2JE. Registered company number: 872828

www.pearsonschoolsandfecolleges.co.uk

Edexcel is a registered trade mark of Edexcel Limited

Text © Pearson Education Ltd, 2010

This edition first published 2010

14 13 12

10 9 8 7 6 5

British Library Cataloguing in Publication Data
A catalogue record for this book is available from the British Library.

ISBN 978 0 435016 95 1

Typeset by HL Studios

Cover design by Creative Monkey

Printed in Spain by Graficas Estella

Acknowledgements
The publisher would like to thank the following for their kind permission to reproduce their photographs:

(Key: b-bottom; c-centre; l-left; r-right; t-top)

Alamy Images: Andrew Jankunas 172l, Brian Yarvin 126bc/c, Clint Farlinger 13tl, Danita Delimont 129t, David Hoffman 67t, dbphots 37c, Ekaterina Minaeva 119c, foodpix 126t, GP Bowater 135t, Greg Balfour Evans 156t, Holmes Garden Photos 251br, Ian Francis 260cl, imagebroker 260tl, Linda Kennedy 148c, Mark Sunderland 156br, Mike Goldwater 185, Mike Robinson 172r, NASA 13b, Pacific Press Service 83br, Paul Thompson Images 174b, Peter Casolino 208t, Phil Degginger 74bl, RIA Novosti 210, Rick Dalton 127bl, The Print Collector 174t, UrbanImages 171c, Wayne Hutchinson 260bl; **Camera Press Ltd:** 84bl; **Corbis:** All Canada Photos 41b, Benjamin Rondel 60tl, epa / Narong Sangnak 260br, Joe Cornish 53tl, Jonathan Blair 81tl, Julia Waterlow 220t, Justin Stumberg 89tl, Paulo Fridman 160t, Reuters / Damir Sagolj 89tr, Robert Harding World Imagery 40t, Sygma / Sergio Dorantes 65cr; **©Fairtrade www.fairtrade.org.uk:** 262; **FLPA Images of Nature:** Ariadne Van Zandbergen 228t, Gary K Smith 120b, John Eveson 126tc/b, Keith Rushforth 229t, Khalid Ghani 136b, Minden Pictures / Konrad Wothe 193b, Nicholas and Sherry Lu Aldridge 127tl, Nigel Cattlin 125c; **Getty Images:** AFP / David Ralphson 153b, AFP / Toru Yanamaka 208b, Burton Mcneely 65tr, Chris Jackson 64br,

Christopher Pillitz 251bl, David Goddard 39br, Richard Martin-Roberts 27b, Time & Life Pictures / Vernon Merritt III 166c, Universal Images Group 24cl; **iStockphoto:** Duncan Walker 174; **Nature Picture Library:** Dave Watts 180c, Gary K. Smith 142bl, Julia Bayne 156bl, Karl Ammann 138t; **Ordnance Survey:** 164b; **Pearson Education Ltd:** Photodisc. Photolink. L. Hobbs 192; **Peter Facey:** 164bc, Peter Facey 164t; **Photolibrary.com:** 95b, Britain on View 24tl, 43tl, 142cl, Corbis 74tl, Fridmar Damm 203t, Godong Godong 137c, Hubertus Kanus 204b, Mark Boulton 124bl, Martin Bond 108bl, 156tc, Oxford Scientific 39tl, 65br, Patrik Giardino 133br, Paul Nevin 127br, Peter and Georgina Bowater 145c, Phillip Carr 108br, Photodisc 203b, Robert Harding Travel 123t, SGM SGM 176c, Steve Vidler 26t, Terrance Klassen 124br, The Travel Library / Justin Foulkes 56cr, View Pictures 101br, Walter G Allgöwer 127tr, WaterFrame - Underwater Images 45bl; **Press Association Images:** 79t, Chris Ison 55br; **Reuters:** 85c, Jitendra Prakash 215b; **Rex Features:** 97t, Andrew Drysdale 156bc, Jeremy Sutton Hibbert 24l, Kip Rano 133bl, Lou Linwei 218b, Sipa Press 10c, 99c, 170b, The Travel Library / Stuart Black 48tl, Tony Waltham 170t; **Science Photo Library Ltd:** 126bl, Adrian Bicker 53br, Bob Gibbons 47tl, British Antarctic Survey 179t, David Frazier 153t, George Bernard 42t, George Steinmetz 96c, Jan Halaska 11tr, Jeffrey Greenberg 202c, NASA 52t, NOAA 72t, Robert Brook 173c, Simon Fraser 177t; **South American Pictures:** 191b; **Still Pictures:** 76cl, George Mulala 233b, H. Baesemann 192t, M. Henning 191tl, Mark Edwards 169t, 184b, Nazrul Islam 31b, SJ Krasemann 209c; **SuperStock:** Andre Seale 43br, Sylvain Grandadam 201b; **TopFoto:** All Imageworks 160b; **University of Southampton Park:** 164tc; **USDD:** 51br, 76br; **Zomba Action Project:** 159t

Cover images: Front: **Pearson Education Ltd:** Photodisc. Edmund Van Hoorick

All other images © Pearson Education

Every effort has been made to trace the copyright holders and we apologise in advance for any unintentional omissions. We would be pleased to insert the appropriate acknowledgement in any subsequent edition of this publication.

Websites
The websites used in this book were correct and up to date at the time of publication. It is essential for tutors to preview each website before using it in class so as to ensure that the URL is still accurate, relevant and appropriate. We suggest that tutors bookmark useful websites and consider enabling students to access them through the school/college intranet.

Disclaimer
This Edexcel publication offers high-quality support for the delivery of Edexcel qualifications.

Edexcel endorsement does not mean that this material is essential to achieve any Edexcel qualification, nor does it mean that this is the only suitable material available to support any Edexcel qualification. No endorsed material will be used verbatim in setting any Edexcel examination/assessment and any resource lists produced by Edexcel shall include this and other appropriate texts.

Copies of official specifications for all Edexcel qualifications may be found on the Edexcel website, www.edexcel.com

Contents

About this book

This book has several features to help you with your International GCSE Geography.

Introduction
Each chapter has a short introduction to help you start thinking about the topic and let you know what is in the chapter.

End of chapter checkouts
These have three parts:
- a checklist of the topics that you need to revise
- a checklist of the key terms you should understand (more terms are defined in the Glossary in the ActiveBook)
- short questions to help you checkout and test your understanding of the content of the chapter.

Chapter 6: Urban environments

6.1 The nature of urbanisation

The growth of towns and cities which leads to an increasing percentage of a country's population living in urban settlements is called **urbanisation**. Urban settlements (towns and cities) differ from rural ones (hamlets and villages) in terms of (Figure 6.1):

- their economies – they make a living from manufacturing and services rather than agriculture
- their size – they are larger in population and extent
- their densities of people and buildings which are generally high
- their way of life.

Introduction

This chapter is about towns and cities. Worldwide, the process of urbanisation is changing where and how people live and work. For many, urbanisation brings benefits, but there are also serious costs such as congestion, discrimination, pollution and poor housing. Perhaps these costs are greatest in LIC cities. Despite their overall prosperity, HIC cities also have their challenges. These include reducing the amount of deprivation and reviving worn-out parts of the built-up area. At the same time, however, important new developments are taking place around the edges of HIC cities.

Figure 6.1: *A modern central city landscape*

Figure 6.2 shows how the level of urbanisation (the percentage of the population living in urban settlements) varies across the globe. In general terms, it is the middle-income countries (MICs) and higher-income countries (HICs) that show the highest levels of urbanisation. The lowest levels are found in Africa and South-East Asia.

Towns and cities are growing in number and size all over the world. While the world's population is increasing fast, the urban population is increasing even faster. Figure 6.3 shows that the world population more than doubled between 1950 and 2000 but that the urban population more than trebled. Today, the rate of urbanisation has been such that half the world's population is now living in urban areas.

See Figure 5.9 on page 121 which shows the changing balance in the world's population. Clearly we have now reached the point where just over half the world's population lives in urban areas.

145

Margin boxes
The boxes in the margin do one of five things:
- ask short questions to check your knowledge and understanding so far
- set exercises based on some of the figures and tables
- suggest some simple research exercises to back up what is in the chapter
- give you extra information or help
- guide you to linked topics in other parts of the book.

End of chapter checkout

Checklists

Now you have read the chapter, you should know:
- about the nature of the three processes: urbanisation, suburbanisation and counterurbanisation
- the factors that affect the rate of urbanisation
- what megacities are, and why they have developed
- the main problems caused by rapid urbanisation
- the reasons for similar land uses to concentrate in particular parts of urban areas
- the reasons for the segregation of different ethnic and socio-economic groups of people within urban areas
- the consequences of this segregation of different groups of people
- the characteristics and problems of shanty towns
- how attempts are being made to deal with challenges of shanty towns
- the types of change taking place on the edges of cities in HICs (high-income countries)
- the arguments used in the debate about whether it is better to use brownfield rather than greenfield site
- the symptoms and locations of areas of social deprivation and poverty in HIC cities
- about the changing fortunes of the inner areas of HIC cities
- the roles of different managers in regenerating and re-imaging cities

Make sure you understand these key terms:

Accessibility: the ease with which one location can be reached from another; the degree to which people are able to obtain goods and services, such as housing and healthcare.
Brownfield site: land that has been previously used, abandoned and now awaits a new use.
Congestion: acute overcrowding caused by high densities of traffic, business and people.
Counterurbanisation: the movement of people and employment from major cities to smaller cities and towns as well as to rural areas.
Environmental quality: the degree to which an area is free from air, water, noise and visual pollution.
Ethnic group: a group of people united by a common characteristic such as race, language or religion.
Greenfield site: land that has not been used for urban development
Land value: the market price of a piece of land; what people or businesses are prepared to pay for owning and occupying it.
Megacity: a city or urban area with a population larger than 10 million.
Poverty: where people are seriously lacking in terms of income, food, housing, basic services (clean water and sewage disposal) and access to education and healthcare. See also Social deprivation.

Shanty town: an area of slum housing built of salvaged materials and located either on the city edge or within the city on hazardous ground previously avoided by urban development.
Social deprivation: when the well-being and quality of life of people falls below a minimum level
Social segregation: the clustering together of people with similar characteristics (class, ethnicity, wealth) into separate residential areas.
Socio-economic group: a group of people sharing the same characteristics, such as income level, type of employment and class.
Squatter community: see Shanty town.
Suburbanisation: the outward spread of the urban area, often at lower densities compared with the older parts of a town or city.
Urban regeneration: the investment of capital in the revival of old, urban areas by either improving what is there or clearing it away and rebuilding.
Urban re-imaging: changing the image of an urban area and the way people view it.
Urban managers: people who make important decisions affecting urban areas, such planners, politicians and developers.
Urbanisation: growth in the percentage of a population living and working in urban areas.
See the Glossary in the ActiveBook for more definitions.

Questions

Try testing yourself with these questions:

1 a) What is meant by urbanisation?
   b) State three causes of urbanisation.
2 Why are cities in LICs growing faster than those in HICs?
3 What are the distinguishing features of each of the following urbanisation processes:
   - suburbanisation
   - counterurbanisation
   - decentralisation
   - urban regeneration?
4 a) What is a 'dormitory settlement'?
   b) How are conurbations formed?
5 a) What is a megacity?
   b) Describe how the number and distribution of megacities are changing.
6 a) What are 'world cities'?
   b) Name three world cities.
7 What are the main causes of rapid urbanisation in LICs?
8 Describe four problems, other than the growth of shanty towns, created by rapid urbanisation.
9 a) Describe the pattern of urban land values shown in Figure 6.15.
   b) What other features of the city change with increasing distance from the centre?
10 a) Identify the four zones of a city.
   b) Why do similar activities tend to come together at particular locations within the city?
11 Give two typical features of a CBD

12 a) What are the features that distinguish different groups of people within the city?
   b) Why do those different groups live in different parts of the city?
13 a) What is a ghetto?
   b) What are the reasons given for their existence?
14 a) What are shanty towns?
   b) How and why do they develop?
15 Examine some of the ways of improving living conditions in shanty towns.
16 What are the push and pull factors responsible for people moving to the urban fringe?
17 Explain why retailing is moving out of the CBD to out-of-town retailing parks.
18 a) Name three other types of business development found on the edges of HIC cities.
   b) What do they find attractive about the urban fringe as a location?
19 a) Distinguish between brownfield sites and greenfield sites.
   b) What are the arguments that favour using brownfield sites?
20 a) What is meant by deprivation?
   b) What is the 'cycle of poverty'?
21 Using Figure 6.27, identify those parts of Birmingham with low levels of deprivation.
22 a) What were the reasons for the decline of the inner city in the 20th century?
   b) What are the reasons for its revival in the 21st century?
23 a) What is meant by:
   - gentrification
   - gated communities?
   b) Who has benefited most from these two developments? Give your reasons.

175

Section C of the specification (Practical geographical enquiry) is covered on the ActiveBook CD which accompanies this book. This section involves the practical work required in the investigation of specific topics in Sections A and B.

Chapter 1: River environments

1.1 The hydrological cycle

Fresh water is essential for life on Earth. This water is constantly being recycled as it moves through a cycle known as the **hydrological cycle** or **water cycle**. This is a global circulation of water – it is a giant **closed system** (Figure 1.1). This means that there is a fixed amount of water in the system because water neither enters nor leaves the Earth and its atmosphere.

Introduction

This chapter is about rivers. They are a vital part of the global circulation of water. They are responsible for the creation of landforms found throughout the world. They are valuable to us because they supply much of the water we use in our everyday lives. At the same time, because of the risk of flooding, they can become hazards that threaten people and their settlements.

Figure 1.1: *Stores and flows in the hydrological cycle*

Key

Stores

Flows (transfers)

Stores

During the hydrological cycle, water is held in a number of **stores** and then moves between them by means of a series of **flows** or **transfers**. The stores in the cycle are:

*   the atmosphere – here the water exists either as water vapour or as minute droplets in clouds

*   the land – here water is stored on the surface in rivers, lakes and **reservoirs**. Water is also taken in by plants and temporarily stored in vegetation. It is also stored below ground in the soil or bedrock. This is known as the **groundwater** store. Generally speaking, water exists in these stores in a liquid form. However, it can also exist in a solid form as snow and ice, as for example in ice sheets, glaciers and snowfields.

- the sea – it is estimated that over 95% of the Earth's water is stored in the sea. This is overwhelmingly held in liquid form (water), but also in the form of ice, for example the icebergs in high-latitude seas.

While the amount of water in the global hydrological cycle cannot change, the proportion held in the different stores can. The latter changes are triggered by changes in the Sun's energy. For example, an increase in the Sun's energy will lead to more evaporation and possibly to the melting of ice sheets and glaciers.

Flows (or transfers)

The transfers of water that take place between stores do so by means of a variety of flows as follows (Figure 1.2):

- **evaporation** – we might say that the hydrological cycle starts with evaporation by the heat of the Sun. Water is converted from a liquid into a gas (water vapour). This takes place from the surface of the sea and from water surfaces (ponds, lakes, etc.) on land. Evaporation is particularly important in the transfer of water from the sea store into the atmosphere

- **transpiration** – plants take up liquid water from the soil and 'breathe' it into atmosphere as water vapour

- **condensation** – this is the change in the atmosphere when water vapour cools and changes to liquid. The liquid takes the form of water droplets that appear in the atmosphere as clouds

- **precipitation** – this is the transfer of water in any form (rain, hail or snow) from the atmosphere to the land or sea surface

Locate and name the stores on a tracing or copy of Figure 1.2.

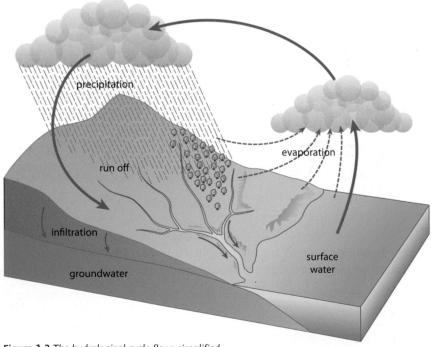

Figure 1.2 *The hydrological cycle flows simplified*

- **overland flow** – most of the precipitation that hits the ground moves under gravity and eventually enters a stream, river or lake. This is also known as **run off**

- **infiltration and percolation** – this is the transfer of water downwards through the soil and rock into the **aquifer** or groundwater store

- **throughflow** – this takes place between the ground surface and the top of the groundwater store. Under the influence of gravity, water moves slowly through the soil until it reaches a stream or river

- **groundwater flow** – this takes place in the aquifer and is the underground transfer of water to rivers, lakes and the sea.

All of these transfers fit together to form a circle involving the three major stores (the atmosphere, the land and the sea). We might imagine that the cycle starts and finishes in the sea. However, some of the water that falls as rain on the land may never reach the sea. Instead it may be returned directly back to the atmosphere from the land by the transpiration of plants and evaporation from both soil and water bodies.

Be sure you know the difference between these 8 flows and where they fit into the hydrological cycle.

1.2 Drainage basins and their features

Every river has its own **drainage basin** or **catchment area**. Each drainage basin is a system. There is a movement of water within it that is rather like a small-scale hydrological cycle. The drainage basin cycle involves stores and flows (see Figure 1.3). However, the important difference between the drainage basin and the hydrological cycle is that the former is an **open system**. A drainage basin has external inputs and outputs. The amount of water in the system in the basin varies over time. In the hydrological cycle the amount of water remains exactly the same.

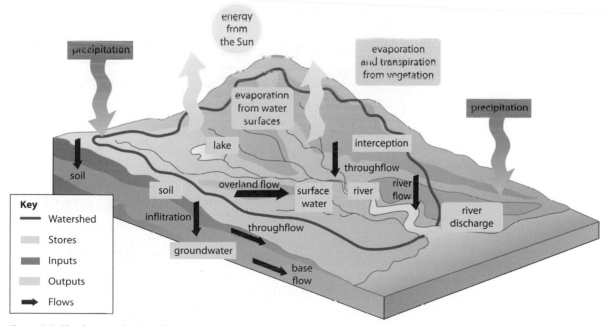

Figure 1.3: *The drainage basin cycle*

The inputs of a drainage basin are:

- energy from the Sun

- precipitation formed from moisture picked up outside the basin

- possibly water from tributary drainage basins – this is not shown in Figure 1.3; an explanation is given below.

Most of the flows and stores are broadly the same as in the hydrological cycle.

The outputs are:

- the river's **discharge**

- the water in its basin from which evaporation and transpiration take place and which eventually falls as precipitation in another drainage basin.

Why is the hydrological cycle a closed system and the drainage basin cycle an open system?

For more on systems, see:

· Chapter 2.6 (page 54)

· Chapter 5.2 (page 116)

· Chapter 5.5 (page 123)

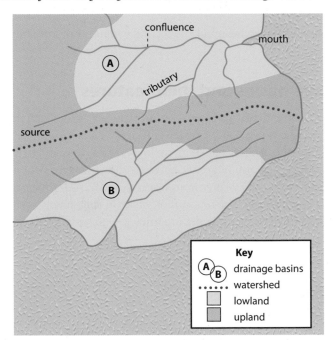

Figure 1.4: *Basic features of the drainage basin*

As Figure 1.4 shows, it is possible to draw a dividing line between neighbouring drainage basins. It follows the tops of the hills and is called the **watershed**. The main river has its source in the higher parts of the basin close to the watershed. This is where most precipitation falls. Smaller streams or **tributaries** enter the main river channel at locations known as **confluences**. The mouth or **estuary** of the river is where it flows out into the sea.

Drainage basins can be of at least three broad types. Not all of them simply collect and deliver water directly to the sea. Some of them are just parts of much larger drainage basins. For example, the basin of the River Negro in Brazil is a tributary or part of the huge drainage basin of the River Amazon. The water it collects is conveyed to the Amazon and then eventually to the sea. Some drainage basins do not lead, either directly or indirectly, to the open sea. Rather they lead to 'inland' seas or lakes such as the Caspian Sea, the Aral Sea or Lake Victoria in Kenya.

The **drainage** or **channel network** is the system of surface and underground channels that collect and transport the precipitation falling on the drainage basin.

Figure 1.4 shows the channel networks of two drainage basins, A and B. Basin A's network is less dense (has fewer channels) than B's, though the main channel is shorter. Channel networks can be mapped and their lengths and densities (number of channels per unit area) measured. The network can change over short periods of time. For example, during flooding drainage basins often have many more and longer channels than they do in periods of low or normal rainfall.

Each drainage basin is unique in its combination of a range of features. These features include size, shape, rock type, relief and land use. The features become factors that determine how quickly or slowly water moves through the basin.

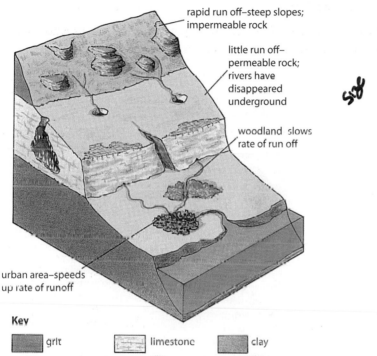

rapid run off–steep slopes; impermeable rock

little run off–permeable rock; rivers have disappeared underground

woodland slows rate of run off

urban area–speeds up rate of runoff

Key

grit   limestone   clay

Figure 1.5: *Factors affecting run off*

Are you sure you know the difference between permeable and impermeable rocks?

Figure 1.5 shows how some of these features can affect overland flow or run off. Rock type and relief are physical factors over which people have little control. However, land use can be easily changed by people. Woodland can hold water and slow overland flow. However, once it is cleared for cultivation, run off will speed up. The built-up areas of towns and cities can speed up run off even more. Rainwater hits solid surfaces such as roofs, pavements and roads. It is then quickly channelled into drains which speed its delivery into a stream or river.

1.3 Hydrographs and river regimes

It can be important to know how quickly any rain falling in a drainage basin or catchment area will reach the drainage network. It is also important to know how much a river's channel can hold. If the rainwater reaches the river quickly, the channel may not be able to cope and flooding will occur. The amount of water carried by a river at any one time is known as its **discharge**. This is measured in **cumecs** – that is, in cubic metres of water per second moving past a particular point along the river's course.

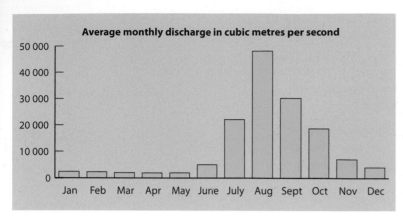

Figure 1.6: *A hydrograph of the River Ganges in Bangladesh*

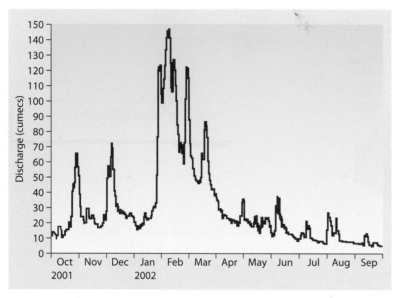

Figure 1.7: *Hydrograph showing the regime of the Thames at Reading, 2001–2002*

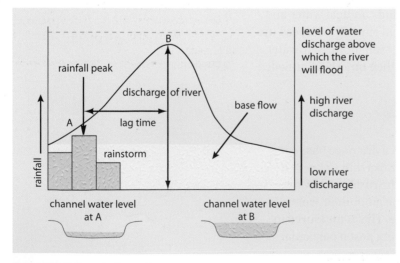

Figure 1.8: *A storm hydrograph*

River discharges vary throughout the year, from month to month, from day to day. These variations make up what is termed the **river regime**. In most rivers, the regime closely reflects local climatic conditions, particularly the rainfall regime. Figure 1.6 shows the average monthly discharge of the River Ganges as it passes through Bangladesh. This diagram is a **hydrograph**. Clearly, mean (average) discharge is high between June and October. This period of high discharge from the river coincides with the monsoon season, during which total rainfall can exceed 275 cm.

Figure 1.7 shows the regime of the River Thames (England) during one year. Unlike the Ganges, the highest discharges generally occur in the winter, in February and March. Another feature of the hydrograph is its 'jaggedness'. Discharge clearly varies from day to day. The peaks reflect the impact of passing showers and short periods of heavy rainfall.

The majority of the world's drainage basins are home to many people. The big attraction of such areas to people was their fertile soils and the ability to grow food. Today much money is invested, not just in farmland, but also in homes, businesses and transport in these drainage basins. Thus it is important that we know how rivers will behave following a period of heavy rainfall. How great will be the risk of flooding – and over what area? This is where a storm hydrograph comes in useful.

A **storm hydrograph** records the changing discharge of a river after a passing rainstorm. The bars in the left-hand corner of Figure 1.8 show the input of rain. It takes time for the rain to reach the river and cause river levels to rise once it has hit the ground. This delay between peak rainfall and peak discharge is called the **lag time**. The shorter the lag time, the quicker the water reaches the river channel. A short lag time will cause the river discharge to rise steeply. The steeper the rise in discharge, the greater the chances of flooding. It is possible to mark on the storm hydrograph the level of discharge above which the river will flood. Once the storm and its peak discharge have passed, the amount of water in the river starts to decrease.

The storm hydrograph shows that discharge of the river as being made up of two flows:

- the **base flow** – the 'normal' discharge of the river

- the **storm flow** – the additional discharge of the river directly related to the passing of the rainstorm.

There are a number of factors affecting the critical time lag of a storm and hydrographs generally. These include:

- the amount and the intensity of the rain – heavy rain will not sink into the ground; instead it will become overland flow or run off and quickly reach the river

- temperatures are significant because they affect the form of precipitation. For example, if temperatures are below freezing, precipitation will be in the form of snow. This can take weeks to melt. If the ground remains frozen, melting snow on the surface can reach the river quickly

- land use – trees and plants will intercept and delay the rain reaching the ground. Bare soil and rock will speed up runoff and reduce the time lag. So too will urban areas covered by tarmac and concrete

- steep slopes will cause rapid surface runoff, so water will reach the river more quickly. Flat and gently sloping land may lead to water sinking into the soil. This will delay it reaching the river

- rock type – impermeable rocks will not allow rainwater to sink into it, so will speed up runoff. Permeable rock will allow infiltration and percolation of water into the bedrock. This in turn will slow the delivery of the water to the river

- dams and reservoirs regulate and even out discharges. They hold back discharge and so reduce the risk of flooding downstream (Figure 1.9).

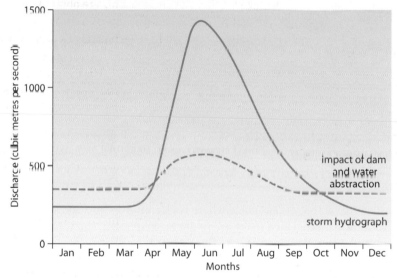

Figure 1.9: *The impact of a dam and water abstraction on a river's storm hydrograph*

In your own words, describe the differences between the two hydrographs in Figure 1.9. Try to explain those differences.

1.4 River processes

Weathering and mass movement

Rivers play a major part in shaping landforms. They do this work by means of three processes – erosion, transport and deposition. These river processes act in a sort of partnership with two other processes – weathering and mass movement. Let us take a look at these two processes before looking more closely at the work that rivers actually do.

Weathering involves elements of the weather, particularly rainfall and temperatures (Table 1.1).

Physical weathering	This breaks rock down into smaller and smaller pieces. It is done by changes in temperature and by rainfall freezing and thawing in rock cracks.
Chemical weathering	This causes rock to decay and disintegrate. It is largely done by slightly acidic rainfall seeping into porous rock.
Biological weathering	The roots of plants, especially trees, growing in cracks in the rocks gradually split the rock apart.

Table 1.1: Different types of weathering

Figure 1.10: A landslide – a hazardous form of mass movement

What made the landslide in Figure 1.10 into a serious hazard and natural disaster?

For more on hazards, see Chapter 3.

All this destructive activity takes place where rocks outcrop (are above the surface of the surrounding land). Once rocks are really broken down, the weathered material starts to move down the slope under the influence of gravity. This is **mass movement**. It takes several different forms. In river valleys, there are two main types of mass movement:

- **slumping** – this occurs when the bottom of a valley side slope is cut away by the river flowing at its base. This makes the slope unstable and weathered material slumps down towards the river. Slumping is also helped when the weathered material on the slope is saturated by heavy rain. The water does two things. It makes the weathered material heavier and acts as a lubricant. Figure 1.10 is an example of sudden slumping leading to a major landslide.

- **soil creep** – weathered material moves slowly down slope under the influence of gravity. It collects at the bottom of the valley side and is eroded by the river.

Erosion

There are several different ways in which rivers erode their channels and valleys (Table 1.2).

Hydraulic action	Water hits the river bed and banks with such force that material is dislodged and carried away. This is particularly important during periods when the river's discharge is high.
Abrasion	The material being carried by a river is rubbed against the the sides and floor of the channel. This 'sandpaper' action widens and deepens the channel.
Corrosion	Minerals in the rocks forming the sides of the river channel are dissolved by the water flowing past them.

Table 1.2: The processes of river erosion

Attrition is another river process. It involves particles of material being carried by a river becoming rounder and smaller as they constantly collide with each other. This process doesn't erode river channels and valleys.

Why is attrition not included in Table 1.2?

Transport

This is the movement of material (known as the **load**) by the river. The load is made up of material that has been washed or fallen into river. It also made up of materials eroded by the river itself from the sides of the channel. The load can be transported in a number of different ways (Figure 1.11).

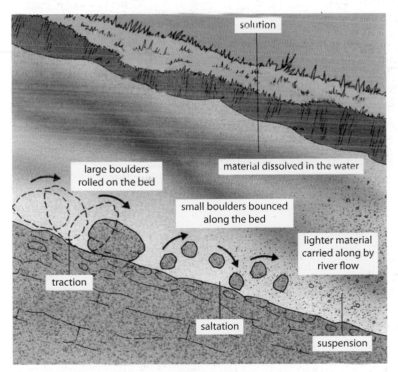

Figure 1.11: Ways in which rivers transport their load

Explain why the size of load material affects the way it is transported by a river.

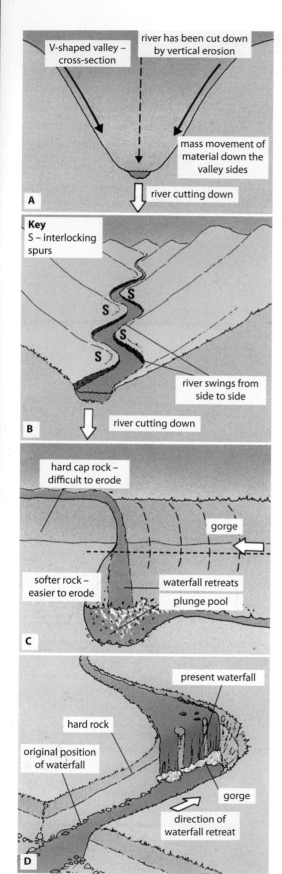

Figure 1.12: *The origin of river landforms in upland areas*

Deposition

Deposition is the laying down of material transported by the river. This occurs when there is a decrease in the energy, speed and discharge of the river. This is most likely to happen when a river enters a lake or the sea. It will also happen wherever there is a decrease in the gradient of the river's channel.

These three processes are affected by a number of factors. A wetter climate means more discharge and therefore more erosion and transport. Softer rocks are more easily eroded and transported. Gentle slopes encourage deposition.

1.5 Downstream changes in river channels and landforms

The **long profile** of a river runs from its source to the point where it enters the sea, a lake or joins another and larger river. The character of the long profile changes downstream. Overall it has a smooth concave shape. It is steep and in places irregular where the river is flowing well above sea level in upland country. The irregularities occur where hard rock outcrops run across the valley. Natural lakes and reservoirs can also disrupt the smoothness of the long profile. However, the profile becomes much gentler and smoother as the river runs through lowland country and reaches its destination. Changes in the character of river landforms are associated with these changes in the long profile. For this reason, we should distinguish between upland and lowland river landforms.

Upland landforms

The main river landforms found in upland areas are: steep V-shaped valleys, **interlocking spurs**, waterfalls and gorges (Figure 1.12). They have all been formed mainly by the processes of river erosion already described in Part **1.4**. The processes of weathering and mass movement have also played a part.

In the uplands, the long profile is steep and the river flows fast. Much of the river's energy is spent cutting downwards. The processes of hydraulic action (erosive force exerted by water) and abrasion, in particular, erode the river bed and thus make the valley deeper (Figure 1.12A). Because of the steepness and deepness of the valley, there is mass movement of material down the sides of the valley. Some of this material becomes river load and helps the abrasion process. The valley floor is narrow and often completely occupied by the river.

Interlocking spurs are formed where the river swings from side to side (Figure 1.12B). Again the main work of the river is vertically downwards into its bed. This means that the river cuts down to flow between spurs of higher land on alternate sides of the valley.

Waterfalls occur where a band of hard rock outcrops that is much more resistant to erosion than the softer rock below it (Figure 1.12C and D). This softer rock is readily eroded by the force of the water as it falls over the hard cap rock. Gradually, the falling water excavates a **plunge pool** at the bottom of the falls. Slowly the hard rock is eroded back by the river and so the waterfall gradually retreats upstream leaving a **gorge** below it. The gorge is protected from being widened by its capping of hard rock. The Iguaça Falls in South America are a spectacular example and attract many tourists (Figure 1.13).

Figure 1.13: *Map and photograph of the Iguaçu Falls*

Lowland landforms

The river and its landforms change when the river leaves the uplands and flows across lowlands (Figure 1.14). The river channel becomes wider, deeper and smoother. Because of this, both the **velocity** (speed) and discharge of the river continue to increase, despite the gentler gradient. The river course in plan (map) view becomes less straight and is characterised by a series of **meanders**. The valley cross section is wider and flatter. The floor is occupied by a floodplain with its distinctive **levees**, meanders and ox-bow lakes (Figure 1.15). Near the end of its course, the **flood plain** spreads out to become either a **delta** or an **estuary**.

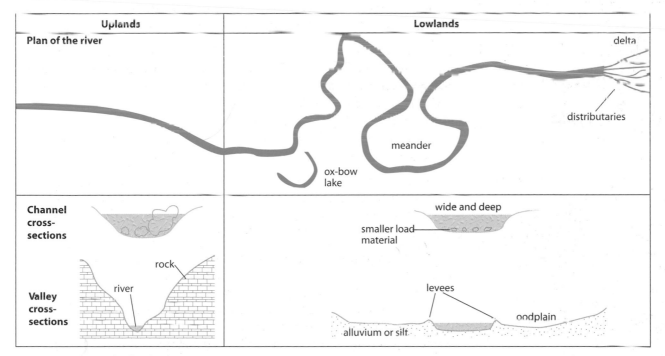

Figure 1.14: *River and valley features*

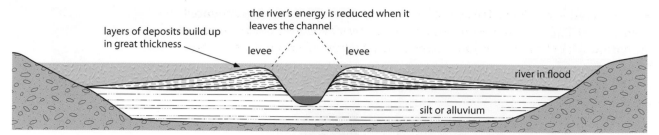

the river's energy is reduced when it leaves the channel

layers of deposits build up in great thickness

levee   levee

river in flood

silt or alluvium

Figure 1.15: *The formation of a floodplain and levees*

During its lowland course, the river is still an agent of erosion. However, vertical erosion is less important because the river is too close to sea level. More important is **lateral erosion** where the river wears away the sides of the channel, especially on the outside of meanders. The river becomes an agent of **deposition** as well. Such a large load of material has been picked up that, once the river loses energy, it drops some of that load, usually mud, stones and other organic matter. The greatest thickness of river-deposited material, known as **alluvium**, is on the **flood plain**. As its names suggests, the flood plain is an area of flat land formed by flooding. Every time the river leaves its channel, its velocity (speed) decreases. Once this happens, alluvium is deposited across the valley floor. A great thickness of alluvial material builds up. The largest amount of deposition is always on the banks of the channel, which builds up to a greater height than the rest of the floodplain to form levees (Figure 1.15).

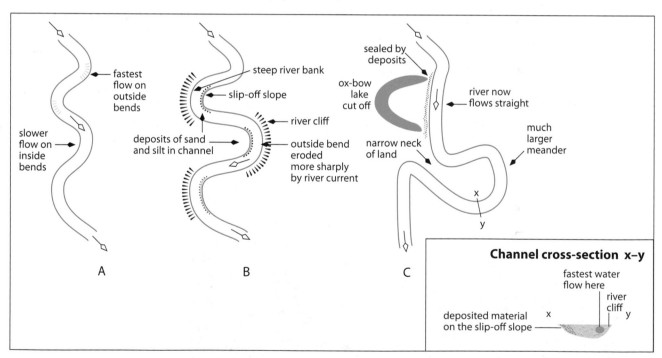

Figure 1.16: *Formation of meanders and oxbows*

A study of the formation of **meanders** and **ox-bow lakes** shows how the river both deposits and erodes laterally (Figure 1.16). The force of the water undercuts the bank on the outside of a bend to form a steep bank to the channel, called a **river cliff** or **bluff**. An underwater current with a spiral flow carries the eroded material to the inside of the bend where the flow of water is slower. Here the material is deposited to form a gentle bank, called a **slip-off slope** or **point bar**.

As lateral erosion continues, the bend of a meander becomes even more pronounced (Figure 1.16). Especially in times of flood, when the river's energy is much greater, the narrow neck of the meander may be breached (broken and crossed) so that the river flows straight again. The redundant meander loop retains some water and becomes an ox-bow lake. Deposition during the flooding helps to seal off the edges and ends of the lake.

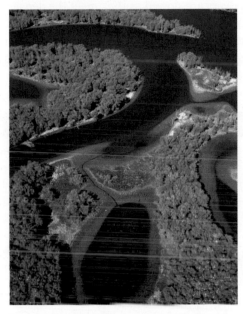

Figure 1.17: *Mississippi meanders and ox-bow lakes*

Lateral erosion on the outside banks of meanders helps to widen the flood plain. Flood plains have great value for people. Flat land with rich, thick alluvial soils and nearby, plentiful water is attractive to agriculture, industry and urban settlements. Rivers meander naturally. The meanders migrate across the flood plain as the outside of the meander erodes laterally (sideways). Figure 1.17 shows a small part of the complicated meander pattern of the Mississippi River.

Try researching two facts about the Mississippi River:

• the actual length of the river from its source to the sea

• the straight-line distance from its source to the sea.

What does this tell you about the amount of meandering the river does?

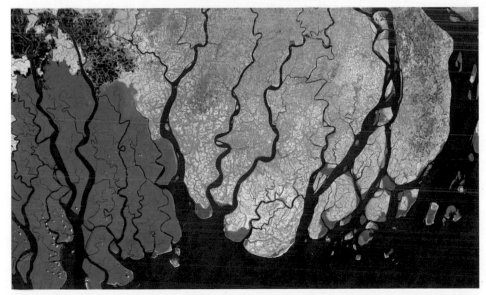

Figure 1.18: *Satellite image of part of the Ganges–Brahmaputra delta. It also shows huge amounts of silt being deposited in the waters of the Bay of Bengal.*

The **delta** is the final landform of the river's journey from its source to the sea or lake. Deltas are vast areas of alluvium at the mouths of rivers. The Ganges–Brahmaputra delta is one of the largest in the world (Figure 1.18). It is located at the head of the Bay of Bengal. The rivers that have built it up carry huge quantities of sediment, derived mainly from the Himalayas, down to the delta. It is estimated that they deliver about 1.7 billion tonnes of sediment each year. The flows of the combined rivers are slowed as they meet the denser sea water in the Bay. The result is that much of the load being carried is dropped. In fact, it is deposited faster than the tides can remove it out to sea. The river flow is blocked by so much deposition that the rivers split up into smaller channels known as **distributaries**. These distributaries help deposit sediment over a wide area, creating new land where there was once sea.

For more information about deltas, see Case studies on pages 30 and 51.

Not all rivers build up deltas as they enter the sea. Many have open mouths or estuaries.

Look at an atlas map of the British Isles to locate the drainage basin of the River Tay.

Case study: The River Tay (UK) and its valley

In the uplands

The River Tay is fed by streams which drain the slopes of the Grampian Mountains in the Highlands of Scotland. Precipitation in the upland parts of the drainage basin is high (well over 1000 mm a year) and slopes are steep.

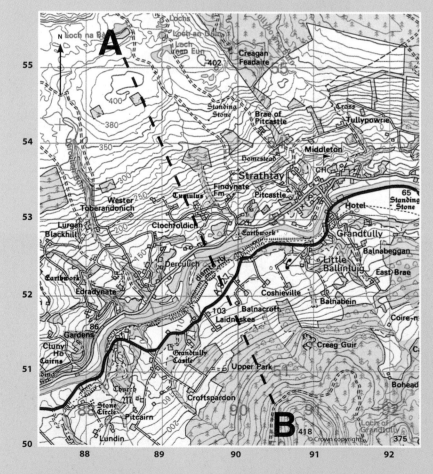

Figure 1.19: *Part of the upland course of the River Tay*   0 ———— 1 km

The height of the drainage basin and the steep slopes result in large amounts of run off. The Tay is already about 100 metres across in that part of its course as shown on the Ordnance Survey map extract (Figure 1.19). The curving nature of the river course suggests that it is flowing between interlocking spurs.

The valley cross-section is shown in Figure 1.20A. It is V-shaped and steep-sided. The river fills the valley floor. The cross-section shows that the river is still flowing at some height above sea level. Erosion by the river appears to be vertical rather than lateral.

In the lowlands

Figure 1.20B shows the valley cross-section near the sea. The flat and low-lying land is the flood plain. It is 0.6 km wide where the tributary River Earn meets the main River Tay. Notice the big meander loop on the tributary through grid squares 1718 and 1717 (Figure 1.21). The black dashes marked around its banks show the levees.

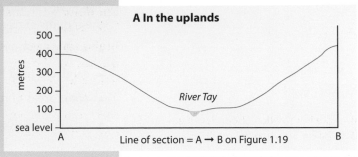

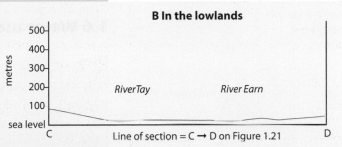

Figure 1.20: Cross sections across the Tay valley

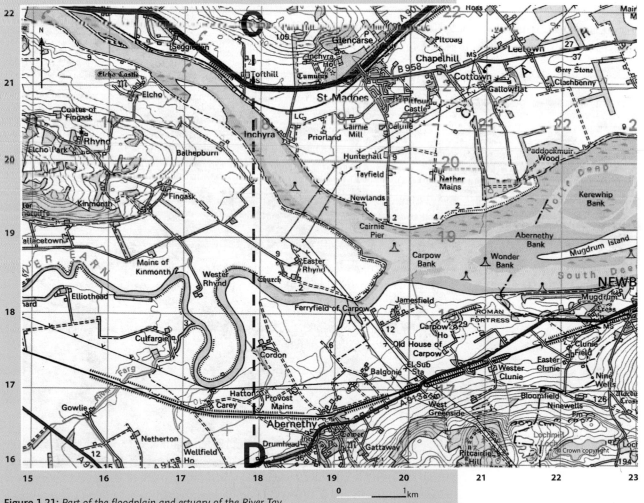

Figure 1.21: Part of the floodplain and estuary of the River Tay

The River Tay shows many of the typical estuary features that can be found at the mouths of rivers (Figure 1.21). They include:

- a wide channel – up to 2 km
- sand and mud banks (Abernethy Bank)
- some areas of marsh (in grid square 2119)
- channels of deeper water (North Deep).

1.6 Water uses, demand and supply

Uses

Only 3% of all the water on Earth is fresh water; the rest is saltwater in the seas (Figure 1.22). Over 75% of the fresh water is locked up in glaciers and ice sheets, and 20 per cent is groundwater. The world's remarkably small amount of fresh water is:

- essential to all life,
- vital to the process of economic development,
- unevenly distributed with some areas 'water-rich' and others 'water-poor'.

Freshwater is needed for the following purposes:

- domestic use – e.g. bathing and showering; flushing toilets; drinking and cooking; washing clothes and dishes; watering the garden
- industrial use – e.g. producing a litre of beer uses 300 litres of water; producing a hamburger uses on average 2400 litres of water; the production of one tonne of paper uses 400 000 litres of water. See also Figure 1.29 on page 21
- agricultural use – e.g. irrigating crops; providing drinking water for livestock
- **leisure** use – e.g. sport fishing on rivers; sailing on lakes and ponds; watering golf courses.

All forms of water use involve two key elements:

- **demand** – this is the need for water for a range of uses. It is also often referred to as **consumption**. In other words, the amount of water consumed reflects the level of demand
- **supply** – that is meeting the demand for water by tapping various sources, such as groundwater, lakes and rivers.

For any country or area within it, it is possible to compare water demand and water supply. This comparison is known as the **water balance** (Figure 1.25 on page 18).

Demand

Water demand and consumption have increased dramatically during the last 100 years with global demand doubling every 20 years (Figure 1.23). The major factor behind the rising demand has been the continuing growth of the world's population. Between 1990 and 2010, the world population grew from 5.3 billion to an estimated 6.8 billion. However, the rise in the demand and consumption of water is not just due to growing numbers of people. Development also plays an important part.

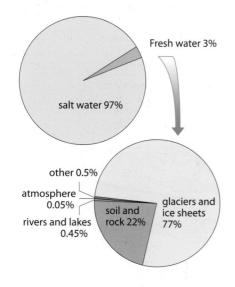

Figure 1.22: *The world's water*

salt water 97%

Fresh water 3%

other 0.5%

atmosphere 0.05%

rivers and lakes 0.45%

soil and rock 22%

glaciers and ice sheets 77%

How might global warming change Figure 1.22?

- The rising standard of living that is part of development increases the domestic use of water. More houses with piped water, flush toilets, showers and baths, washing machines, and even swimming pools mean much higher water consumption.

- The rise in agricultural productivity needed to feed a growing population increases the use of water, particularly for irrigation.

- Industrialisation is a key part of development. Most factories are large consumers of water. Water is used for cooling machinery. It is also used in the generation of electricity for powering industry.

Given the link between development and water consumption, we can recognise two 'worlds of water'. There are big differences between water consumption in high-income countries (HICs) and in low-income countries (LICs). Water consumption in HICs is very high. On average, each person in an HIC uses about 1200 cubic metres of water each year. This is about three times as much as a person in a LIC where consumption is around 400 cubic metres per year.

There are also some big differences in the use of that water (Figure 1.24). In LICs most water is used by agriculture and relatively little by industry or in the home. In HICs industry uses the most water followed closely by agriculture. Domestic use of water is relatively small, but the percentage is over three times greater than in LICs.

Supply

Having looked at one side of the water equation, let us now look at the other – water supply. In many parts of the world, the water needed to meet the increasing demand comes from three main sources:

- **rivers and lakes** – possibly this was the source of supply used by the earliest humans

- **reservoirs** – these are artificial lakes created by building a dam across a valley and allowing it to flood. The water collected and stored behind the dam can become an important water supply

- **aquifers** and wells – much of the world's fresh water supply lies underground. It is stored in porous rocks known as aquifers. This groundwater can be extracted by drilling wells or boreholes down to the aquifer. The water is then raised to the surface by buckets, pumps or under its own pressure.

Water surplus and deficit

If we were to draw up two world maps, one showing the distribution of water demand or consumption and the other, water supply, we would find that the two maps show quite different patterns. If we laid one map on top of the other, we would be able to pick out three types of area:

- areas where the water balance is negative – in other words where water demand exceeds supply. These are referred to as **water-deficit areas**

- areas where the water balance is positive – in other words **water-surplus areas** where the supply or availability of water exceeds demand

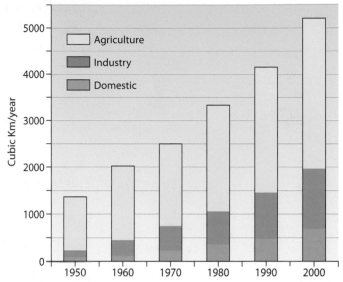

Figure 1.23: *World water consumption, 1950–2000*

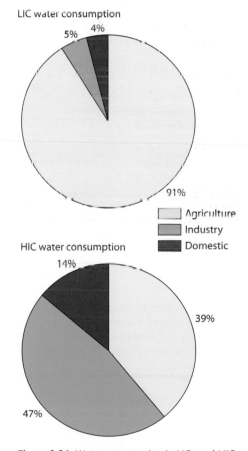

Figure 1.24: *Water consumption in LICs and HICs*

- areas where water demand and supply are roughly the same – water-neutral areas where the water balance is literally evenly balanced.

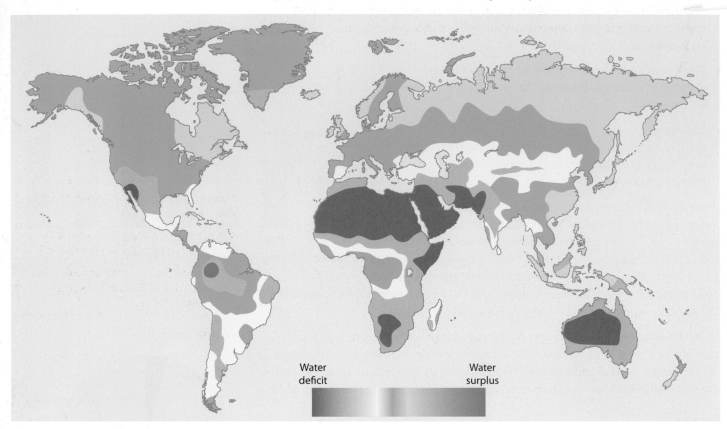

Figure 1.25: *Water-surplus and water-deficit areas of the world*

Figure 1.25 shows the results of overlaying the two world maps – one of demand and the other of supply. Once again we see that there are 'two worlds of water'. There are, in fact, very few truly water-surplus areas. However, there are large areas where the water balance is slightly in surplus. These are typically remote, mountainous regions with high annual rainfall, few people and low water demand. On the other hand, there are many water-deficit areas. These are most obvious in Africa and the Middle East, in Australia and parts of North and South America. Many of these areas are in deficit because they receive little precipitation during the course of a year. Others are in deficit because of large populations and rising development. Good examples of such an area is India.

The various shades of green in Figure 1.25 show those parts of the world where water supply just about meets water demand. Describe the main areas where this is the case.

There are ways of moving water from surplus to deficit areas. The most widely used way is by long-distance pipelines. However, water can also be transported by motor vehicles and even tanker ships.

Case study: Meeting the rising demand for water in England and Wales

Daily water consumption in England and Wales is about 120 litres per person per day. That is not a particularly high figure. It compares with 309 litres for France and 185 litres for Germany.

Water consumption in Britain has been rising in harmony with the growth of population. However, it has been given a number of pushes over the last 200 years. First, it was the growth in manufacturing in the early 19th century. With deindustrialisation in the second half of the 20th century, manufacturing uses less water (now 14%) (Figure 1.26). Other consumers now account for more water use. Most notable is the use of water in the generation of electricity (now 43%). More water is being used today to irrigate crops (14%) and British citizens are using more water in their homes (20%). More homes today have washing machines, dishwashers and swimming pools.

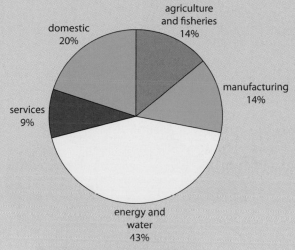

Figure 1.26: *Water use in the UK*

Water is important in making electricity in two ways:

- it is used directly to turn the turbines that generate the electricity, as in HEP
- it is converted into steam by the burning of fossil fuels and the steam turns the turbines.

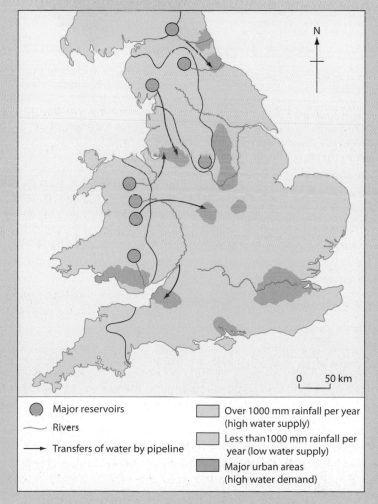

Major reservoirs

Rivers

Transfers of water by pipeline

Over 1000 mm rainfall per year (high water supply)

Less than 1000 mm rainfall per year (low water supply)

Major urban areas (high water demand)

Figure 1.27; *Water demand and supply in England and Wales*

It would be wrong to think that there are no reservoirs in the drier parts of England. For example, London has a number of them on its northern and western outskirts. These are used both to collect water and store recycled water.

Research the names of some large reservoirs in 'dry' England.

Water stress can be a seasonal or temporary condition, as during a climate's dry season or during occasional droughts.

Conversely, water stress can be relieved temporarily by periods of unusually heavy rainfall.

Suggest some ways of saving water and using it more efficiently.

Figure 1.28: *England – levels of water stress*

The problem that faces England and Wales is that the distribution pattern of water demand is different from that of water supply (Figure 1.27). The highest water demand is in SE England which happens to be the driest part of the country. Water is most readily available (the rainfall is highest) in upland areas that are mainly located in Wales and the north of England. The mismatch between demand and supply creates different levels of **water stress** (Figure 1.28). Clearly the greatest water stress lies in the south-east of England. It is being tackled as follows:

- extracting as much water as possible from the aquifers of SE England

- constructing reservoirs in the north and west of the country to collect as much rainfall as possible. Famous reservoirs schemes include Lake Vyrnwy in Wales and Kielder in NE England

- transfering this collected water by pipeline to the main areas of water deficit, i.e. the major cities of the Midlands and South.

There is no doubt that meeting the rising demand for water is a challenge for the UK. Attempts are being made to reduce water consumption by encouraging a much more efficient use of the available water and to eliminate water wastage (see Part **1.7**).

1.7 Water quality

In Part **1.6**, we looked at water demand and supply simply in terms of quantities. Quantity is important. Figure 1.29 below shows how much water is used to provide things that we need or use in everyday life.

It takes ...

10 litres of water to make one sheet of **PAPER**

40 litres of water to make one slice of **BREAD**

140 litres of water to make one cup of **COFFEE**

40 litres of water to make one pair of **JEANS**

1 300 litres of water to make one cup of **WHEAT**

15 500 litres of water to make one kilogram of **BEEF**

4 800 litres of water to make one kilogram of **PORK**

16 600 litres of water to make one kilogram of **LEATHER**

200 litres of water to make one kilogram of **PLASTIC**

40 litres of water to make one glass of **WINE**

70 litres of water to make one **APPLE**

80 litres of water per dollar of **INDUSTRIAL PRODUCT**

Figure 1.29: *The amount of water it takes...*

Select one of the high water consumers in Figure 1.29 and research the reasons for its high consumption.

However, in producing most of the items shown, water quality is also significant. This is obviously the case where water is being used for domestic purposes such as drinking, cooking and washing. It also applies to the growing of crops and rearing of livestock. Clean water is a priority. Polluted water threatens human health and is the cause of diseases such as cholera, bilharzia, typhoid and diarrhoea.

Water quality varies from place to place for a variety of reasons. For example, water quality is generally poorer in dry climates or where the climate has a marked dry season. During dry periods, any water that remains on the surface becomes stagnant and can be a breeding ground for diseases. **Pollution** is another key factor that affects water quality, and this varies greatly from place to place. Levels of pollution are particularly high in urban areas and especially in LIC cities.

Sources of water pollution

There are many sources of water pollution. It is helpful to group them under the headings of the three main water users – agriculture, industry and domestic uses. Figure 1.30 shows some of them in what we might call the 'cycle of water pollution'.

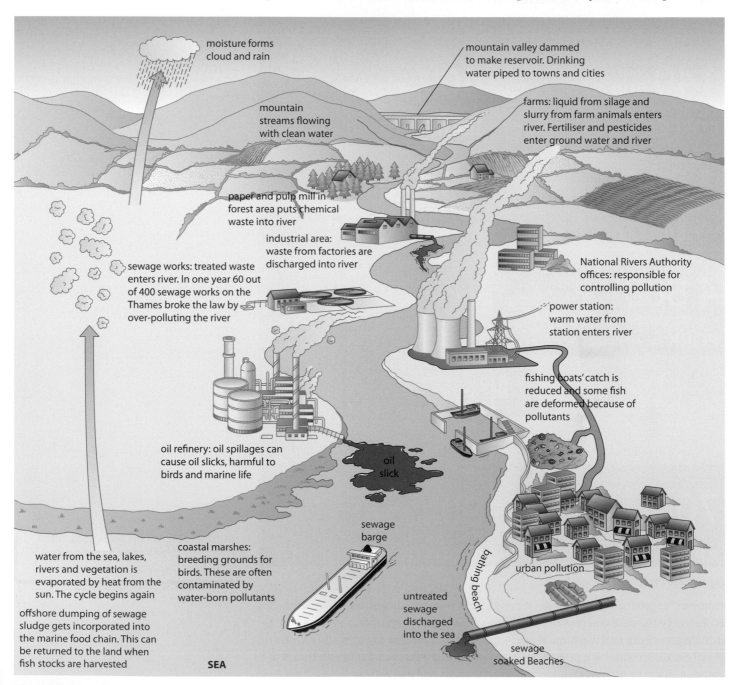

Figure 1.30: *The cycle of water pollution*

Agriculture

- Liquid from farm silage and slurry from farm animals enters rivers

- Fertilisers and pesticides seep into the groundwater

- Deforestation – run off carries soil and silt into rivers, with serious effects on aquatic life and humans who drink the water

Industry

- Taking cooling water for an electric power station from a river and returning it to the source at a higher temperature upsets river ecosystems

- Spillages from industrial plants such as oil refineries

- Working of metallic minerals and the heavy use of water in processing ore – toxic substances eventually find their way into rivers

Domestic purposes

- The discharge of untreated sewage from houses – even treated sewage pollutes

- Use of river for washing clothes and bathing

- Emptying highly chlorinated water from swimming pools

Access to safe water

Safe water is water that is safe for human consumption. It is not contaminated by pollutants and is free from disease. It is estimated that more than 1 billion people in the world do not have access to safe water.

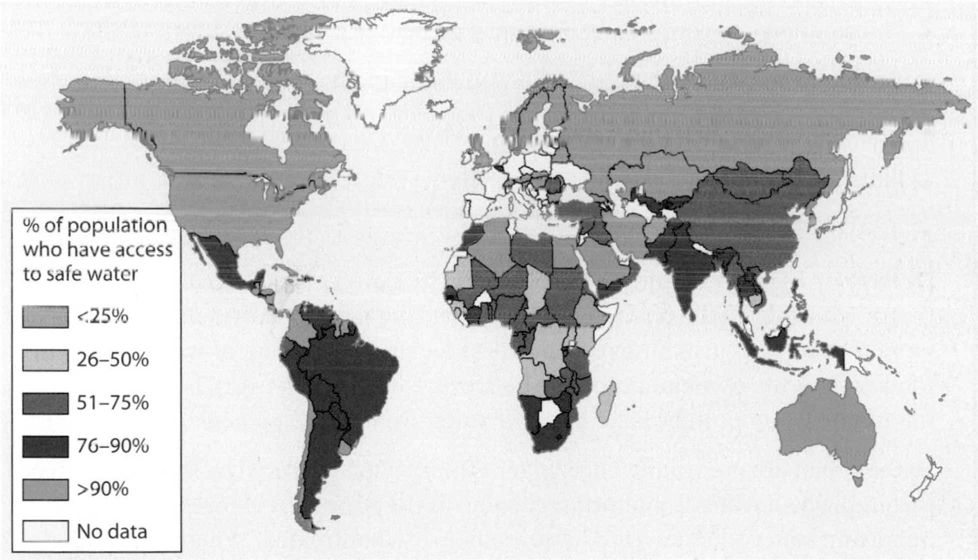

Figure 1.31: *Access to safe water*

Figure 1.31 shows that the countries with the lowest access to clean water (i.e. less than 50% of the population enjoying safe water) are mainly located in Africa and in parts of southern Asia. As a consequence, many people suffer ill health and an early death. In most HICs, more than 90% of the population have access to clean water. It is surprising that the map shows there is no data about clean water for a number of European countries.

Can you think of ways in which recreation and tourism pollute water?

Describe the main features shown by Figure 1.31.

Figure 1.32: *Three stages in the supply of clean water – collection (reservoir), treatment (waterworks) and delivery (standpipe)*

Managing the supply of clean water

Managing the supply of clean water involves three main stages (Figure 1.32):

Collection – Reference has already been made in Part **1.6** to the main sources of water, namely:

- rivers
- reservoirs and lakes
- aquifers and wells.

This is where water is collected from.

Treatment – It is very rare to use water that does not need some form of purification. Rivers are often highly polluted. Reservoir water can be polluted by falls of acid rain and the seepage of pollutants from surrounding hillsides. Groundwater used to be thought of as being pure. However, it is now known that such water can be badly contaminated by chemicals in the rocks. In parts of Bangladesh, groundwater is contaminated by arsenic, a highly toxic chemical.

Water treatment aims to remove pollutants from the 'raw' collected water and so produce water that is pure enough for human consumption (Figure 1.32). Substances that are removed during the process of drinking water treatment include suspended solids (e.g. silt, soil), bacteria, algae, viruses, fungi, minerals (e.g. iron, manganese and sulphur), and synthetic chemical pollutants (e.g. fertilisers).

A combination of processes is used worldwide in the treatment of water for human consumption. The combination varies according to the nature of the raw water. The processes include:

- chlorination – to control any biological growth (e.g. algae)
- aeration – to remove dissolved iron and manganese
- sedimentation – to remove suspended solids
- filtration – to remove very fine sediments
- disinfection – to kill bacteria.

Delivery – In many countries, particularly HICs, water is delivered from the treatment works to the point of consumption (the home, factory, etc.) by means of pipes. The costs of installing pipe networks for the distribution of water are high, so too are the costs of maintaining the network. Unless the network is properly maintained, there can be large losses of water from leaking pipes.

In the urban areas of many LICs, water is more often delivered by standpipes (pipes through which water is pumped vertically) in the streets. In villages, wells are important water sources. Often well water is used untreated. Where water is collected in buckets and carried from a well or standpipe into the home, there are further risks of pollution. Buckets and plastic containers may be dirty. Water left in open buckets in the home are vulnerable to pollution by dust, insects and animals. A universal problem with the delivery of water by standpipes and wells is the time spent collecting the water (Figure 1.32).

There is a fourth and relatively new way of delivering water – in plastic bottles filled at a source such as a spring. This is a very expensive way to deliver water because of the cost of the plastic containers, and of filling and transporting them to the point of sale. It is interesting to note that the biggest sales of bottled water occur in HICs. Some people are worried that drinking piped domestic water might be risky. In other words, they are concerned about water quality and the efficiency of water treatment, even in HICs.

Water management is not just about ensuring a good supply of clean water. Dams and reservoirs can serve a number of different purposes, such as generating electricity, supplying irrigation water, flood control and improving navigation. This multi-purpose use of water, or river management is well illustrated by the Three Gorges Dam project in China.

What do you think are the advantages and disadvantages of bottled water?

Case study: The Three Gorges Dam project (China)

The project, started in 1997, has been undertaken mainly for electricity production and flood control. Figure 1.33 shows the location of the project in the middle of China and on its longest river, the Yangtze. The dam was finished in 2009 and is the largest in the world. It is 185 m high and almost 2 km wide. The reservoir of water that will build up behind the dam is expected to be up to 600 km long. Hydro-electric generators at the dam will produce about 10% of China's present electricity needs. China badly needs this electricity if it is to continue to industrialise. In the interests of reducing global warming, China needs to burn less coal.

In what ways will the Three Gorges Dam project help the growth of industry in China?

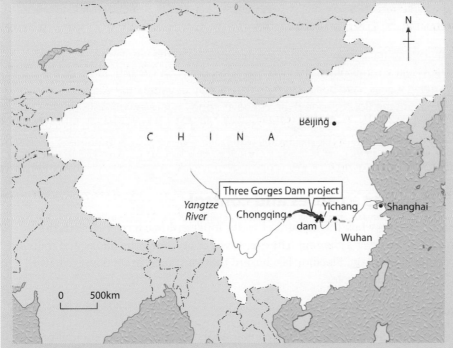

Figure 1.33: *The location of the Three Gorges Dam project*

The major disadvantage of building such a massive reservoir is that more than 1 million people have lost their homes and had to be resettled. By the time it is full, the reservoir will have drowned 13 cities, 140 towns and 1350 villages. The flooding of the Yangtze valley has meant losing some of the country's best and most fertile farmland. It is also likely that silt will be trapped behind the dam, making the farmland lower down the Yangtze less fertile over time.

Chapter 1: River environments

25

Tonnes of industrial and human waste will also be trapped behind the dam. A major concern is whether the dam will be able to withstand the earthquakes that often occur in this part of China. If the dam were to collapse many millions of people would die.

Figure 1.34: *The completed Three Gorges Dam*

Environmentalists have questioned the wisdom of the whole project. They argue that a series of smaller hydro-electric dams on the tributaries of the Yangtze would have been a more efficient way of generating electricity and managing the flood-prone river. However, one long reservoir does offer improved, year-round navigation, as well as water for industry and agriculture. Any domestic use of the reservoir's water will require proper treatment.

Make a list of the disadvantages of the Three Gorges Dam project.

1.8 Flooding – causes and control

Flooding occurs when the amount of water moving down a river exceeds the capacity of the river's channel. The excess water overflows the banks and spills out across the flood plain. Flooding is a hazard that can cause great damage to the environment and people.

Causes

Rivers usually flood as a result of a combination of causes. This combination can involve both natural (physical) and human factors. In many cases, natural flooding is made worse by people and their activities.

Most flooding is related to spells of very heavy rainfall. The critical factor is how quickly this rainfall reaches the river from where it falls on surrounding land and mountains. The shorter the lag time (see Figure 1.8 on page 6) and therefore the faster it does so, the greater the chances of flooding.

FACTOR	
Physical	**Impact**
Weather	Intense rainfall greater than the infiltration capacity of the ground. Prolonged rainfall leading to saturation of the ground. Rapid snow melt as temperatures suddenly rise above freezing
Rock	Impermeable rocks limiting percolation and encouraging rapid surface run off or overland flow
Soil	Low infiltration rate in certain soils, e.g. clays
Relief	Steep slopes causing fast run off
Drainage density	High drainage density means many tributary streams carry the rainwater quickly to the main river
Vegetation	Low density vegetation absorbs little water and does not seriously impede run off
Human	
Deforestation	Cutting down trees reduces interception and speeds up run off
Urbanisation	Concrete and tarmac surfaces together with drains mean quicker delivery of rainwater to the river
Agriculture	The risk of flooding increased by leaving the soil bare, overgrazing, monoculture and ploughing down rather than across slopes
Climate change	Increasing temperatures, partly due to the burning of fossil fuels, cause more melting of ice sheets and glaciers, as well as more rainfall and more frequent storms

Table 1.3: *Factors causing flooding*

Which of the factors in Table 1.3 are likely to have the greatest effect on lag times? It would help if you were to look back to page 6 about the storm hydrograph.

Table 1.3 lists some of the factors that reduce the lag time and therefore increase the chances of flooding.

Reduction in lag time

Flooding can also result from persistent rain over a relatively long period of time. Gradually, the water table (level of water underground) rises and the soil becomes saturated. Downward infiltration ceases and water simply accumulates in shallow depressions and on low-lying land.

Figure 1.35: *Floods in Sheffield, June 2007*

The difference between these three floods is that the Sheffield flood resulted from several days of persistently heavy rainfall. The Lynmouth and Boscastle floods resulted from much more intense rainfall occurring over an upland area in a shorter time.

In June 2007, the city of Sheffield in the UK received 269 mm of rain. The average total rainfall for that month is normally 67 mm. Sixty percent of that June rainfall fell in just three days. The fact that this rainfall fell on an impermeable urban surface located in a hollow at the foot of the steep-sided Pennine Hills greatly increased the seriousness of the flooding when the River Don burst its banks (Figure 1.35). Summer floods are relatively uncommon in the UK, but those that do occur seem to have a greater impact. Notable examples include the floods at Lynmouth, Devon (August, 1952) and Boscastle, Cornwall (August, 2004).

Consequences of floods

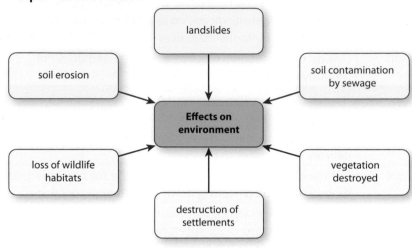

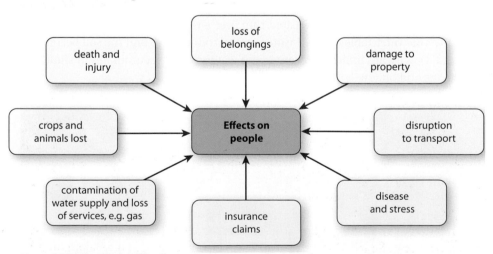

Figure 1.36: *The effects of flooding on the environment and people*

Figure 1.36 shows some of the more common impacts of flooding. River floods can certainly cause a lot of damage. As with all natural hazards, there are both immediate and long-term effects. The immediate effects of a flood on people include loss of life, destruction of property and crops, homelessness, the disruption of transport and communications and the loss of water supply and sewage disposal services.

In the longer term, there is the cost of replacing what has been lost and damaged. One particular challenge is removing the huge amounts of silt deposited by the floodwaters as they go down. In HICs the risks may be covered by insurance. In the case of the Sheffield flood in 2007, the estimated repair bill was £30 million. Two-thirds of this was needed for repairing damaged roads. Repairing some 1200 damaged homes cost over £3 million. The sums involved in fixing up the damage caused by this localised flood are nothing like the estimated costs of the great Mississippi flood in the same year. The cost of repairs here amounted to around $150 billion.

The poor in LICs, however, may lose everything in floods. With cropland ruined and animals lost, widespread famine can result. Stagnant floodwater polluted by human excrement can also become a serious health hazard. It is in these conditions that diseases like typhoid and cholera thrive. The need for emergency food and health aid in these circumstances becomes urgent. The best hope of recovery lies in the help provided by international aid organisations.

> Suggest reasons why floods in HICs are often more costly than those in LICs.

Control

Flood control and flood management can involve three different types of action (Figure 1.37).

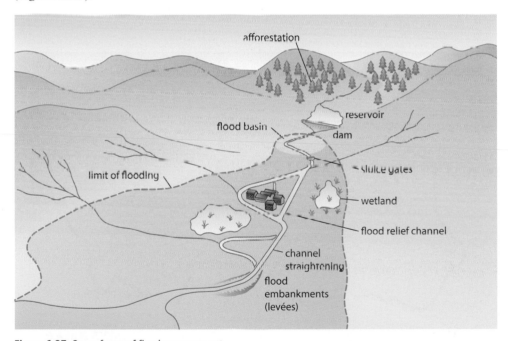

Figure 1.37: *Some forms of flood management*

Construction – This is the building of **hard-engineering** structures such as dams, flood embankments (raised artificial banks), sluice gates and relief channels (spillways). Basically these structures either hold back or help to safely dispose of flood water. These structures are generally expensive to build.

Adjustment or **mitigation** – There is an increasing trend towards flood control schemes that try to avoid or minimise potential flood damage. In other words, it requires working with nature rather than against it. This is sometimes referred as the **soft-engineering** approach to flood control. For example, it might involve

> It is important that you are clear about:
>
> - the difference between hard engineering and soft engineering
> - why soft engineering is more environmentally friendly.

restoring a river to its natural state or preserving marshes and wetlands on flood plains to act as valuable temporary stores of floodwater (like sponges). Other actions include stricter planning controls to ensure that there is little building on the flood plain. People in flood-risk areas should be encouraged to take out flood insurance. Putting in place better flood warning systems would help; so too would publicising what to do in an emergency.

Prediction – Prediction of river floods (their extent and depth) is important to flood control. Knowing how high, or wide a river can flood, helps people to decide, for example, how high river embankments need to be built. It also helps to avoid building houses, factories and services in areas of where there is a high risk of flooding.

The problem with prediction is that floods vary. Small floods are likely to occur fairly regularly – say, once every five years. Large floods may be expected less frequently – possibly once every 50 years. Perhaps once every 1000 years there will be truly exceptional flood of a huge scale. The question for river managers is to decide for which level of flood they should provide protection. This is known as **risk assessment**. Protecting against the regular five-year flood is going to be relatively cheap and easy. However, is it worth investing huge sums of money to provide protection against the hugely damaging 'once-in-a-1000-years flood'? In many cases, river managers will take a middle course and aim to be able to deal with the medium threats of the 50 to 100-year floods. Clearly, where the risk is under assessed, protection is likely to prove inadequate.

How might improved weather forecasting help the prediction of floods?

Case study: Flood management in Bangladesh

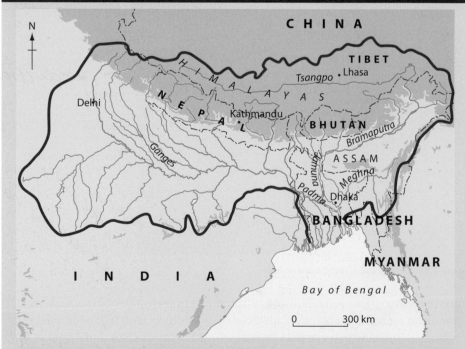

Figure 1.38: *Catchment area of the rivers of Bangladesh*

Eighty percent of Bangladesh and 90% of its over 150 million people live less than one metre above sea-level on the floodplains and delta of three very large rivers – the Ganges, Brahmaputra and Meghna (Figure 1.38). Bangladesh is the world's most flood-affected country. Flood management in this LIC is literally a matter of life or death. Major causes of the annual flooding include the monsoon climate with its heavy summer rainfall and tropical storms with the tidal surges that they cause. Melting Himalayan snow in summer and deforestation in Nepal are two other flood risk factors.

The Bangladeshi Flood Action Plan (FAP) funded by the World Bank began in 1990 and involves:

- building up embankments to protect the main cities, towns, roads and farmland (Figure 1.39)
- dredging channels that have been silted up so that they hold more floodwater
- straightening river channels to prevent erosion of banks or meanders
- constructing dams upstream to control flood waters before they reach the delta
- allowing controlled release of floodwater from river channels via spillways that have been constructed to allow the controlled release of flooding waters
- building huge reservoirs to hold some of the floodwater
- improving flood forecasting and public warning transmission systems
- building emergency shelters on areas of slightly higher ground.

The FAP involves a mix of hard- and soft-engineering action, but more of the former. It is a long-term project and will continue to require more funds than the Bangladeshi government can afford. Achieving effective flood management there is being made more challenging by two developments:

- the threat of global warming – it only needs a slight rise in sea level in the Bay of Bengal and much of Bangladesh will be flooded by the sea. Bangladesh badly needs to improve its coastal defences. On top of that, any rise in sea level will make it even more difficult for Bangladesh to get rid of its floodwater

- the three rivers of the Bangladesh's delta area all flow for considerable distances through neighbouring India (Figure 1.38). Relations between Bangladesh and India are not always good. India could help Bangladesh by improving control of the floodwaters of these rivers before they reach Bangladesh. Equally India could pass the floodwaters on at an even faster rate and increase even more the flood risks in Bangladesh.

causes

Prone to flooding stopping is impossible we need a balance.

ending Increased urbanisation they need to learn how to deal with this

In your own words, suggest a definition for the term ' flood management'.

Figure 1.39: *Mud embankments being built by hand*

End of chapter checkout

Checklists

Now you have read the chapter, you should know:

- ✓ how water moves between the land, sea and air in the hydrological cycle
- ✓ the main features of a drainage basin
- ✓ how to interpret what a hydrograph shows
- ✓ what a river regime is, and the factors affecting it
- ✓ how running water affects the development of landforms through the processes of erosion, transport and deposition
- ✓ how valleys and their distinctive features are formed
- ✓ the importance of water in our everyday lives
- ✓ the reasons for the rising demand for water
- ✓ why there are areas of water shortage and water surplus
- ✓ the reasons why water quality varies
- ✓ the main sources of water pollution
- ✓ how water is treated and delivered to consumers
- ✓ the causes of flooding
- ✓ how the risk of flooding is controlled

Make sure you understand these key terms:

Abstraction: the taking of water from rivers, lakes and from below the watertable.

Base flow: the usual level of a river.

Channel network: the pattern of linked streams and rivers within a drainage basin.

Dam: a large structure, usually of concrete, sometimes earth, built across a river to hold back a large body of water (reservoir) for human use.

Discharge: the quantity of water flowing in a river channel at a particular location and time.

Erosion: the wearing away and removal of material by a moving force, such as running water.

Deposition: the dropping of material that was being carried by a moving force, such as running water.

Flood plain: the flat land lying either side of a river which periodically floods.

Hydrograph: a graph showing the discharge of a river over a given period of time.

Hydrological cycle: the global movement of water between the air, land and sea.

Interlocking spur: a series of ridges projecting out on alternate sides of a valley and around which a river winds.

Levee: a raised bank of material deposited by a river during periods of flooding.

Mass movement: the movement of weathered material down a slope due to the force of gravity.

Meander: a winding curve in a river's course.

Oxbow: a horseshoe-shaped lake once part of a meandering river, but now cut off from it.

Pollution: the presence of chemicals, dirt or other substances which have harmful or poisonous effects on aspects of the environment, such as rivers and the air.

Reservoir: an area where water is collected and stored for human use.

River regime: the seasonal variations in the discharge of a river.

Stores: features, such as lakes, rivers and aquifers, that receive, hold and release water.

Stormflow: the increase in stream velocity caused by a period of intense rainfall.

Stream velocity: the speed at which water is flowing in a river channel at a given location and time.

Transfers: the movement of water between stores in the hydrological cycle.

Transport: the movement of a river's load.

Waterfall: where a river's water falls vertically, as where a band of hard rock runs across the river channel.

Watershed: the boundary between neighbouring drainage basins.

Weathering: the breakdown and decay of rock by natural processes, without the involvement of any moving force.

See the Glossary in the ActiveBook for more definitions

Questions

Try testing yourself with these questions:

1. Draw a simplified labelled diagram of the hydrological cycle.
2. a) What is the difference between a 'store' and a 'flow'?
   b) Name the three main stores of the hydrological cycle.
   c) Name six different types of flow.
3. a) Name two inputs and two outputs of the drainage basin cycle.
   b) What is:
      - a watershed
      - a confluence?
4. Explain how each of the following affects the drainage network:
   - rock type
   - land use.
5. a) What is meant by the term 'lag time'?
   b) Describe how lag time is affected by each of following factors:
      - slope
      - temperature
      - precipitation
      - vegetation.
6. Referring to Figures 1.6 and 1.7, compare the regime of the Ganges with that of the Thames.
7. a) What is the difference between 'weathering' and 'mass movement'?
   b) Describe the four main ways that rivers transport load.
8. a) How does a river change when it leaves an upland area?
   b) Why is deposition greater along the lowland section of a river?
9. a) What processes are responsible for the formation of a V-shaped valley?
   b) Describe three other landforms produced by rivers in upland areas.
10. Draw a simplified, labelled diagram to show how meanders and ox-bows are formed.
11. Compare estuaries and deltas in terms of the way they are formed.

12. a) Using Figure 1.21, draw a sketch map of the River Tay estuary east of easting 20.
    b) On your sketch map, show and label four features commonly found in a river estuary.
    c) What are the advantages and disadvantages of this estuary for shipping?
13. a) What are the five main uses of fresh water?
    b) What are the main sources of fresh water?
14. Why has the demand for water increased so much over the last 100 years?
15. Why is water quality so important?
16. Explain how *a)* industry and *b)* agriculture pollute water.
17. Give four other causes of river pollution.
18. Draw a labelled diagram to show the stages in managing the supply of clean water.
19. a) Make a two-column list of the benefits and costs of the Three Gorges Dam project in China.
    b) Which of the two columns do you think is more important? Give your reasons.
20. a) Identify four physical factors that help cause flooding.
    b) Explain how deforestation and urbanisation also cause flooding.
21. Give examples of *a)* the short-term and *b)* the long-term consequences of flooding.
22. a) What is meant by the term 'flood adjustment'?
    b) What is the difference between 'soft' and 'hard' engineering in the management of floods?

Chapter 2: Coastal environments

2.1 The coast as a system

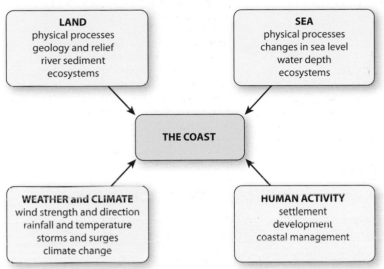

Figure 2.1: Factors affecting the coast

Introduction

This chapter looks at the coast, its landforms and the processes that produce them. Vital parts of the coast are its ecosystems. They are rich in biodiversity and resources. The exploitation of these resources is threatening their survival. This is just one of number of conflicts occurring as development and conservation come face to face. The need for proper management of the coast is great.

The coast, like the drainage basin, is an open system. It involves inputs, flows (processes), stores and outputs (for more on this, see Figure 2.31 on page 54). The coast is the transition zone between the land and the sea. The **coastline** is the actual frontier between the two. The coast is therefore made up of two parts – onshore and offshore – located either side of the coastline. The onshore zone can extend up to 60 km inland. The offshore zone reaches as far as 370 km out to sea.

Beyond the offshore zone lie what are known as 'international waters'. They belong to, and are shared by the global community of all nations.

The coasts of the world are very diverse in terms of their landscapes and **ecosystems**. Figure 2.1 identifies the main factors behind these differences. The diagram reminds us that coasts are the meeting point of not just land and sea, but also the atmosphere. Because of this, weather and climate are important factors. Human **settlement** and **development** add to the coastal diversity.

The physical processes shaping the landforms of the coastline fall into two groups: **marine** (sea) and **terrestrial** (land).

Marine processes

Waves do much of the work of marine processes. They erode, transport and deposit materials. Waves are created by winds as they blow over the surface of the sea. It is the friction between the wind and the water that sets waves in motion. The strength of waves depends on the strength of the wind. It also depends on the length of time and distance over which the wind has been blowing (**the fetch**).

As waves near the coast, they enter into shallower water. Friction with the sea bed causes the wave to tip forward so that it eventually breaks. The resulting forward movement of water, called the **swash**, runs up the **beach** until it runs out of energy. The water then runs back down the beach under gravity. This is called the **backwash**.

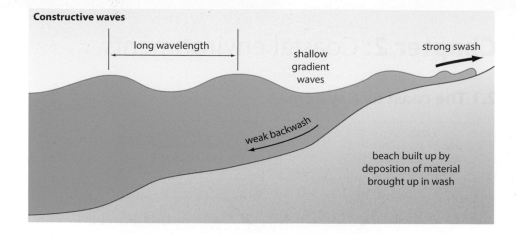

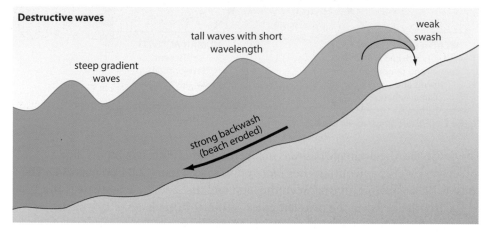

Figure 2.2: *Constructive and destructive waves*

The balance between the swash and backwash of waves creates the difference between **constructive** and **destructive** waves (Figure 2.2). In **constructive waves**, the swash is stronger than the backwash. As a result, material is moved up the beach and much is left there (deposition). In **destructive waves**, the backwash is stronger. Material is dragged back down the beach (**erosion**) and moved along the coast by **longshore drift** (transport).

It is destructive waves that do much of the erosion along a coast. They cut away at the coastline in a number of different ways:

- **hydraulic action** – this results from the force of the waves hitting the cliffs and forcing pockets of air into cracks and crevices
- **abrasion** – this is caused by waves picking up stones and hurling them at cliffs and so wearing the cliff away
- **corrosion** – the dissolving of rocks by sea water.

Attrition is a process whereby the material carried by the waves becomes rounded and smaller over time as it collides with other material. It does not erode the coast as such but does form small pebbles and sand.

Be sure you know the difference between the following pairings:

- marine and terrestrial
- swash and backwash
- constructive and destructive waves
- abrasion and attrition.

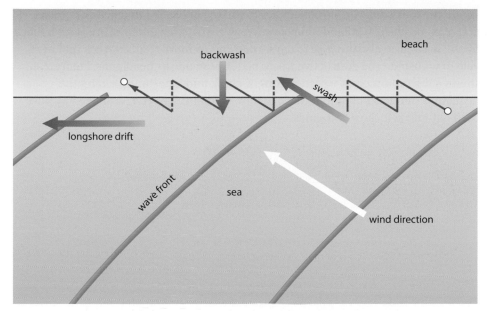

Figure 2.3: *The process of longshore drift*

Once rocks and sand are detached from the cliff, waves can move them along the coastline for quite long distances. This process is known as **longshore drift** (Figure 2.3). Generally speaking, the smaller the material, the further it is likely to be moved by waves as it is lighter. Eventually, the waves are unable to move so much material and the material will be deposited to create new landforms.

Smaller or lighter materials will be moved further by waves because they need less wave energy to transport them

Land processes

There are three main processes at work on the landward side of the coastline:

- **weathering** – the breakdown of rocks which is caused by freeze-thaw and the growth of salt crystals, by acid rain and by the growth of vegetation roots
- **erosion** – the wearing away of rocks by wind and rain
- **mass movement** – the removal of cliff-face material under the influence of gravity in the form of rock falls, slumping and landslides.

2.2 Coastal landforms

The interaction of the processes described in Part **2.1** produces a variety of different coastal landforms. These landforms are broadly divided into those that result from coastal erosion and those due to coastal deposition.

Erosional landforms

By far the most common coastal landforms are the alternations of **headlands** and **bays** which give many coastlines their irregular appearance. Destructive waves clearly play an important role in their formation. The nature of the coastal rocks also plays a part. The direction in which rocks occur in relation to the coastline affects the resulting landforms. Coasts where the rock outcrops run parallel to the sea are called **concordant coasts** and often produce straighter coastlines. Coasts where the rocks outcrop at right angles to the sea are called **discordant coasts** and often produce headlands and bays. Weak rocks, such as clays, are easily eroded by the sea and so also give rise to bays. Outcrops of more resistant rock that are able to withstand the destructive waves better protrude as headlands. Figure 2.4 shows a discordant coast with outcrops of chalk and limestone forming the headlands (land jutting into the sea), whilst Studland Bay and Swanage Bay have been cut into soft clays and sands.

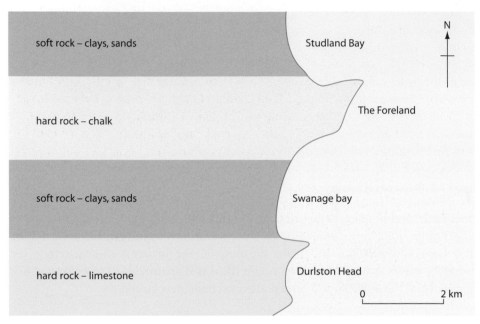

Figure 2.4: *Sketch map of part of the Purbeck coast, southern England*

What is the difference between a concordant coast and a discordant coast?

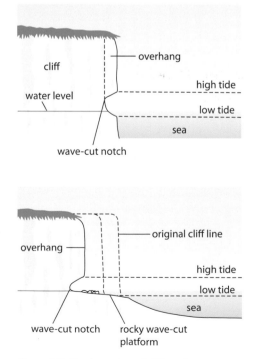

Figure 2.5: *The formation of cliffs and wave-cut platforms*

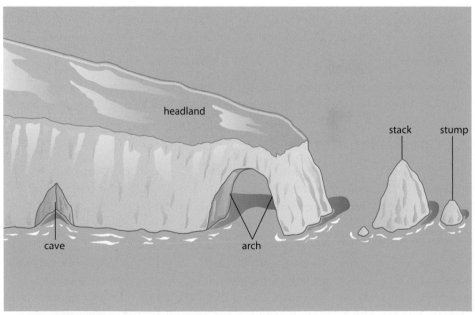

Figure 2.6: *The formation of caves, arches, stacks and stumps*

Most headlands are defined by **cliffs**. Where these cliffs rise steeply from the sea, the repeated breaking of destructive waves leads to them being undercut at the base. A **wave-cut notch** is formed (Figure 2.5). Undercutting weakens the rock above the notch and it eventually collapses. Thus the cliff face retreats but its steep face is maintained. The retreat of the cliff leads to the formation of a gently sloping **wave-cut platform** at the base.

Caves, **arches**, **stacks** and **stumps** also form on the sides of headlands as a result of constant attack on the rocks of the headlands by destructive waves (Figure 2.6). Any points of weakness in the headland's rocks, such as faults or joints are attacked, particularly by hydraulic action and abrasion. This is likely to lead to the opening up of a **cave**. If the cave is enlarged and extends back through to the other side of the headland, possibly meeting another cave, an **arch** is formed. Continued erosion by the sea widens the arch. As the sea undercuts the pillars of the arch, the roof is weakened and eventually collapses. This leaves a **stack** separated from the headland. Further erosion at the base of the stack may eventually cause it too to collapse. This will leave a small, flat portion of the original stack as a **stump**. It may only be visible at low tide.

Figure 2.7: *Old Harry Rocks, southern England*

On Figure 2.7 identify:

- a cave
- an arch
- a stack.

An excellent example of these erosional features is Old Harry Rocks (Figure 2.7) at the end of the chalk headland separating Swanage Bay from Studland Bay in southern England (Figure 2.4).

Depositional landforms

Depositional landforms are produced on coastlines where mud, sand and shingle accumulate faster than they can be moved away by the waves. This usually happens along stretches of coastline dominated by constructive waves (where the swash of water coming onto the beach is stronger than the backwash).

Beaches are the most common depositional landform. They result from the accumulation of material deposited between the storm- and low-tide marks. The sand, shingle and pebbles come from a number of sources. Much of it is material that has been eroded elsewhere and that is being moved along the coast by longshore drift. Some comes from offshore as a result of waves picking it up from the sea bed and rolling it in towards the land. From the opposite direction, rivers feed mud and silt into the coastal zone via their estuaries (mouths). The deposition of this river material then takes place at the heads of sheltered bays.

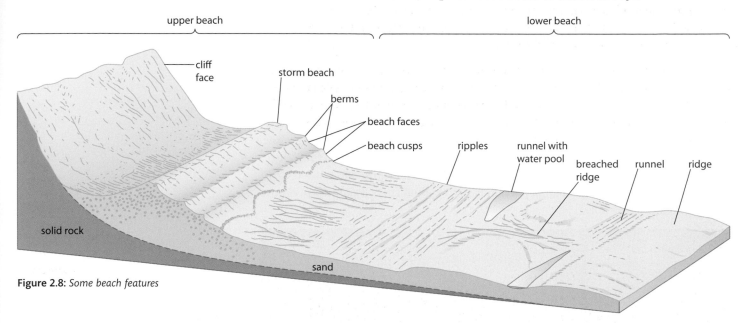

Figure 2.8: *Some beach features*

Many beaches show a number of very small features (Figure 2.8). For example, at the top end there will be a **storm beach** made up of large material thrown up during storm conditions. A series of small ridges, known as **berms**, mark the positions of mean (average) high-tide marks. Beach cusps – small semicircular depressions – are formed by the movement of the swash and backwash of waves up and down the beach. In general, the finer the beach material, the more gently inclined the overall beach.

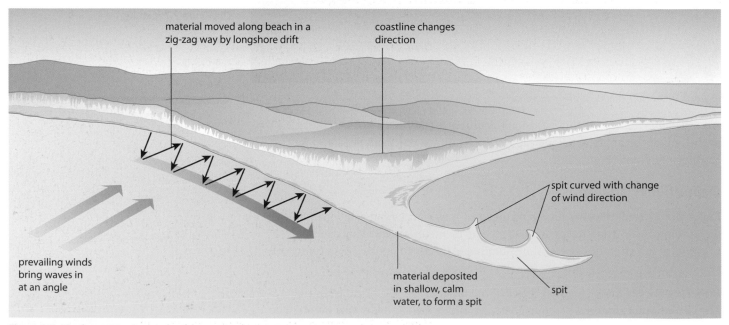

Figure 2.9: *The formation of a spit*

Spits are long narrow beaches of sand or shingle that are attached to the land at one end. They extend across a bay, an **estuary** or where the coastline changes direction. They are generally formed by longshore drift in one dominant direction (Figure 2.9). At the end of the beach, the material being transported by longshore drift is deposited. At a river estuary, the growth of the spit also causes the river to drop its sediment. This occurs mainly on the landward side (rather than the seaward side) of the spit and salt marshes may form. The waves and wind may curve the end of the spit towards the land.

If a spit develops in a bay, it may build across it and link the two headlands to form a **bar**. The formation of a bar is only possible if there is a gently sloping beach and no sizeable river is entering the bay. In this way, bars can straighten the coast and any water on the landward side is trapped to form a **lagoon**. A classic example is to be found at Slapton in southern England (Figure 2.10).

Figure 2.11: Chesil Beach, southern England

Figure 2.10: Slapton Ley showing the lagoon to the left of the bar

Tombolos are spits that have continued to grow seawards until they reach and join an island. The 30km long Chesil Beach on the south coast of England links the isle of Portland to the mainland (Figure 2.11). The formation of this tombolo was due, not only to longshore drift, but also by offshore sediments being rolled towards the coast.

Cuspate forelands are triangular-shaped accumulations of sand and shingle that extend seawards (Figure 2.12). It seems likely that many of them develop as a result of longshore drift occurring from two different directions. At a change in the direction of a coastline, sediment will be brought from both directions, causing the cuspate foreland to develop.

Figure 2.12: The cuspate foreland at Dungeness, southern England

Sand dunes are depositional landforms in coastal areas. However, their formation is only indirectly related to coastal processes. Beaches are the source of the sand which, when dry, is blown inland by the wind to form dunes. Over long periods of time, the wind blows the sand up into a series of ridges running parallel to the coastline. Gradually the older ridges become colonised by vegetation and this helps to stabilise them (see Figure 2.23 on page 47).

Figure 2.13: *A stretch of the Jurassic coast*

Make a simple tracing of Figure 2.13. Identify and label as many coastal features you are able to recognise. Do look closely at the beach.

Research why the Jurassic coast of southern England has been recognised as a World Heritage Site.

Finally, we need to realise that many of these coastal landforms are put to good use by people. They offer opportunities that are exploited by various economic activities. For example, sandy beaches and the many stretches of fine scenery are exploited by tourism, as along the Jurassic coast of southern England (Figure 2.13). This is now designated a World Heritage site. Some of the world's most famous golf courses are laid out on sand dunes. Marinas are being built on the shores of estuary mouths sheltered by spits. Exposed coasts are now being used by wind farms. Nuclear and thermal power stations at the coast are further evidence of the energy industry exploiting these areas (Figure 2.12). More examples of human use of the coast follow in Part **2.3**, and the resulting conflicts are explored in Part **2.6**.

2.3 Factors affecting coasts

Figure 2.1 on page 33 showed that there are other factors besides coastal and land processes affecting the coast, particularly the coastline and its landforms.

Geology

As shown in Figure 2.4 on page 36 the difference between hard and soft rocks is a strong influence on the shape of the coastline. A coastline made up of weak rocks, such as clays and sands, will be easily eroded back by destructive waves. Bays will be created. Coastlines of more resistant, harder rock will not be eroded so quickly.

They often jut out into the sea, often as headlands. The difference between hard and soft rocks will also have an impact on the shape and characteristics of cliffs (Table 2.1).

	Hard rocks	Soft rocks
Shape of cliffs	High and steep	Generally lower and less steep
Cliff face	Bare rock and rugged	Smoother; evidence of slumping
Foot of cliff	Boulders and rocks	Few rocks; some sand and mud

Table 2.1: Contrasts between cliffs made of hard and of soft rocks

So geology affects the coastline in two different ways:

- in plan view – headlands and bays
- in vertical section – the height and shape of cliffs.

Vegetation

In general, the longer a coastal landform, such as a sand dune, has existed, the greater the chances that it will be colonised by vegetation. In order to survive, the vegetation has to be able to cope with the particular conditions, such as high levels of salt in both the air and the soil. The major impact of vegetation is to help protect and preserve coastal landforms. This is well shown in the cases of sand dunes (see Figure 2.24 on page 48) and mangrove swamps (see Figure 2.20 on page 45).

Sea-level changes

One of the obvious effects of global warming and climate change is that low-lying coasts will be drowned by rising sea levels. This problem will be made worse by the fact that many of the world's most densely populated areas are located on coastal lowlands (see also Chapter **7.8** on page 200). In fact, rising sea levels are nothing new. During the Ice Age, sea levels also changed, but to a much greater extent. They fell as more and more of the world's water was locked up in ice sheets and glaciers. The sea levels then rose again as the ice sheets and glaciers melted.

Figure 2.14: A fjord in Norway

Figure 2.15: *A raised beach*

A rising sea-level gives rise to what is called a **submergent coastline**. The main features are **rias** (drowned river valleys) and **fjords** (drowned glacial valleys) (Figure 2.14).

An **emergent coastline** is associated with a falling sea level. The most common landforms are **raised beaches** (Figure 2.15). These are areas of wave-cut platform and their beaches now found at a level higher than the present sea level. In some places, **relict cliffs** with caves, arches and stacks are found where there are raised beaches.

Human activities

Human activities can have significant effects on sea processes and also on the character of the coast. At this stage, we need only identify the main ones. They will be explored and explained in more detail in later sections of this chapter. The main ways include:

- **settlement** – coastal lowlands have proved attractive to people and their settlements throughout history and throughout much of the world. Many of the world's most densely populated areas are located on the coast,

- **economic development** – people have taken advantage of the particular economic opportunities that the coast offers, such as land for agriculture and industy (Figure 2.16). Fishing and the chance to trade either along the coast or overseas lead to the building of ports and harbours. As was illustrated at the end of Part **2.2**, the coast is often used for tourism and in the energy business,

- **coastal management** – for many centuries, people have sought to control the coastline, for example, by protecting stretches of coastline from high rates of either erosion or deposition by building sea walls and groynes (see Figure 2.37 on page 59).

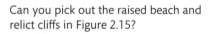

Can you pick out the raised beach and relict cliffs in Figure 2.15?

Why is the coast attractive to human settlement and development?

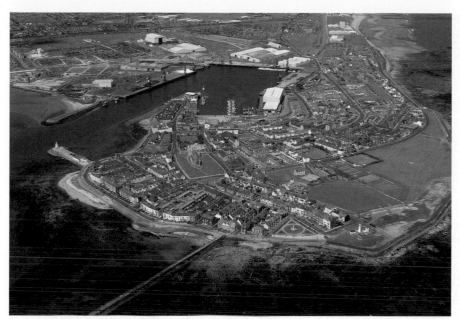

Figure 2.16: *Coastal development*

Look closely at Figure 2.16. What different land uses can you identify?

As a result of these and other human activities, the natural landscapes and features of the coast can be greatly changed. So too the actual shape of the coastline.

2.4 Coastal ecosystems and their distributions

Given the large amounts of development and settlement which have taken place in the coastal areas of the world, it is easy to forget that the coast is home to a variety of ecosystems. In their natural state, coasts can be very rich in **biodiversity**. In this section, we will look at four different ecosystems. Two of them, coral reefs and mangroves, have tropical distributions. The other two, salt marshes and sand dunes are common across the world.

Coral reefs

Coral reefs are a unique marine ecosystem. They are built up entirely of living organisms (Figure 2.17). Reefs are huge deposits of calcium carbonate made up mainly of corals. Their global distribution is shown in Figure 2.18. It is mainly controlled by four factors:

- **temperature** – coral growth needs a minimum water temperature of 18°C. They grow best between 23°C and 25°C

- **light** – is needed for the coral to grow; because of this need, corals grow only in shallow water

- **water depth** – because of the need for light, most reefs grow where the sea is less than 25 metres deep

- **salinity** – since corals are marine creatures, they can only survive in salt water.

Figure 2.17: *Section of a coral reef*

At a local level, there are other factors affecting where coral reefs develop:

- **wave action** – corals need well oxygenated salt water; this occurs in areas of strong wave action

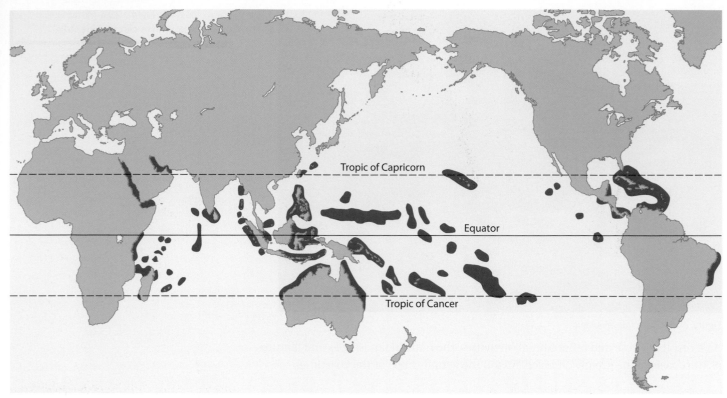

Figure 2.18: *The global distribution of coral reefs*

Many coral reefs take the form of horseshoe-shaped rings enclosing a lagoon. In this form, they are known as 'atolls'.

- **exposure to air** – whilst corals need oxygenated water, if they are exposed to the air for too long they die

- **sediment** – corals need clear, clean water. Any sediment in the water blocks their normal ways of feeding. Sediment also reduces the amount of light.

Coral reefs with the highest biodiversity occur in South-east Asia and northern Australia. The Great Barrier Reef is in Australia and is renowned not just for its great **biodiversity**, but also its extent and excellent condition.

Mangroves

Mangroves are most common in South-East Asia (Figure 2.19). It is thought that they originated here and subsequently spread around the globe. Today, most mangroves are found within 30 degrees latitude of the Equator, but a few hardy types have adapted to temperate climates. They reach as far as the North Island of New Zealand.

Mangroves literally live on the coastline – they have one 'foot' on the land and the other in the sea. Because they grow in the intertidal zone, they live in a constantly changing environment. They are regularly flooded by the sea. At low tide, especially during periods of high rainfall, there may be floods of fresh water. This quickly alters the salt levels, as well as temperatures. Mangroves are not only able to survive these changing water conditions, they can cope with great heat and choking mud.

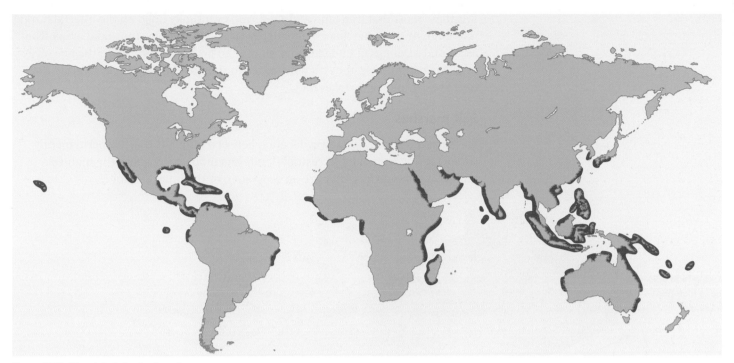

Figure 2.19: *The global distribution of mangroves*

Despite these environmental difficulties, the mangrove ecosystem is among the most successful ecosystems on Earth. South-East Asia also boasts mangroves with the highest biodiversity in the world. There are many species of mangrove. They range in size from small shrubs to trees over 60 metres in height. They are all clever at adapting to their environment. Each mangrove has an filtration system to keep much of the salt out and a complex root system that is adapted for survival in the intertidal zone. Some have snorkel-like roots that stick out of the mud to help them take in air; others use prop roots or buttresses to keep their trunks upright in the soft sediments at tidal edge, as in Figure 2.20.

Identify the main features of the global distribution of mangroves shown in Figure 2.19. In what ways is the distribution similar or different to that of coral reefs (Figure 2.18)?

Figure 2.20: *A belt of mangrove*

It is these roots that trap mud and sand, and eventually build up the intertidal zone into land. At the same time, the mangrove is colonising new intertidal areas. The fruits and seedlings of all mangrove plants can float. As they drift in the tide away from the parent trees, they become lodged in mud where they begin to grow. So a new area of mangrove takes root.

Salt marshes

Salt marshes occupy a midway location between mudflats that are permanently submerged by water and terrestrial (land) vegetation lying above the high-tide mark. Like mangroves, they are an ecosystem of the intertidal zone.

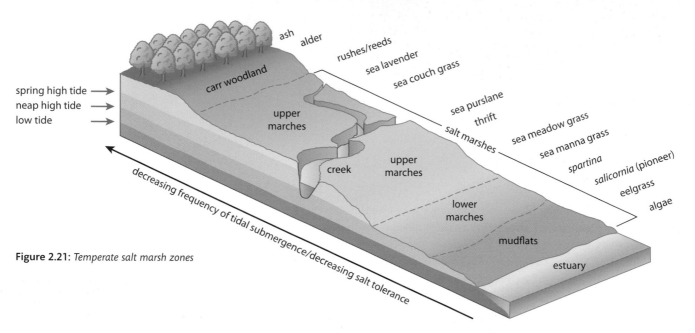

Figure 2.21: *Temperate salt marsh zones*

Coastal salt marshes develop in locations sheltered from the open sea, namely at the heads of bays and in estuaries. Since estuaries are where a river meets the sea, the water is brackish (partly salty and partly fresh). In bays, the water is salty.

Salinity (how salty the water is), and the frequency and extent of flooding of the marsh determine the types of plants and animals found there (Figure 2.21). In some cases, the low marsh zone floods twice daily while the high marsh floods only during storms and unusually high tides. These different environmental conditions result in differences in the types of plants and animals found in different parts of the same marsh area.

Salt marshes are criss-crossed by meandering creeks, which allow tidal water to drain in and out (Figure 2.22). The creeks slow down tidal energy and the marsh plants slow down wave energy. As a result, there is an almost continuous deposition of silt and mud. Over time, this means that the salt marsh gradually extends seawards.

Research the difference between spring tides and neap tides. What is the significance of the difference in terms of salt marsh ecosystems?

Figure 2.22: *A typical area of salt marsh*

Which of the salt marsh zones is shown in Figure 2.22? Refer to Figure 2.21 to see the possible choices. Give reasons for your choice of zone.

Coastal sand dunes

Coastal sand dunes are accumulations of sand shaped into mounds and ridges by the wind. They develop best where:

- there is a wide beach and large quantities of sand
- the prevailing wind is onshore (from the sea to the shore)
- there are suitable locations for the sand to accumulate.

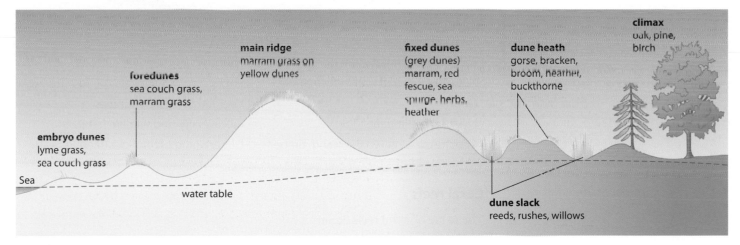

Figure 2.23: *A typical coastal sand dune cross-section*

When the beach dries out at low tide, some of the sand is blown to the back of the beach by the onshore wind. The sand accumulates there, often around a small obstacle such as a piece of driftwood or dry seaweed. As the accumulation grows, an **embryo dune** is formed. It continues to grow and becomes more stable. Another dune may eventually develop on the seaward side of the original dune. The original dune is now further inland and relatively sheltered from the prevailing onshore wind. If this sequence continues, a series of dunes will develop in the form of ridges running parallel to the shore (Figure 2.23).

Figure 2.24: *A belt of embryo and foredunes*

Over time, the ridges of the dunes will be colonised and 'fixed' by vegetation. The older the ridge and the further inland, the greater the vegetation cover. The first plants, such as sea twitch and sea couch grass, have to be able to cope with the following conditions:

- salinity

- a lack of moisture as sand drains quickly

- wind

- temporary submergence by wind-blown sand.

Once some plants become well established, environmental conditions improve and other plants begin to appear. Eventually, in temperate areas, dune heath will become established (Figures 2.23 and 2.24).

2.5 Coastal ecosystems under threat

In this section, we return to the same four ecosystems examined in Part **2.4**. We will look at them at in terms of their value to people and how this, in turn, threatens their existence. All ecosystems offer people a range of opportunities. These opportunities are referred to as **goods and services**. Table 2.2 shows the main goods and services provided by coastal ecosystems.

> A 'good' is a specific material resource that can be extracted and used.
>
> A 'service' is more difficult to define. It is a general benefit, advantage or opportunity.

Goods	Services
Fish and shellfish	Protection from storms
Fishmeal and animal feed	Harbours
Seaweed for food and industrial use	Shelter
Salt	Recreational opportunities
Land for settlement	Biodiversity and wildlife habitats
Construction materials – sand, timber	Dilution and natural treatment of wastes

Table 2.2: Goods and services provided by coastal ecosystems

Coral reefs

The value of coral reefs lies in:

- their biodiversity – within the Great Barrier Reef there are 700 species of coral; 1500 species of fish and 4000 species of mollusc

- the protection they give to low-lying coasts from the impact of tropical storms

- their rich fish stocks – they supply the basic food requirements of many LICs

- their appeal to tourists and the recreational opportunities they offer such as snorkelling and scuba diving. Over 150 million people each year take holidays in areas with coral reefs.

Coral reefs are easily stressed by human actions. Any contact with the human body is likely to kill the coral immediately around the point of contact. Reefs are also

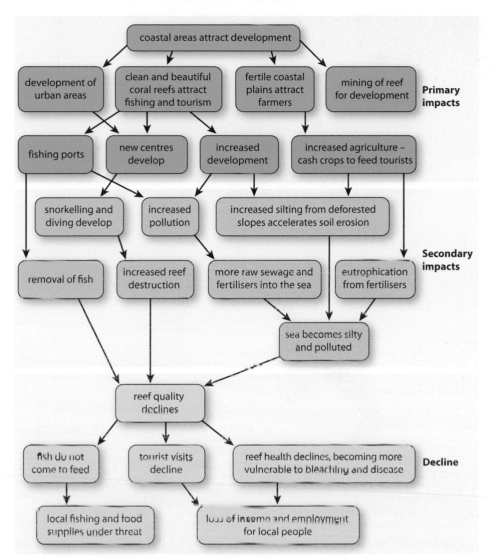

Figure 2.25: *A model of coral reef decline*

threatened by pollution, overfishing and the quarrying of coral for building stone. If the stress persists, the death of the reef soon follows. Figure 2.25 above shows the sequence of coral reef decline that follows from the development of the coastal area nearby. The development involves the spread of urban areas, the growth of a fishing industry, the coming of commercial farming and the rise of tourism. These have a range of secondary impacts that eventually lead to the decline and possible death of the coral reef.

A recent survey of the world's coral reefs showed that 27% of them were highly threatened by human activities. Another 31% were classified as being under 'medium threat'.

Referring to Figure 2.25, suggest reasons for the following links:

- increased development > increased pollution

- sea becomes polluted > reef quality declines

- reef health declines > loss of income and employment.

Case study: Coral reef management in St Lucia

The Caribbean island of St Lucia is fringed with coral reefs. A survey has identified 90 km² of those reefs as seriously threatened by human activities, particularly by overfishing, tourism and coastal development, marine pollution and sedimentation from the land.

Marine reserves
Allows fish stocks to regenerate and protects marine flora and fauna. Access to the area is by permit and can be enjoyed by divers and snorkellers.

Fishing priority areas
Commercial fishing has precedence over all other activities in these areas.

Yachting areas
Yachting is not allowed in the SMMA. Moorings are provided in these areas only.

Multiple use areas
Fishing, diving, snorkelling and other legitimate uses are allowed.

Recreational areas
Areas for public recreation, sunbathing, swimming.

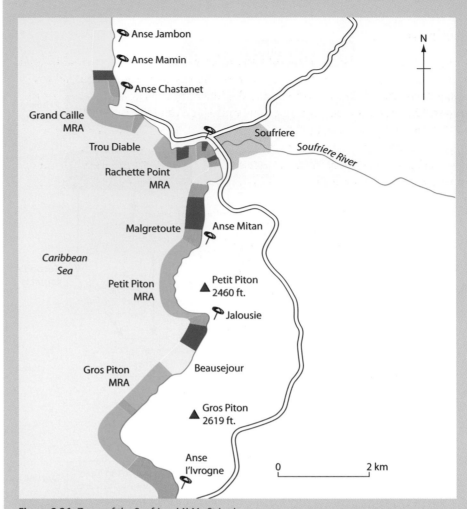

Figure 2.26: *Zones of the Soufriere MMA, St Lucia*

Both fishermen and divers damage the reef areas in a variety of ways, such as lowering metal anchors and chains and climbing over and touching the coral.

Moored yachts pollute the sea and this has an adverse impact on fish stocks.

On the west coast, particularly in the vicinity of Soufriere, the growth of tourism and urban development have resulted in conflicts between user groups – for example between fishermen and divers over reef areas, and between fishermen and yachts anchoring in fishing zones. In response to these conflicts, the Soufriere Marine Management Area (SMMA) was set up to try to resolve the conflicts and to reduce the threats to the coral reef.

The solution the SMMA came up with was an apparently simple one – divide the 11 km length of coast into five different zones (Figure 2.26):

- **marine reserves** – all uses forbidden, so future of coral reefs protected

- **fishing priority areas** – no diving or yachting

- **recreational areas** – mainly for diving and various water sports

- **yacht mooring areas** – mooring of yachts allowed

- **multiple-use areas** – open to all users.

The segregation of different users of the coral reefs has resolved the conflicts. However, the plan does little to protect the coral reefs outside the marine reserves. The best hope is that each of the user groups will do their utmost to minimise their impact on the reefs.

Mangroves

Mangroves are valuable nurseries of fish and crustaceans (shellfish), and are rich in wildlife. Mangrove roots, which are exposed at low tide, trap silt and help to create new land. Mangrove timber provides fuel and building material. However, perhaps the greatest value of mangroves in this age of rising sea levels is the protection from storm surges they give to low-lying coastal areas. The World Conservation Union compared the death tolls in two Sri Lankan villages of the same size that were hit by the 2004 tsunami. Two people died in the settlement protected by dense mangrove, whilst up to 6000 people died in the village without such protection.

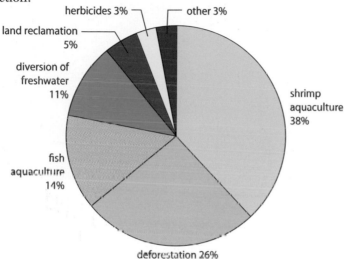

Figure 2.27. The global destruction of mangroves

It is widely believed that mangrove swamps are disease-ridden. For this reason, they are being cleared at a fast rate. Figure 2.27 shows the causes of this destruction at a global scale. Just over half of the mangrove swamps are being cleared to make way for aquaculture – the farming of fish and shrimps. A quarter is being cleared (deforestation) to provide timber for fuel and building purposes. The land reclamation is being undertaken to provide sites for the building of tourist hotels and other amenities. The diversion of freshwater is intended to meet the needs of tourists and expanding agriculture. The latter (farming) requires the application of herbicides to prepare cleared areas for cultivation.

> What are the arguments for and against protecting mangroves from human use?

Case study: Management of the mangrove

Bangladesh is one country in the world that understands the value of the mangrove. It is a low-lying country. Its long coastline is vulnerable to tropical storms and storm surges. Bangladesh also has a huge population and a shortage of land. The mean population density is around 1000 persons per km². Up to 25 million people live less than 1 metre above sea level.

As part of its Coastal Zone Policy, the Bangladesh government is taking advantage of the fact that mangroves trap sediment and stabilise shores. By deliberately planting mangroves on delta sediments washed down from the Himalayas, it has gained over 120 000 hectares of new land in the Bay of Bengal. The plantings are relatively new, but there have been mangroves here for as long as the Ganges, Brahmaputra, and Meghna Rivers have been draining into the Bay. The vast tidal woodland they form is known as the Sundarbans – it literally means 'beautiful forest'. Today, it is the largest surviving single tract of mangroves in the world (Figure 2.28).

Figure 2.28: *Satellite image of the Sundarbans*

The management of the Sundarbans is not only creating new land and protecting Bangladesh from coastal flooding, it is also permitting local people to make use of its resources. The only real threat is the clearance of some mangroves to allow the aquaculture of shrimps and fish. The former is a valuable export; the latter an important food to help feed a large and hungry population.

There is more information about Bangladesh to be found in:

- Chapter 1.5 (page 14)
- Chapter 1.8 (page 30)
- Chapter 4.3 (page 99)
- Chapter 5.6 (page 128)
- Chapter 7.8 (page 205)

Salt marshes

On the face of it, areas of salt marshes appear to be of little obvious value. However, the reality is that many salt marshes are among the most used and therefore the most threatened ecosystems in today's world. Specific threats include:

- reclamation to create farmland and sites for industrial and port developments – this is based on the perception that marshes are wasted spaces that need to be put to some good use

- industrial pollution – particularly of water, as many marshes occur in estuaries which are favoured as sites for ports, power stations and oil refineries (Figure 2.29)

- agricultural pollution – heavy applications of fertilisers and pesticides on adjacent farmland lead to eutrophication (an increase in the concentration of chemical fertilizers in an ecosystem) of marshland waters

- pressure from developments such as marinas and other recreational facilities.

Salt marshes are also threatened by changes associated with global warming such as more storms and higher water levels.

Figure 2.29: *Industrial development on a salt marsh*

Why are salt marsh areas attractive to industry?

Coastal sand dunes

Of the four ecosystems, coastal sand dunes are probably the least threatened at a global level. This perhaps reflects the fact that they have little to offer people other than coastal protection. In the UK, however, they are put at risk by the density of people using them as recreational spaces. Various forms of recreation – such as trail biking and horse riding– are doing great damage. Sand dunes are delicate ecosystems and easily disturbed (Figure 2.30). Disturbance of dunes often leads to a loss of vegetation and to **blow-outs**. Because of their nearness to urban and industrial areas, whole tracts of coastal sand dune are at risk of being built over. Because of their nearness to the coastline, they are under pressure from tourism to provide amenities such as golf courses and caravan sites. In many parts of the world, areas have been planted with trees to help stabilise mobile dunes. The net effect of this has been to destroy the coastal sand dune ecosystem.

Figure 2.30: *An area of degraded sand dune*

2.6 Coastal conflicts

The coastal system

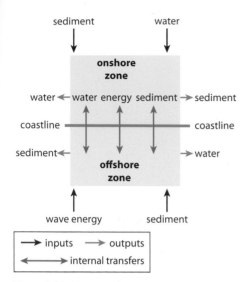

Figure 2.31: *The coastal system*

For information on other systems, see:

- Chapter 1.1 (page 1)
- Chapter 1.2 (page 3)
- Chapter 5.2 (page 117)
- Chapter 5.5 (page 123).

Find the location of Southampton Water on an atlas map of the British Isles.

The coast is often described as being a **system** as with the drainage basins (see page 3) and the ecosystem (see page 117) (Figure 2.31). To understand what this means, think of the sea as an invisible box. Things enter that box (**inputs**) and either remain there (**stores**) or pass through it (**transfers**) and eventually leave it (**outputs**). One input is sediment. This comes from rivers and the weathering and erosion of cliffs. The stores of sediment are beaches and sand dunes. The transfer of sediment is mainly the movement of sand and shingle along the coast by longshore drift. The loss of sediment from the coast to the open sea is an output.

Where there is a balance between inputs and outputs, the system is said to be in **equilibrium**. However, the system can have a positive **sediment budget**. In other words, inputs are greater than the outputs. In which case, it is likely that beaches and other depositional features will increase in size. If the sediment budget is negative, with outputs exceeding inputs, then those features are likely to be declining.

Today, coastal management is based on identifying **coastal cells**. These are sections of the coast which are self-contained in terms of the movement of sediment. In other words, these coastal cells are systems (see Figure 2.39 on page 61).

An important point is that the equilibrium of coastal systems can easily be upset by a whole range of human activities. As we saw in Part **2.5**, human activities can seriously disrupt coastal ecosystems. Equally, in this part, we will see that most forms of human intervention in the coastal system can give rise to a whole range of conflicts.

Conflict between development and conservation

Each of the threats considered in Part **2.5** creates a specific conflict. Many of those conflicts are about human needs versus the well-being of coastal ecosystems. They all raise the basic questions – should those ecosystems be protected and conserved? Or should people be encouraged to make the fullest use of their resources and opportunities, that is exploit them? In short, the overriding coastal conflict is between **conservation** and **development**. The case study of Southampton Water below is a tale of land reclamation, of marshes being turned into sites for a variety of activities.

Case study: Southampton Water, southern England

Southampton, on the English south coast, is one of the UK's leading ports. It is a port with a very long history. One of the attractions was that it was located at the head of a very sheltered and secure stretch of water – Southampton Water (Figure 2.32). In its natural state, the shores of Southampton Water were fringed by mudflats and salt marshes. These two habitats provided feeding for huge numbers of wildfowl and wetland birds. However, over the centuries these wildlife havens have been much reduced by development.

In the 19th and 20th centuries, because of Southampton's success as a port, mudflats were reclaimed on which to build new docks – first the Eastern Docks and then the Western Docks. The latter were built for the large ocean-going liners carrying passengers to all parts of the world. These docks were subsequently extended upstream to provide the large terminal facilities needed for handling containerised cargo. Southampton is now the UK's second busiest container port.

In the middle of the 20th century, land was reclaimed on the southern shore close to the entrance to Southampton Water to provide the site for a large oil refinery. Later, more land was reclaimed for an oil-fired electric power station. At the same time, salt marshes were being reclaimed at Dibden Bay to accommodate a planned further expansion of the port (Figure 2.33). However, in the interests of nature conservation, it has been decided not to go ahead with the plan. A small area at the southern end has been used as the site for a residential marina at Hythe. Hamble, on the other side of the water, is renowned as a yachting centre.

Most of the salt marshes have now been reclaimed and other sections of the Southampton Water shores have become built up, not just by the expansion of Southampton, but also by urban settlements such as Fawley, Hamble and Hythe. In fact, the development of the Southampton Water coastline has led to a range of different land uses being accommodated.

Unfortunately, the natural environment and conservation have taken a back seat. It is only recently that the western shore has received some official protection. The stretch of shore to the north of Hythe is now a Special Protection Area (SPA) and that to the south is now a Special Area of Conservation (SAC). However, this protection has come far too late. It was needed 100 years ago!

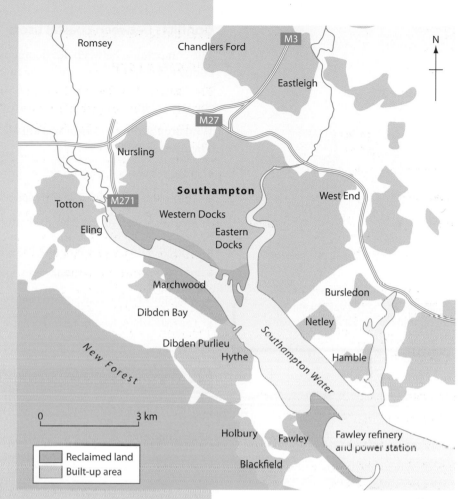

Figure 2.32: *Southampton Water*

Figure 2.33: *The reclaimed land at Dibden Bay*

Conflicts between coastal users

The competition between development and conservation is just one cause of conflict in coastal areas. There are many other conflicts. These conflicts are between the various users (sometimes called **stakeholders**) of the coast. In many respects, these users are competing with each other because of their particular needs.

Who are the main users of coastal areas and what are their special needs? The users include:

- local residents – good choice of housing; clean environment

- employers – access to labour; space for shops, offices and factories

- farmers – well-drained land; shelter from strong onshore winds

- fishermen – harbours; unpolluted waters

- port authorities – harbours and space for port-side services and terminals

- transport companies – good roads and terminals such as ports and airports

- tourists – beaches, hotels, recreational amenities, heritage sites

- developers – greenfield sites.

Which two of the coastal stakeholders do you think are most in conflict. Give your reasons.

Case study: The Mediterranean coast under pressure

The mainland coast of the Mediterranean coast is over 19 000 km long and home to over 160 million people living in the 22 countries that share the coastline. It is reported to hold 584 coastal cities, 750 yachting harbours, 286 commercial ports, 68 oil and gas terminals, 180 power stations and 112 airports.

Figure 2.34: *A highly-developed stretch of the Mediterranean coast*

Tourism is the major economic activity of the Mediterranean region. Since it is of the 'sun, sea and sand variety', it has put great pressure on coastal areas (Figure 2.34). Much coastal space is taken up by the infrastructure of tourism – hotels, restaurants, bars, recreational amenities and so on. The growth of coastal tourism has also encouraged the development of roads, airports and ports for ships, boats and liners. It is estimated that an additional 200 km of coastline is being developed each year and that by 2025 over half of the Mediterranean coastline will be built upon.

See also the Case study in Chapter 8.5 (page 225).

The growth of tourism is clearly damaging and destroying the natural environment. Equally, there are developments taking place that are damaging tourism. For example, inshore waters are being polluted by:

- the ships serving the oil and gas terminals
- discharges from industrial plants
- the run off of agricultural chemicals into the sea.

The success of tourism depends on clean beaches and clear seawater. So in terms of marine pollution, tourism is in conflict with at least three other activities. It is also in conflict with these same activities because:

- they are all competing for coastal sites
- no upmarket hotel wants to be located close to an oil refinery or a power station. It would be bad for their image and their visitor appeal!

Similar problems and conflicts also occur in the UK as can be seen in Figure 2.35 below.

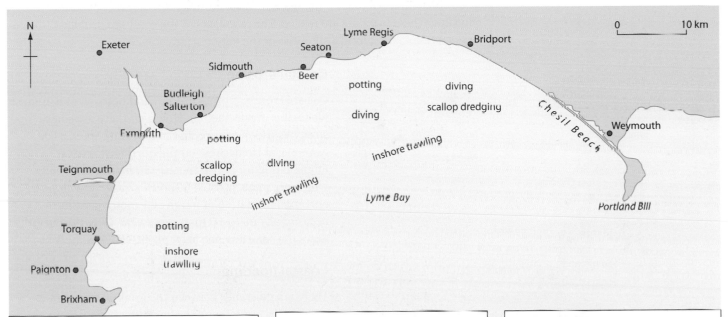

Wildlife lovers
The key habitats are the rocky reefs and the areas that support seagrass and maerl. These act as a nursery ground for commercially valuable invertebrates and fish, which provide food for large numbers of seabirds, such as auks, divers, gulls, terns and grebes. All three habitats are sensitive to physical damage.

Scallop dredgers
Boats operating out of the bay's ports bottom-trawl for scallops in inshore waters. The industry generates around £180 000 a year. Dragging heavy fishing gear across the seabed causes high levels of physical damage, stirs up sediment and smothers sensitive species. This is likely to have long-term negative effects on all the other users of the bay. If it were to be continued to the sand and gravel areas close to the shore, the impact would be even worse.

Trawlers
Three areas in Lyme Bay are important to trawlers: the central area, where red mullet, skate, squid and cuttlefish are found between June and November; a winter run of lemon sole from Portland Bill moving west across the bay; and sprat and herring in the late summer in the southwestern part. Fishing gear has an adverse impact on habitats.

Potters
Crab and lobster potting in the main reef areas generates nearly £180 000 a year for the local economy, but is incompatible with scallop dredging because pots can get tangled in the lines of a scallop dredger. Female edible crabs travel far along the coast to spawning grounds and it is important to protect their migration routes from damage.

Divers and anglers
Diving is a low-impact activity and generates about £87 000 a year, mainly through dive companies in Torbay, Exmouth and Lyme Regis visiting the wreck sites and rocky reef area. Angling trips are made across the bay for species such as cod and bass. Angling generates nearly £250 000 a year for the local economy. The impact on marine habitats is low, but fishing lines may snag sensitive species such as pink sea tans.

Tourists
Tourism contributes to the economy of the entire southwest region, as well as that of local communities. Sightseeing, sailing, water-skiing, jet-skiing, power-boating, windsurfing and wildlife watching are all popular but depend on a healthy, attractive environment.

Figure 2.35: *Key stakeholders in Lyme Bay, southern England*

The conflicts that occur in coastal areas are on the landward side of the coastline and between different users of the inshore waters. This was the case with the coral reefs of St Lucia (see Part **2.4**). It is also illustrated in the waters of Lyme Bay on the south coast of England. Here there are at least six stakeholders or users of its waters (Figure 2.35). It is important to note that one of these stakeholders is wildlife. Again, the only solution to the conflict is to separate the different uses by allocating specific areas of water to particular users. This solution is not as simple as it might seem. It is quite difficult to mark out areas of the sea. It is also difficult to police these areas to check that they are being used as they should be.

2.7 Coastal management

Coastal management is about two things. The first is resolving the conflicts, as we saw in the previous part, between different users of the coast and between those users and the well-being of coastal ecosystems. The second is taking action to meet big changes that threaten long stretches of the coast. The changes can present risks. Two risks stand out today – the risk of coastal erosion, and the risk of coastal flooding. These two risks are related. The managers of the coast are usually employees of either local authorities or the national government.

Coastal erosion

Coastal erosion is quite normal and natural, and in most places it is unspectacular. However, there are some stretches which are eroding at alarming speeds. For example, at Holderness on the northeast coast of England (Figure 2.36), the 20–30 metres high cliffs which are made up of soft sands, gravels and clays are currently retreating at a rate of 1 metre per year – occasionally up to 10 metres per year. Over the last 2000 years the coastline has been pushed back some 4 km.

Coastal flooding

There is a difference between the gradual retreat of a coastline by erosion and the flooding of a low-lying coastline by occasional, abnormally high sea levels. **Storm surges** are the greatest flood threat. These are caused by very low air pressure, which raises the height of the high-tide sea. Strong onshore winds then drive the 'raised' sea towards the coast and are capable of breaching coastal defences and flooding large areas. **Tsunamis** generated by earthquakes can also lead to widespread coastal flooding as was the case with the 2004 tsunami.

Storm surges and tsunamis are periodic events. However, there are some stretches of coastline where the risk of flooding is both constant and increasing. This is the case with the city of Venice at the head of the Adriatic Sea. Global warming and its associated rise in sea levels is also increasing the coastal flood risk in many parts of the world.

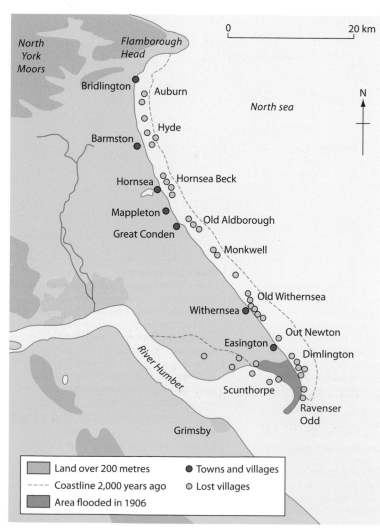

Figure 2.36: *Retreat of the Holderness coast, England*

Over the last 150 years or so, people have taken steps to protect valued stretches of the coast from erosion and flooding. Much concrete, rock and timber have been used in the belief that these materials might help people win the endless battle against the sea. All the management strategies used so far in this battle have involved either **hard engineering** or **soft engineering**.

For more on tsunamis, see Chapter 3.2 (page 69).

Hard-engineering management

Hard engineering involves building some type of sea defence, usually from rocks or concrete. It aims to protect the coast from erosion and the risk of flooding by working against the power of waves. Figure 2.37 illustrates some of the techniques used at the foot of cliffs and on beaches. Each has its strengths and weaknesses. For example, rip rap is effective and cheaper to install than either sea walls or revetments. However, it may shift in heavy storms and be undercut by the backwash of waves.

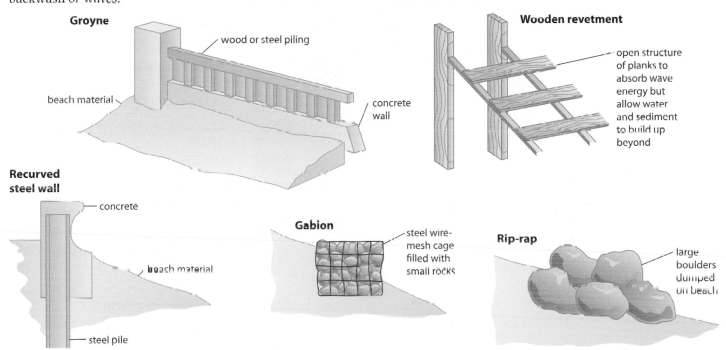

Figure 2.37: *Examples of coastal hard engineering*

Hard engineering as a whole has several disadvantages:

- most structures are expensive to build and maintain – to repair a sea wall can cost up to £3000 a metre

- effective defence in one place can have serious consequences for a nearby stretch of coastline, particularly in the direction of longshore drift. For example, groynes trap beach material that is being moved by longshore drift on their upstream side. Downstream of the groyne, the lack of beach material increases the exposure of the coast to the forces of erosion

- defence structures like sea walls, gambions and rip-rap cannot keep pace with rising sea levels

- structures can spoil the natural beauty of a coastline.

Which form of hard engineering shown in Figure 2.37 would be best for:

- reducing the effects of longshore drift

- protecting the base of a cliff from erosion?

Soft-engineering management

Soft engineering methods of coastal management try to work with natural processes. It also makes use of elements of the coastal system, such as beaches, sand dunes and salt marshes. The following are examples of soft engineering:

- **beach replenishment** – pumping or dumping sand and shingle back onto a beach to replace eroded material (Figure 2.38)

- **building bars** – underwater bars located just offshore reduce wave energy

Figure 2.38: *Beach replenishment in progress*

- **fencing, hedging and replanting vegetation** – this helps to preserve a beach or sand dune by reducing the amount of sand that is blown inland

- **cliff regrading** – the angle of a cliff is reduced so that it is not so steep because this reduces the likelihood of cliff retreat by mass movement (a large part of the cliff suddenly falling down as a result of water erosion).

All but the last of these actions are used to absorb wave and tidal energy. They do not disfigure the natural appearance of the coast. They are more environmentally-friendly than hard-engineering solutions. Soft-engineering strategies are generally much less expensive than hard-engineering ones.

Managed retreat

In recent years, another type of coastal management has appeared. It is probably a response to the rising sea levels of global warming. Some see this as yet another form of soft engineering. Others see it as a distinct form. It involves abandoning existing coastal defences and allowing the sea to flood inland until it reaches higher land or a new line of coast defence. Allowing low-lying coastal areas to flood and develop into salt marshes produces a good natural defence against storms. It also increases the amount of salt marsh – an increasingly scarce and threatened ecosystem. It is a relatively cheap method of coastal defence. The main cost is one of compensating people for the loss of 'drowned' homes and livelihoods. Because of this particular cost, managed retreat is not suitable in coastal areas where there is urban development and high quality farmland.

For more on salt marshes see Part 2.4 (page 46)

Shoreline management plans

Today in the UK and other HICs, the approach to coastal management has become much more comprehensive. It assesses all the possible risks such as the risk of flooding and cliff erosion. Those risks are then considered from the perspective of different groups of people (stakeholders) in the coastal community. Who is likely to be most threatened by a particular problem? What do they stand to lose if the particular situation takes place?

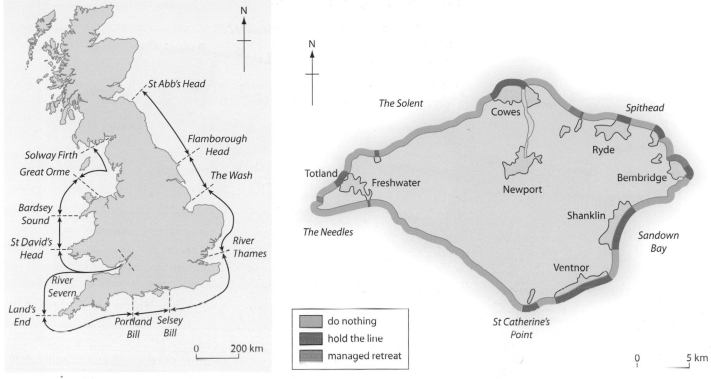

Figure 2.39: *The coastal cells of England and Wales*

do nothing

hold the line

managed retreat

Figure 2.40: *Coastal management of the Isle of Wight*

A plan of action is then drawn up that tries to minimise the risks and costs. In the UK, the long coastline is divided up into cells (Figure 2.39) and these into smaller sub-cells. A management plan is prepared for each sub-cell. Figure 2.40 shows the management plan for the Isle of Wight. You will see that the coastline is divided up into three different types of action:

- **do nothing** – this means that along these stretches there are few if any risks. In short, the coast is safe and secure

- **hold the line** – in other words, hard engineering will be needed to continue to protect these stretches of coast because much money is invested in urban development, for example in the tourist resorts of Cowes, Shanklin and Ventnor

- **managed retreat** – three low-lying areas are recognised as being threatened by flooding. Clearly the retreat at the resort of Bembridge is going to need very careful management.

Study Figure 2.40. What do you notice about the occurrence of 'hold the line' coastal management?

Case study: Abbots Hall Farm, Essex

The east coast of England is 'sinking' into the sea at a rate of over 6 mm a year. This is beginning to threaten large areas of low-lying coast. Many kilometres of sea wall have been built over the last few centuries as protection. In Essex, about 40% of its salt marshes have been lost as a result of the rising sea level, coast erosion and land reclamation. The mudflats and salt marshes here are important feeding and nesting areas for huge numbers wading birds.

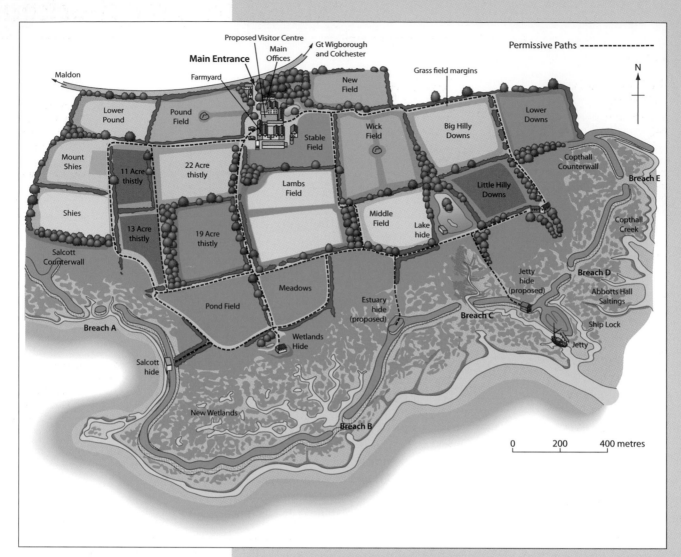

Figure 2.41: *Abbots Hall Farm managed retreat*

The Royal Society for the Protection of Birds (RSPB) owns Abbots Farm on the north side of the Blackwater estuary (Figure 2.41). In 2002 it started a programme of managed retreat. Five breaches were made in the old sea walls. This has allowed the sea to cover some 80 hectares of arable fields. The flooded land will gradually revert to what it was before it was cultivated – salt marsh.

It should be said that not everyone is a nature lover and supports this or other programmes like it. Many argue that it is a government's responsibility to protect land and people when they are being threatened by the sea. But what about the financial costs, especially in an age of global warming and rising sea levels?

Research two other examples of managed retreat, preferably outside the UK. Are there conflicting views about such management?

It will take time for people to accept that not all of the present coastline can be held against the sea in an era of rising sea levels. Managed retreat at Abbot Hall Farm was easy in that the land being lost was of no great monetary value. Now other authorities need to see that managed retreat is not just good for wildlife. Managed retreat ensures the supply of sediment that builds up the natural coastal defences of other areas of coastline, by forming marshes or beaches, shingle bars or mud flats. It is much cheaper than building sea walls and leaves the coast looking as it used to.

End of chapter checkout

Checklists

Now you have read the chapter, you should know:

✓ the physical processes that affect the coast

✓ the landforms resulting from these processes

✓ how these landforms are affected by geology, vegetation, sea-level changes and people

✓ about coastal ecosystems and their biodiversity

✓ the factors affecting their distribution

✓ why these coastal ecosystems are valuable

✓ how they are being threatened by tourism and other developments

✓ that there are conflicts along the coast, particularly between development and conservation

✓ the coast is changing as a result of natural processes and human activities

✓ the reasons for and against protecting stretches of changing coast

✓ the different methods used in the protection of the coast

Make sure you understand these key terms:

Arch: a coastal feature formed by the meeting of two caves cut into either side of a headland.

Bar: a ridge-like accumulation of coastal sediments exposed at low tide.

Bay: a wide, coastal inlet that is open to the sea.

Beach: an accumulation of coastal sediments, most often occurring in sheltered areas along the coast, such as bays.

Biodiversity: the number and variety of living species found in a given area or ecosystem.

Headland: an area of land jutting out into the sea.

Cave: a hollow cut by the sea into the base of a cliff.

Cliff: a steep rock slope, usually facing the sea.

Conservation: the protection of aspects of the environment for the future benefit of people.

Deposition: the dropping of material that was being carried by a moving force, such as the waves.

Development: making use of the coast for a variety of purposes, such as tourism, housing, shipping and industry.

Ecosystem: a community of plants and animals that interact with each other and their physical environment

Erosion: the wearing away and removal of material by a moving force, such as the sea. .

Estuary: the mouth of a river as it enters the sea.

Hard engineering: protecting the coast by building such structures as sea walls and groynes.

Longshore drift: the movement of sediments along the coast by wave action.

Mass movement: the movement of weathered material down a slope or cliff due to the force of gravity.

Raised beach: a former beach now standing above sea level and some metres inland.

Soft engineering: protecting the coast by working with nature.

Spit: material deposited by the sea that grows across a bay or estuary.

Stack: a detached column of rock located just off-shore and usually caused by the collapse of an arch.

Sub-aerial: occurring on land, as opposed to underwater or underground

Wave: a ridge of water formed by the circular movement of water near the surface of the sea.

See the Glossary in the ActiveBook for more definitions

Questions

Try testing yourself with these questions:

1. a) Name the two zones of the coast.
   b) Describe the four main marine processes.
2. Why is it important to distinguish between constructive waves and destructive waves?
3. a) With the aid of a sketch diagram, describe the process of longshore drift.
   b) What part does longshore drift play in the development of coastal landforms?
4. With help of Figure 2.13, suggest why the Jurassic coast is such a popular tourist location.
5. a) What is the difference between a storm beach and a berm?
   b) With the help of an annotated diagram, explain how spits are formed.
6. Describe the conditions necessary for the formation of sand dunes.
7. a) What is the name given to a coastline that has experienced a rise in sea level?
   b) Describe the main coastal features produced by changes in sea level.
8. Describe some of the ways in which people can affect the character of the coast.
9. a) Using Figure 2.18, describe the main features of the global distribution of coral reefs.
   b) Name six physical factors controlling the growth of coral.
10. a) What is meant by the term intertidal?
    b) In what ways are mangroves a very tolerant ecosystem?
11. What are the conditions favouring the growth of salt marshes?
12. How and why does the vegetation change as one moves inland across a belt of sand dunes?
13. a) What is meant by the 'goods and services' of ecosystems?
    b) Give examples of goods and services that coastal ecosystems provide.

14. Why is it so important that mangroves should be protected?
15. Describe the main threats to salt marshes.
16. a) Why are sand dunes reckoned to be the least threatened of the coastal ecosystems?
    b) In what ways do tourism and recreation threaten the well-being of sand dunes?
17. a) With the aid of an annotated diagram, explain what is meant by the phrase 'the coast is a natural system'?
    b) What is a 'coastal cell' in the UK?
18. a) What is involved in conserving the coast?
    b) Use examples from the Southampton Water case study (page 54) to illustrate the conflict between conservation and development.
19. In what ways does tourism threaten the coast?
20. a) Who are the 'coastal stakeholders'?
    b) Give examples of the conflicts that can exist between coastal stakeholders.
21. a) With the help of examples, distinguish between hard and soft coastal engineering.
22. a) Explain what is meant by 'managed retreat'.
    b) In what circumstances does this become the preferred coastal management option?
23. Briefly describe the steps involved in making a coastal management plan.
24. What are the coastal management options in dealing with global warming?

Chapter 3: Hazardous environments

Introduction

This chapter is about three different natural hazards that threaten people in many parts of the world. They are earthquakes, volcanic eruptions and tropical revolving storms (hurricanes and typhoons). They have the power to cause great damage to settlements and to injure and kill many people. Is it possible to predict when and where they will occur? What can be done to minimise their destructive impacts, both before and immediately after the event?

For information about another hazard not covered in this chapter – flooding – see Chapter 1.8.

3.1 Different types of hazard

A **hazard** is defined as an event that threatens, or actually causes damage and destruction to people, their property and settlements. A **natural hazard** is one produced by environmental processes and involves events such as storms, floods, earthquakes and volcanic eruptions. There are also hazards that are created by people. These range from industrial explosions to nuclear warfare, from air and road crashes to fire and the collapse of buildings. Most of these are the outcome of mishaps to do with human technology. The important point to remember with is that, if there were no people, there would be no hazards because hazards in this context means hazards to people.

Geological	Climatic	Biological	Technological
Earthquakes	Storms	Fires	Nuclear explosion
Volcanic eruptions	Floods	Pests	Accidents
Landslides	Drought	Diseases	Pollution

Table 3.1: Four major categories of hazard with examples

Table 3.1 above classifies hazards into four main categories based on their causes and gives some examples of each. This may look neat and tidy, but we need to realise that some hazards have more than one cause and therefore do not fit easily into this classification. For example, floods are not only caused by heavy rainfall. A stream of volcanic lava running down into a valley can easily block the flow of a

Figure 3.1: *Malnourished children in a desertified area*

river and cause flooding upstream. Floods in coastal areas can be caused by the tidal waves (tsunamis) associated with **earthquakes**. Coastal flooding also results from storm surges caused by low atmospheric pressures and not from heavy rainfall (see Figure 3.13 on page 73).

Another point is that some **natural events** only become hazards in an indirect ways. For example, drought mainly becomes a hazard because of its effect on food production. Crops and livestock lacking water will not yield so much food. Food shortages mean malnutrition and possibly death by starvation (Figure 3.1).

Diseases are an interesting group of hazards. Are diseases natural events or are they caused by humans? Some are certainly natural hazards. For example, malaria is a 'vector' or biological hazard carried from one human to the next by a mosquito. In contrast, there are many contagious diseases associated with human pollution of the environment. Typhoid and cholera are just two examples. An interesting aspect of all diseases is that the hazard threat is very focused on people. The outcomes are illness and death for people.

In this chapter, we are going to focus on three natural hazards: tropical storms, earthquakes and volcanic eruptions (Figure 3.2). Tropical storms are a climatic hazard in which two weather elements, wind and rain, threaten human life and property. Earthquakes and volcanic eruptions are geological hazards.

Before we look more closely at these three hazards, a point needs to be made about hazards in general. An important aspect of all hazards is **risk**. Risk is about the probability of a particular event happening and the scale of its possible damage. Risk is also what people take knowing that they are 'exposed' to a natural event that might prove hazardous. The greater the probability of a natural event occurring in a particular location and causing damage, the greater is the risk that people are taking. This is particularly so if they remain in that location or do not take evasive (preventative) or precautionary actions, known as **adjustment** or **mitigation**.

So it is important to remember these three aspects of hazards:

- **distribution** – where do they occur on the Earth's surface?

- **frequency** – do they occur regularly?

- **scale** – do the events vary in their hazardousness?

To these, we might add a fourth and important question about **prediction**. Can we predict when these events will occur and their likely scale of damage?

Figure 3.2: *Three natural hazards: tropical storms, earthquakes and volcanic eruptions*

3.2 Earthquakes and volcanic eruptions

In this part of the chapter, we look at three aspects of two tectonic (tectonic means pertaining to the structure and movement of the earth's crust) hazards, earthquakes and volcanic eruptions:

- their global distributions
- their causes
- their hazard characteristics.

Since earthquakes and volcanic eruptions both result from plate tectonics, they are closely linked in terms of both their distributions and causes. They differ, however, in terms of the sort of damage they do.

Tectonic plates

The tectonic plates shown in Figure 3.3 are constantly moving. But they do so at a rate that is almost imperceptible on a human time scale.

The crust of the Earth is made up of a number of **tectonic plates** which are the rigid blocks that make up the surface of the earth (Figure 3.3). These plates move over the surface of the globe. Their movements create four different types of plate margin.

When two plates are moving apart, for example in the oceans, the margin between them is called a **constructive** or **divergent plate margin**. It is called this because magma (molten rock) rises to the crust to fill the gap and create new crust through submarine volcanoes. This is happening, for example, along the mid-ocean ridge in the Atlantic Ocean.

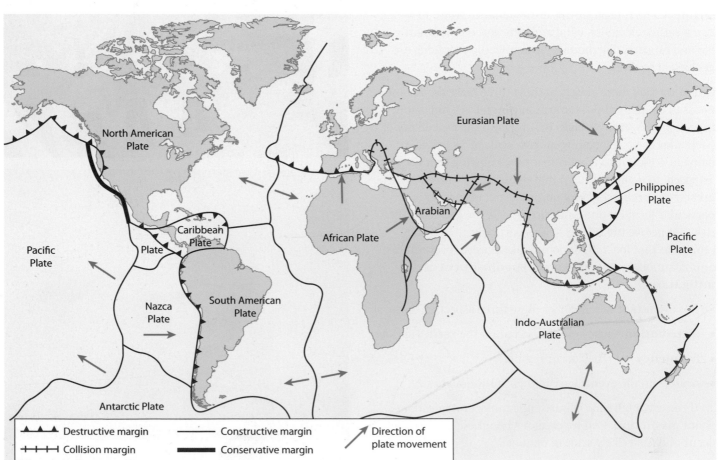

Figure 3.3: *The world's tectonic plates and their margins*

When two plates are moving towards each other, like the Nazca plate and the South American plate, the margin between them is called a **destructive** or **convergent plate margin**. The edge of one plate margin is being destroyed as it plunges beneath the other plate it is meeting head on. This is known as **subduction**. Molten rocks rises to the surface to form volcanoes. The friction between the two plates creates earthquakes.

A **collision plate margin** occurs where two plates meet head on and are of equal density and strength. The sediments between the two plates are squeezed upwards. The result is the formation of fold mountains, such as the Himalayas that were created by the collision between the Eurasian and Indo-Australian plates. Earthquakes are created by the pressure and friction.

There is a fourth type of plate margin referred to as a **conservative plate margin**. This occurs where two plates are sliding past each other. Since there is neither rising magma here nor subduction, there are no volcanoes. Instead the friction gives rise to earthquakes as in California between the Pacific and North American plates.

Tectonic plates shape the landscape by creating new rocks and forming mountains and rift valleys. They do this by the processes of volcanic activity, folding and faulting. These are the most powerful natural forces on the planet. It is not surprising that they should give rise to the most awesome natural hazards.

> Make a list of the different types of plate margin and write brief notes about what is happening at each of them.

Distribution

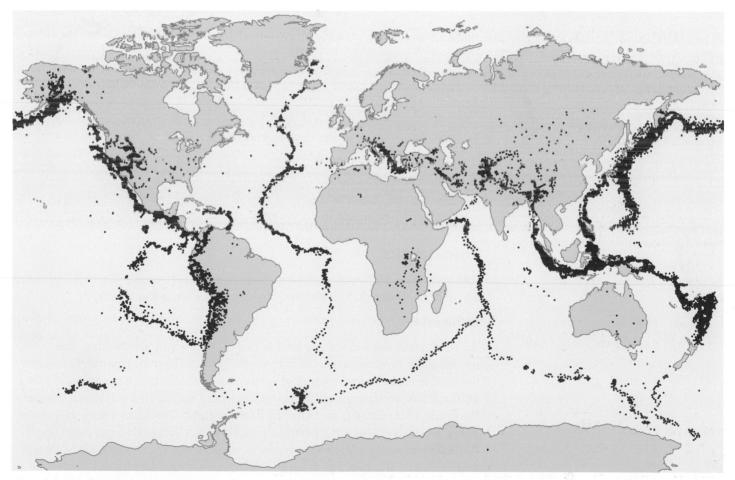

Figure 3.4: *Global distribution of earthquakes*

The distributions of earthquakes and volcanoes are similar in that they occur along tectonic plate boundaries. A comparison of Figure 3.4 and Figure 3.5 shows how similar the distributions are. There is an impressive density of earthquakes along the destructive plate margins that fringe the Pacific Ocean (Figure 3.4). The occurrence of earthquakes under the Atlantic, Indian and Pacific Oceans should be noted. When it comes to the distribution of volcanoes, again the concentration around the shores of the Pacific Ocean is noticeable (Figure 3.5). Another concentration occurs along the African Rift Valley formed by a constructive plate margin.

Underwater volcanic eruptions can cause tidal waves (tsunamis). See page 69.

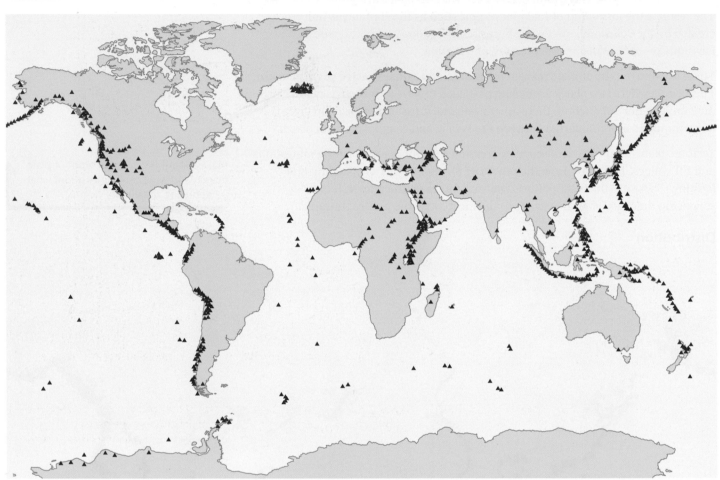

Figure 3.5: *Global distribution of volcanoes*

Characteristics

Although their distributions and causes are similar, earthquakes and volcanoes are very different hazards. Their hazard characteristics are not at all alike.

Earthquakes

An earthquake is a sudden and brief period of intense ground-shaking. The movement of the ground can be both vertical and horizontal. Two different scales are used to measure the strength of earthquakes. The Richter Scale measures an earthquake's strength according to the amount of energy that is released during the event. That energy is measured by a seismograph. The Richter scale runs from 2.4 or less to over 8.0. It is a logarithmic scale which means that one point up on the scale represents a 30 times increase in released energy. The Mercalli Scale is quite different. It is based on what people experience and the amount of damage done (Figure 3.6).

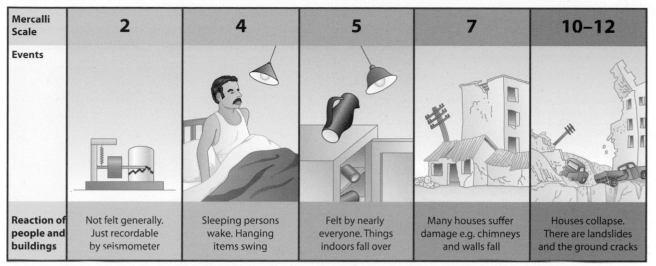

Mercalli Scale	2	4	5	7	10–12
Events					
Reaction of people and buildings	Not felt generally. Just recordable by seismometer	Sleeping persons wake. Hanging items swing	Felt by nearly everyone. Things indoors fall over	Many houses suffer damage e.g. chimneys and walls fall	Houses collapse. There are landslides and the ground cracks

Figure 3.6: *Some examples from the Mercalli Scale*

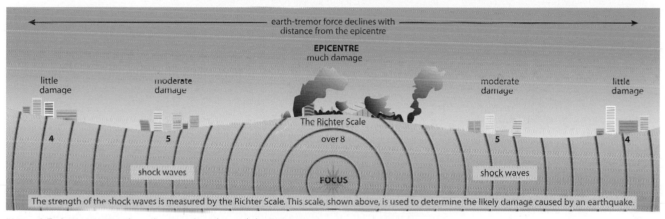

Figure 3.7: *A cross section through an earthquake, and the Richter Scale*

Which of the two earthquake scales do you prefer? Give your reasons.

Figure 3.7 shows what happens during an earthquake, depending on the strength of the shockwaves as measured on the Richter Scale. The centre of the earthquake underground is called the **focus**. Shock waves travel outwards from the focus. These are strongest close to the **epicentre** (the point on the surface directly above the focus). The amount of damage caused depends on the depth of the focus and the type of rock. The worst damage occurs where the focus is closest to the surface and where rocks are soft. Shock waves 'liquefy' soft rocks so that they behave like a liquid. This means that such rocks lose their load-bearing ability. The foundations of buildings and bridges simply collapse.

The hazard threat of earthquakes lies in their ability to shake buildings so vigorously that they fall apart and collapse. Often this damage is worse than it should be because of poor building design. There is a saying that 'earthquakes do not kill people, buildings do!' It is falling masonry that traps, crushes and kills people. Earthquakes rupture gas pipes and break electricity cables. It is not surprising therefore that fire is another aspect of the earthquake hazard.

Another after effect of an earthquake is the tidal wave or **tsunami**. Earthquakes with epicentres under the sea can generate particularly large and destructive tidal waves. The Asian tsunami of 2004 had its epicentre just off the west coast of Sumatra and generated a huge tidal wave up to 30 m high. It caused immense damage in the coastal areas of those countries bordering the Indian Ocean. The casualty list amounted to nearly 300 000. The majority of these victims were drowned. It was one of the deadliest **natural disasters** in recorded history.

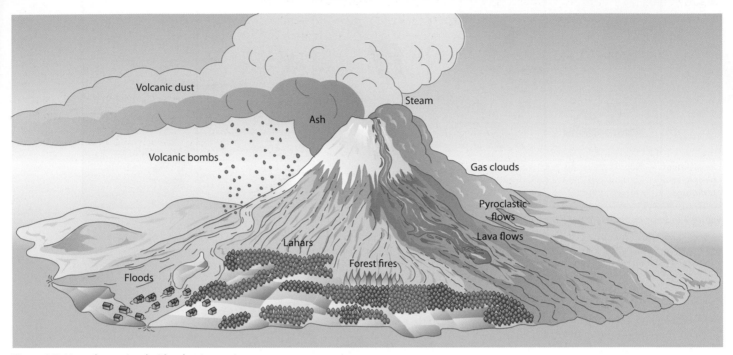

Figure 3.8: *Hazards associated with volcanic eruptions*

Volcanic eruptions

There are several different hazards associated with volcanic eruptions (Figure 3.8):

- **lava flows** – since few lava flows reach much beyond 10 km from the volcanic crater, they do not cause as much death and destruction as you might think. Lava flows may destroy farmland, buildings and lines of transport, but lives are rarely lost

- **ash** – ash may be thrown into the air during a violent eruption. Often this is carried in the wind and therefore can affect quite a large area. This happened over much of Europe in 2010 when a volcano in Iceland erupted. The ash cloud brought air travel to a halt. The further away from the volcano, the thinner will be the deposits of ash. Ash can cause much damage by simply blanketing everything, from crops to roads. Roofs of buildings will collapse if the weight of the deposited ash is great. Air thick with ash can asphyxiate humans and animals

<table>
<tr><td>Under the heading of gas emissions, remember to include pyroclastic flows (see page 84).</td></tr>
</table>

- **gas emissions** – sulphur is not the only gas to be emitted during an eruption. Other gases emitted, notably carbon dioxide and cyanide, can kill. Being dense, they keep close to the ground

Volcanic eruptions can also generate tsunamis. The huge eruption of Krakatoa in 1883 created waves up to 35 m high. These waves drowned over 36 000 people.

3.3 Tropical storms

In this part of the chapter, we focus on a third and very different natural hazard – the tropical storm. As in Part **3.2**, the same three aspects will be investigated, namely distribution, causes and hazard characteristics.

Distribution

Tropical storms or cyclones are large areas of low air pressure. They bring torrential (fast and heavy) rain and very strong winds to tropical regions. Figure 3.9 shows their distribution and what they are called in different parts of the world. For example, severe tropical storms are called hurricanes in North and Central America and the North Atlantic. Depending on the location, there may be from six to over 20 each year, but most occur between mid-summer and early autumn when the sea is warmest.

> Look closely at Figure 3.9. What do you notice about the limits to tropical storms in the two hemispheres?

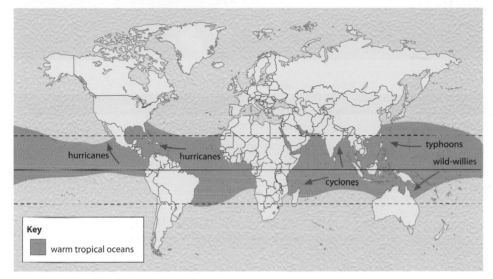

Figure 3.9: *Global distribution of tropical storms*

Causes

Tropical storms need warm water over 27°C to form. The water heats the air above it, (Figure 3.10), creating an area of very low pressure in the centre or 'eye'. In the northern hemisphere, the storm winds rotate anti-clockwise; in the southern hemisphere they rotate clockwise. The rising air quickly cools down, forming thick, dense cumulo-nimbus clouds which bring very heavy rainfall.

This area of rotating low pressure (wind) can be over 100 km wide and travel at up to 50 kph. Inside wind speeds can reach over 250 km/h around the edges of the central eye. The eye itself is calm. Figure 3.11 is a satellite image showing the swirling mass of cloud and the clear 'eye' at the centre of a hurricane in the Atlantic Ocean off Florida in the USA. Tropical storms need warm water for energy – once they reach land they quickly lose power.

[handwritten annotations: warm seas / deep seas, low pressure]

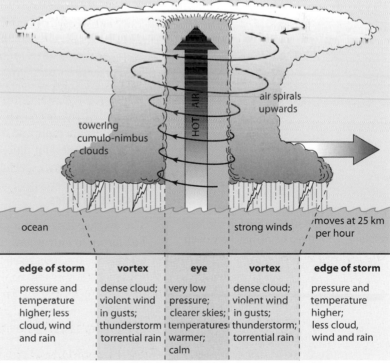

edge of storm	vortex	eye	vortex	edge of storm
pressure and temperature higher; less cloud, wind and rain	dense cloud; violent wind in gusts; thunderstorm; torrential rain	very low pressure; clearer skies; temperatures warmer; calm	dense cloud; violent wind in gusts; thunderstorm; torrential rain	pressure and temperature higher; less cloud, wind and rain

Figure 3.10: *Cross-section through a tropical storm*

[handwritten annotations: pressure / eye / ohs]

Figure 3.11: *Satellite view of a tropical storm*

Catergory	Wind speed (kph)	Pressure (mb)	Storm surge (m)	Damage
1	119–153	<980	1.0–1.7	Minor – trees, mobile homes
2	154–177	979–965	1.8–2.6	Roofs and windows of buildings Small boats broken from moorings Flooding
3	178–209	964–945	2.7–3.8	Structural damage to buildings Flooding over a metre up to 10 km inland
4	210–249	944–920	3.9–5.6	Major – destroys buildings, beaches and floods up to 10 km inland
5	<250	>920	Over 5.7	Catastrophic – destruction up to 5 metres above sea level Mass evacuation needed
Note that tropical storms have wind speeds between 55 and 118 km/h.				

Figure 3.12: *The Saffir-Simpson classification of tropical storms*

Once wind speed in a tropical storm reaches 119 km/h, it is classified as a hurricane, measured on the five-point Saffir-Simpson scale (Figure 3.12). The critical features that cause the most damage are the wind speeds and the scale of the storm surges.

Tropical storms are given names by meteorologists. These are from alphabetical lists, with alternate male and female first names over a six-year cycle. There are different lists (and names) for different parts of the world. Names help to identify and track individual storms, especially as there may be more than one happening at a time.

Characteristics

The average length of a tropical storm or hurricane is 10 days, but the biggest can last for up to four weeks. They cause three main types of damage – wind, **storm surges** (in coastal areas) and floods. Winds can destroy trees, crops, buildings, transport, power and communications. Storm surges along coastal areas can be devastating as huge waves hit the land (Figure 3.13). Torrential rainfall can last for several hours or several days, causing widespread flooding inland. This can cause potentially deadly landslides and mudslides.

Storm surges are sudden rises in sea level resulting from the passing of a very deep low pressure weather system. The low pressure allows the sea to 'expand'. See page 78 for an example.

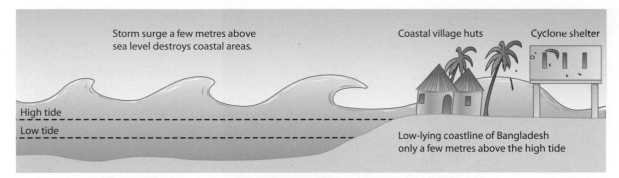

Figure 3.13: *The effects of a storm surge*

The long-term impact of a tropical storm or hurricane often depends not just on its ferocity, but whether it hits an HIC or LIC. Damage cannot be prevented. However, people in wealthier HICs can board-up properties and be evacuated in time. Warnings are broadcast in advance of approaching storms being monitored via satellite. People are also more able to cope with clearing up the damage and restoring business and economic activities after the event. LICs can be devastated by the effects of a tropical storm. With buildings and farmland ruined and little money available to rebuild, it can take years for the people and economy to recover. Even then, an LIC may often be dependent on international aid both for emergency help and long-term rebuilding.

The three hazards looked at in this chapter all have one thing in common. The scale of their damage and destruction is related to where they occur. Death tolls and damage are almost invariably higher in densely populated areas.

Remember:
- HIC = high-income country
- MIC = middle-income country
- LIC = low-income country

Methods of monitoring weather conditions

Since tropical storms are a moving hazard, it is important that they are tracked and forecasts made of their future progress. This is the work of meteorologists. If meteorologists are able to measure how they are developing, then they will be able to warn people in the predicted path of the storm. This should give those people some time in which to prepare for the storm. Precautionary actions might include moving to higher ground or to an emergency shelter. Homes can be made ready by boarding up windows, moving furniture upstairs. The media (TV, radio, the Internet) have an important role to play in keeping the general public updated about the storm and where it is expected to go.

Hurricane Mitch passed over Central America in October 1998. It proved to be a particularly tricky hurricane. First, the meteorologists could not be sure where the storm would come ashore. Another challenge was predicting the storm's speed of movement. In the event, it moved much slower than most storms. This at least gave areas in the predicted path more time to prepare for the storm. However, those areas beneath the slow-moving storm received much more heavy rainfall than normal (see Part **3.4**).

See the Case study of Hurricane Mitch on page 75.

How do meteorologists track and predict the movement of tropical storms? The data they work on comes from a number of different sources.

Figure 3.14: *Superimposed satellite images showing the progress of a hurricane from right to left*

Weather stations

There is a global network of weather stations that track the movement of tropical storms. Some are manned; others are automatic. Some monitor the weather all the time; others just at set hours during the day and night. Once all this information about pressure, temperature, humidity, winds and so on is collected and put together, it can be used to predict what will happen to the storm. Will it deepen, with an increase in rainfall and wind speeds or will the storm begin to weaken and fizzle out?

Weather satellites

For viewing large weather systems on a worldwide scale, weather satellites are invaluable (Figure 3.14). They show cloud formations, large weather events such as hurricanes, and other global weather systems. With satellites, forecasters can see weather systems such as tropical storms. On each satellite, there are two types of sensor (Figure 3.15). One is a visible light sensor called the **imager**. This works like a camera in space and helps gather information on cloud movements and patterns. This sensor can only be used during daylight hours, since it works by capturing reflected light to create images.

The second sensor is called the **sounder**. It is an infrared sensor that reads temperatures. The higher the temperature of the object, the more energy it emits. This sensor allows satellites to measure the amount of energy radiated by the Earth's surface, clouds, oceans, air and so on. Infrared sensors can be used at night which is helpful for forecasters, considering that the images can only pick up data during daylight hours.

Radar

Doppler radar is another important meteorological tool. Radar works a little differently from satellite sensors. Instead of reading reflected light or energy, radar measures reflected sound waves. When sound waves are broadcast from a radar mast and come into contact with a moving object, such as a rain cloud, radar will give information about the direction and speed of the object's movement. By using radar and getting a 'picture' of precipitation (water falling to the ground) on the radar screen, meteorologists are able to track a storm's progress over time.

Figure 3.15: *A weather satellite*

3.4 The scale and impacts of natural disasters

The amount of damage and destruction caused by a particular natural disaster depends on a whole range of factors. These include:

- the scale of the event in terms of its energy, the area affected and how long it lasts

- the degree to which people are warned in advance of the event. This is one reason why earthquakes are often so devastating. They occur almost anywhere near a plate margin without warning

- the density of human settlement in the area affected. The more people and economic activities there are in a disaster area, the greater will be the potential damage

- the degree to which people are prepared for a possible natural hazard. Are there emergency shelters? Have people been educated in what should be done in an emergency? Are houses, factories and businesses located in areas of low risk? Have buildings been constructed in such a way that they may be able to withstand the hazard?

- the ability of a country to cope with the aftermath of a hazard, both immediately and in the longer term.

It is with respect to the last two points that a basic contrast is so often seen. The contrast is between LICs and HICs in terms of their ability to prepare for hazards and their ability to cope with the damage caused. The next two cases illustrate these two different 'hazard worlds'.

A lack of capital and technology also helps to explain why natural hazards often have a more devastating impact on LICs.

Case study: Hurricane Mitch hits Central America

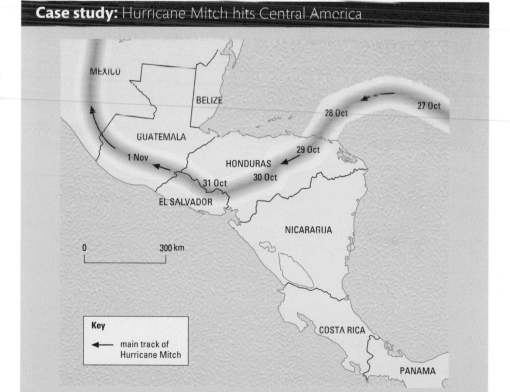

Figure 3.16: *The path of Hurricane Mitch through Central America (1998)*

Check back to Table 3.12 on page 72 to remind you of the features of a Category 5 hurricane.

Look back at page 74 to remind you how meteorologists would have tracked Hurricane Mitch.

Reference has already been made in Part **3.3** to Hurricane Mitch which passed over Central America in October 1998. Its path is shown in Figure 3.16. It was the most destructive tropical storm for 200 years. Mitch began as tropical depression on 21 October to the south of the Caribbean. A day later it became, first, a tropical storm and then a hurricane as wind speeds increased rapidly. By 26 October it had become a category 5 hurricane with speeds of over 250 km/h, moving west across the Caribbean.

Whilst meteorologists could track Mitch via satellite, they could not accurately predict which direction it might eventually take. Even had they known where it would make landfall, very little could be done to protect the area. Nor could people be evacuated in time easily. By 28 October, Mitch had started to move south-west towards Honduras (Figure 3.16). Although wind speeds inside the hurricane were still high, they had started to fall. The main problem for Honduras and neighbouring Nicaragua and El Salvador was the relatively slow movement of the whole system. As a result of this, rainfall was intense and 180 cm fell in just three days.

Figure 3.17: *Damage caused by mudslides*

The huge volume of water created widespread flooding, destroying buildings, roads, bridges, crops and live-stock. It also caused many mudslides which claimed a large number of victims. By the time Mitch turned north to Mexico, at least 10 000 people had lost their lives. Even then it had not finished as winds increased again before it reached Florida in the USA.

In the end Hurricane Mitch entered the record books. It was:

- the second longest-lasting category 5 hurricane (33 hours)
- the third longest period of continuous high winds (15 hours)
- the fourth strongest hurricane on record (winds of 249 km/h)
- the fourth lowest air pressure every measured (905 mb).

Country	Dead or missing	Homeless or evacuated
Honduras	14 000	2 million homeless
Nicaragua	3000	0.75 million homeless
Costa Rica	7	3000 evacuated
El Salvador	400	50 000 homeless
Guatemala	200	80 000 evacuated
Belize	0	10 000 evacuated
Mexico	6	Unknown number evacuated

Table 3.2: The human impact of Hurricane Mitch

For most of the countries hit by Mitch, there was neither much warning nor anywhere to go for shelter. Two million people in Nicaragua were affected by Mitch (Table 3.2). Mudslides triggered by torrential rain destroyed villages, schools, health facilities and farms (Figure 3.17). The final death toll is thought to have been about 20 000 – but many bodies have never been found. In Honduras, even optimistic estimates think it will be at least 2015 before the country will have repaired all the damage caused by a disaster which made 2 million of its 5 million population homeless. The overall cost of damage caused by Mitch was an estimated $10 billion.

After Mitch hit Central America, short-term **emergency aid** in the form of medicines, food, water and shelter came from governments and non-governmental organisations (NGOs) across the world. However, its effects are still being felt today by its peoples, economies and environments. Most of the countries in Central America are relatively poor LICs, with economies based primarily on farming. The money needed to repair the damage is simply not available within the region.

Longer term, much of the funding needed to rebuild homes and **infrastructure** has come from international aid, agencies or organisations like the World Bank. Much of this was organised via a new Central America Emergency Trust Fund and included money for a road-rebuilding project and repairs to schools and clinics. Some of these projects also created jobs for local people.

The impact of natural disasters like Hurricane Mitch in LICs is far greater than in HICs. Long-term recovery is often dependent upon aid outside of the region affected. Some experts believe that Hurricane Mitch caused so much damage that it set back development in Honduras and Nicaragua by 30 years.

Case study: Hurricane Floyd hits the USA

Hurricane Floyd hit the east coast of the USA in September 1999. Heavy rain caused flooding across 13 states and led to the evacuation of 4 million people – a million from Florida alone. Over 70 people were killed, the highest death toll in the USA from a hurricane since 1972. The final bill for damage was estimated at $6 billion.

Floyd started life on 2 September 1999 as a tropical wave off the West African coast. Five days later it had become a tropical depression and was 1500 km east of the Caribbean (Figure 3.18). A day later it had become a tropical storm.

(handwritten note: 2 million homeless)

(handwritten note: Don't have money for the repairs)

(handwritten note: International Aid & the World Bank contributed massive amounts of international aid)

Why has it taken the Central American countries so long to fully recover from the damage caused by Hurricane Mitch?

(handwritten note: Honduras set back 30 years. Honduras on coast. 20% banana crops ruined)

By the time it was 400 km from the Leeward Islands, it had been upgraded to hurricane status. As it turned north-west, the winds started to drop. Turning west once more, it quickly gained strength until winds reached 230 km/h and pressure dropped to 921 mbs (the air pressure of hurricanes is measured in millibars – mbs) . Floyd was now a category 4 hurricane, causing widespread damage to the Bahamas as it passed through on 13–14 September.

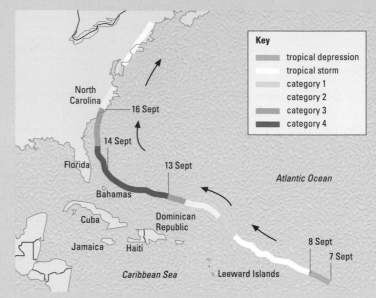

Figure 3.18: *The track taken by Hurricane Floyd*

Still uncertain as to where along the USA coast Floyd would make landfall, the south-eastern states began to evacuate coastal residents inland – Disney World in Florida was shut down for the first time ever. However, Floyd started to move north up the Atlantic coastline, missing Florida. It hit land in North Carolina on 16 September. Wind speeds had dropped as Floyd became a category 2 hurricane. However, it was the rain which did most of the damage, partly because Floyd was a very wide hurricane. Between 16 and 17 September almost 50 cm of rain fell on ground which was still saturated by heavy rain from Hurricane Dennis two weeks earlier.

Storm surges along the coast, up to 3 m high, and exceptionally heavy rainfall caused extensive flooding across 13 states. All were declared major disaster areas, with North Carolina the worst hit. Rivers peaked at over 7 m above normal levels, 51 people were drowned and 7000 homes were completely destroyed. Tens of thousands of homes were damaged and 10 000 inhabitants forced into temporary accommodation. Roads were destroyed and damaged and hundreds of thousands of cattle, pigs and poultry were drowned. Electricity supplies were badly affected.

Despite extensive damage to property and land, the quality and timing of early warning systems and subsequent organised evacuation saved many lives. National agencies monitor and track hurricanes via planes and satellites. If a storm is approaching, a 'Hurricane Watch' is announced 36 hours ahead. A 'Hurricane Warning' is issued 24 hours before expected arrival, usually leading to evacuation orders.

Although it took many months before everyone was re-housed and damage repaired, over $2 billion of government aid was made available by the US

Check back to page 72 for more information on storm surges.

Congress. Individual states, insurance companies and business funding also helped recovery. With sophisticated warning systems in place and the ready availability of emergency funds, the impact of tropical storms in a wealthy HIC like the USA will almost always be far less destructive than in poorer LICs.

Why were most people evacuated by road rather than by air or sea?

Figure 3.19: *The evacuation of almost 4 million people under way*

3.5 Reasons for living in high-risk areas

History tells us where in the world specific types of natural hazard are likely to occur. We have a fairly good idea of where the high-risk areas are. Figures 3.4 (page 67) and 3.9 (page 71) show the global distributions of two natural hazards (earthquakes and tropical storms) that cause the greatest number of deaths and the largest amount of damage. Compare those maps with the map showing the global distribution of major cities and therefore areas with high population densities (Figure 3.20). What we find may be quite surprising. Many of those cities and areas of high population density are located within the risk areas of earthquakes and tropical storms. Why do so many people continue to live and work in what are clearly hazardous areas?

It has been estimated that between 2000 and 2010 close to 1 million people were killed by earthquakes. This is not surprising because there are billions of people living in the world's earthquake zones.

Compare Figure 3.4 (page 67) with Figure 3.20 (page 80).

There are a number of possible explanations.

- A lack of education and information may mean that residents are unaware of the real risks, particularly if the hazards occur only infrequently. This can be the case particularly in poor undeveloped areas

- People may be aware of the risks but decide to live in the area anyway. Perhaps the area offers some tempting benefits (see below)

- It may be that people are unable to move away from hazardous areas, owing to a lack of money or they are concerned about not being able to find a job elsewhere

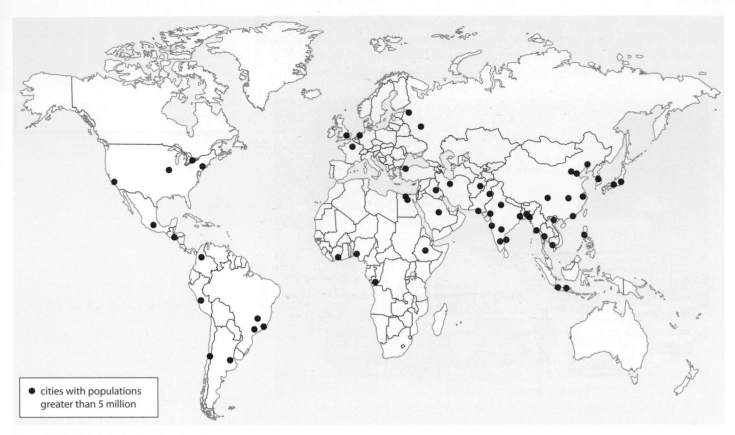

Figure 3.20: *Global distribution of major cities*

cities with populations greater than 5 million

- Human nature is such that many people are optimists and think that they will never be a natural disaster victim. Alternatively they may be resigned to their fate – if they are to be victims, there is nothing they can do about it

- Perhaps the biggest factor is that the areas of high population density have gradually grown up over many centuries. As a result, they have a sort of momentum which keeps them going no matter how many hazards occur. So for millions of people, these high-risk areas are home and as a result have a number of attractions. For example, this is where their family has lived for generations. This is where many of their relatives and friends are living today. This is where they work. This is where, despite the hazards, they feel comfortable

- The cities in these high-risk areas represent centuries of investment – of money and human effort. No human society is rich enough that it can afford to throw away all this investment and abandon these cities.

Unlike earthquakes and tropical storms which are probably the most vicious and costly natural hazards, volcanoes do offer some benefits:

- **minerals** – volcanoes bring valuable mineral resources to the surface. These include diamonds, gold and copper

- **fertile soils** – volcanic ash often contains minerals that enrich the soil. Fine dust is quickly mixed into the soil like an artificial fertiliser

- **geothermal energy** – water running through the Earth's crust is heated by volcanic rock at or near a plate margin. This hot water emerges as hot springs and can be used to heat homes, factories and business premises

It is wrong to think that all volcanoes give rise to fertile soils.

Figure 3.21: *Mount Vesuvius crater: a tourist attraction*

Why do you think tourists like to visit volcanoes?

- **tourism** – volcanoes are features that interest many people and do attract tourists. Mount Vesuvius in Sicily (Italy) is a classic example, drawing hundreds of thousands of tourists each year (Figure 3.21). The hot springs found in volcanic areas around the world also attract visitors.

Finally, you should note that dense populations are also found in the high-risk areas of other natural hazards. Obvious examples are those river valleys and delta areas that suffer from regular and severe flooding. For example, the Ganges, Brahmaputra and Meghna delta where some 90 million people live (see Part **1.8**). Here, as with volcanoes, there are some benefits, such as fertile soils replenished by the regular flooding.

3.6 Mitigating the consequences of hazards

Mitigation (or **adjustment**) involves taking actions before, during and after a hazard event to reduce its possible consequences. It is all about learning to live with hazards and trying to minimise their potential impacts. At least six major steps or actions are involved here (Figure 3.22):

- **Risk assessment** – determining the probability of a particular hazard happening and the scale of its possible damage

- **Prediction** – putting in place monitoring systems that might give warning about an imminent hazard

- **Preparation (adjustment)** – finding ways of reducing the possible death toll and the scale of damage of property. Educating people about the hazards of the areas in which they live and what to do in case of an emergency is important here

- **Hazard event** – the natural hazard that has been anticipated and planned for happens

- **Recovery** – first emergency aid and then repairing the damage

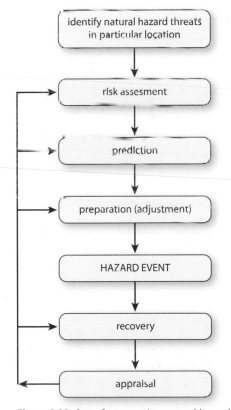

Figure 3.22: *Steps for managing natural hazards*

- **Appraisal** – an examination of what happened after the event with many questions to be asked and answered. Were there emergency plans ready to put into action? How effective were the preparations that had been made before the event? What should be done to make them better in future?

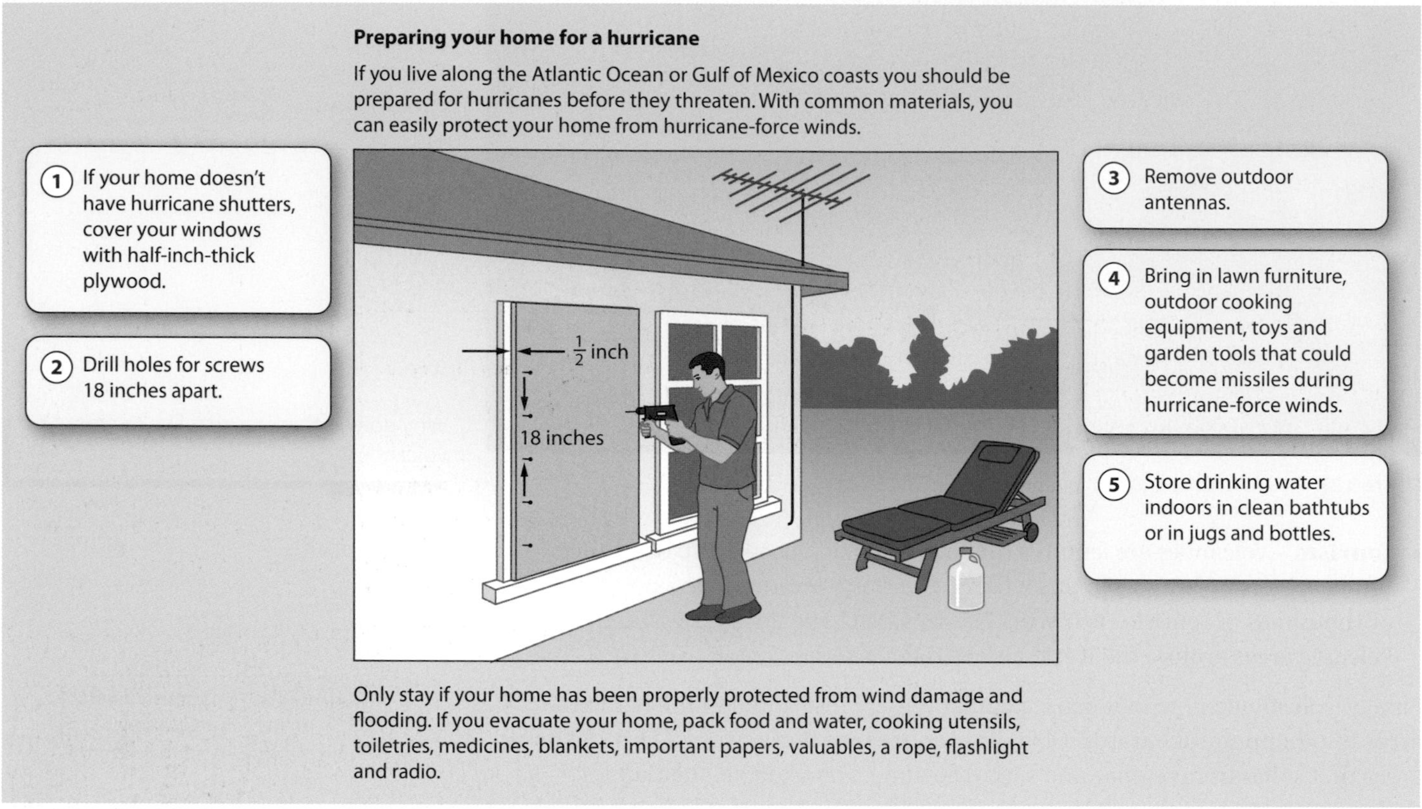

Preparing your home for a hurricane

If you live along the Atlantic Ocean or Gulf of Mexico coasts you should be prepared for hurricanes before they threaten. With common materials, you can easily protect your home from hurricane-force winds.

(1) If your home doesn't have hurricane shutters, cover your windows with half-inch-thick plywood.

(2) Drill holes for screws 18 inches apart.

$\frac{1}{2}$ inch

18 inches

(3) Remove outdoor antennas.

(4) Bring in lawn furniture, outdoor cooking equipment, toys and garden tools that could become missiles during hurricane-force winds.

(5) Store drinking water indoors in clean bathtubs or in jugs and bottles.

Only stay if your home has been properly protected from wind damage and flooding. If you evacuate your home, pack food and water, cooking utensils, toiletries, medicines, blankets, important papers, valuables, a rope, flashlight and radio.

Figure 3.23: *A hurricane preparation leaflet distributed in the USA*

We have already looked at two case studies in Part **3.4** that illustrate the damage done by tropical storms, as well as the general management of those events. In this part of the chapter, we will consider another two case studies but of different hazards – an earthquake in an HIC and a volcanic eruption in a LIC. The focus will be more on management than damage.

Look at an atlas map of Japan and find the location of Kobe.

Case study: Kobe earthquake, 1995

Early in the morning of Tuesday, 17 January 1995 the shock waves of a huge earthquake roared through the port city of Kobe in Japan. Measuring 7.2 on the Richter Scale, it was the worst earthquake to hit Japan for 50 years.

- 6432 people were killed.

- Over 100 000 buildings were destroyed.

- 300 000 people were made homeless.

- Rail links, bridges, the main expressways, docks and port area were badly damaged.

- The cost of the damage was estimated at $200 billion.

- Over 300 fires broke out destroying 7000 homes and responsible for 500 deaths devastating an area of 100 km² in central Kobe.

The epicentre of the earthquake was near Awaji Island. Here only buildings were destroyed (Figure 3.24). The greatest destruction was where most people lived – in the cities of Kobe, Akashi and Ashiya. The famous bullet train tracks, motorways and bridges were all badly damaged (Figure 3.25). Broken gas pipes and electricity lines caused fires to rage throughout the built-up areas – especially among the many wooden houses.

The scale of the damage and the size of the death toll surprised many people. Japan experiences over 1000 earthquakes every year. Fortunately most are quite minor tremors, or occur deep underground or under the sea, and have little impact. However, the Japanese have long been very aware of the danger that major earthquakes bring. They take the earthquake threat very seriously. They have to in such a densely populated country. Their risk assessments are thorough. They spend a considerable amount of time, effort and money designing buildings and transport links to withstand earthquakes.

Japanese earthquake preparations also include holding regular earthquake drills in schools and places of work. Every year armed forces and emergency services are involved in a full-scale practice. It is a vital part of earthquake preparation that everyone should know what to do in such an emergency. The response time is particularly critical in order to rescue trapped and injured people.

No one would doubt that the Japanese are well prepared to face the earthquake hazard. The problem with all earthquakes is not knowing where and when exactly they will occur. It is generally agreed that the Kobe earthquake was well 'managed', but what lessons were learnt? Were there any things that might have been done before the event that would have reduced the death toll and damage?

The worst damage of the earthquake occurred in the old parts of Kobe where many of the buildings were erected before modern anti-earthquake building regulations came into effect. Lessons were learnt about the construction of raised expressways (Figure 3.25). Many lengths were badly damaged. The tracks of the bullet train were designed to be able to withstand earthquakes. However, these were broken in no less than nine places. Overall though, it was felt that the emergency arrangements worked quite well.

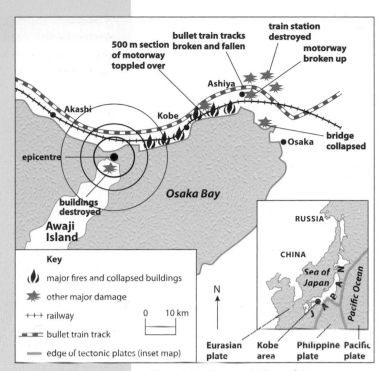

Figure 3.24: *Cause and effects of the Kobe earthquake*

Figure 3.25: *Some of the earthquake destruction*

Case study: The eruption of Mount Pinatubo

Mount Pinatubo is a volcanic mountain located about 100 km north-west of Manila, the capital of the Philippines (Figure 3.26). By June 1991, the volcano had been quiet for more than six centuries. During this time the ash and lava from previous eruptions had weathered into fertile soil which was used to cultivate rice. Then, suddenly, the volcano became active again (Figure 3.27).

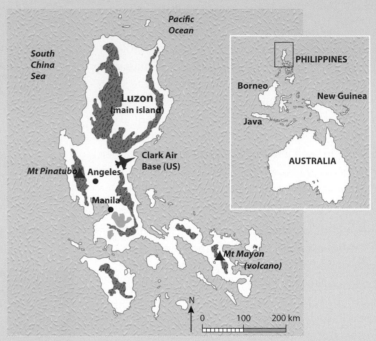

Figure 3.26: *Mount Pinatubo in the Philippines*

Advance warning that the volcano was about to erupt gave the authorities a little time to evacuate thousands of people from the nearby town of Angeles. Some 15 000 American airmen and women also left the nearby Clark Air Base. The level of activity increased and finally on 12 June the volcano sent a cloud of steam and ash some 30 km up into the atmosphere. However, more deadly than this steam and ash were the flows of burning gases that descended from the crater at speeds of over 200 km/h (Figure 3.27). They are known as **pyroclastic flows** and are commonly the main killers of people during a volcanic eruption (see Figure 3.8 on page 70).

Why are pyroclastic flows so deadly?

The eruption caused serious problems:

- Ash fell to a depth of 50 cm near the volcano, and for the 600 km radius around the volcano it was over 10 cm deep.

- The volume of ash in the atmosphere turned day to night and hampered the rescue operations.

- Torrential rain accompanied the eruption, and much of the ash was rained back to earth as mud, causing thousands of buildings to collapse under its weight.

Figure 3.27: *Pinatubo erupts and produces this fast moving pyroclastic flow*

- Power supplies were cut and roads and bridges were left unusable, as was the water supply which was quickly contaminated.

- Some 350 people were killed, mostly by pyroclastic flows.

However, the trail of destruction did not end there. When a volcano erupts, much cinder, ash and lava falls on the slopes around the crater. The lava solidifies, and the cinder and ash remain in a loose and unstable condition on the upper slopes. This is what happened after the 1991 eruption. Some years later, after people had returned to their former homes, heavy rain washed this loose material down the volcano sides. This occurred after typhoons hit the Philippines in 1993 and 1995. The local people were inundated by mud avalanches known as **lahars**. In September 1995, 65 000 people were forced to flee from their homes. One lahar was nearly 3 m high. Bacolor, a town of 20 000 people, was turned into a wasteland by mud and ash. Helicopters had to be called in to rescue people trapped by the lahars (Figure 3.28).

Which is the correct description of a lahar:

- a type of river erosion
- a form of mass movement
- a type of volcanic eruption?

The effects of the 1991 eruption were thus felt long after the volcano became dormant again. Thousands of people found themselves living in refugee camps for the second time in four years. Malaria and diarrhoea quickly spread in those camps. The cost to the Philippines was immense. Crops, roads and railways, business and personal property were destroyed, amounting to over $450 million.

The Philippines is a LIC and had little money to spend on rebuilding the part of Luzon devastated by the eruption. As a result of reviewing the hazard event, the authorities of Central Luzon decided to focus on:

- protecting against further lahars and flash flood damage by building dykes and dams

- establishing new work for the farmers and other workers well away from the danger area

- creating new towns and villages away from the disaster area.

Figure 3.28: *Filipinos flee the lahar, September, 1995*

The great cost of these adjustments could not be borne by the people of Luzon alone. The area benefited from two types of international aid:

- emergency aid after both the eruption and the lahars

- development aid to assist with the three objectives listed above.

These two case studies show that there are 'two worlds' when it comes to natural disasters. The need for adequate preparation in areas where there are hazards was underlined in 2010 with two severe earthquakes. The one in Haiti measured 7.0 on the Richter scale and hit the capital city of Port au Prince. It killed around 250 000 people. The second one was well over 8 on the Richter scale and reckoned to one of the biggest ever recorded. It hit the well-populated central area of Chile and killed up to 1000 people. The casualty difference was partly explained by the fact that Chile had used its previous experience of earthquakes to be better prepared for the one in 2010.

Research the 2010 Haiti and Central Chile earthquakes to compare, in more detail, the damage they caused.

Rank the three hazards in terms of human ability to predict them.

Predicting hazards

Prediction is a key activity when it comes to preparing to cope with (manage) natural hazards (see Figure 3.22 on page 81). It sounds a simple task, but in reality it still lies virtually impossible. We know where earthquakes are most likely to occur. However, those plate margins occupy a large area of the world. We have little idea of where exactly along them the next earthquake is going to take place. Volcanic eruptions are a little easier. We know where most of the world's active volcanoes are located. However, we do not really know which one of them is likely to become the next major volcanic disaster. As for tropical storms, we know where they are most likely to occur and at what time of the year. Once they have been detected, they can, as we saw in Part **3.4**, be tracked and their likely future course plotted.

Let us look a little more closely at predicting the two tectonic hazards. For **tropical storms**, look back at Part **3.3**.

Volcanic eruptions

We think we know where most of the world's active volcanoes are located (see Figure 3.5 on page 68). However, the problem here is that some volcanoes may erupt only after hundreds or thousands of years of being quiet (**dormant**). So it is very difficult to predict eruptions. However, sometimes there are warning signs. Near the time of an eruption, the magma beneath the volcano comes close to the surface. This will cause:

- the escape of gases, particularly sulphur dioxide, which can be monitored with special equipment
- an increase in the number of small earthquakes in the locality which can be measured with special equipment
- a swelling of the sides of the volcano.

The problem is that monitoring equipment is very expensive and could be in place for generations without detecting any signs. Perhaps the best way is for people living near volcanoes to keep a regular watch for any changes which may possibly indicate a coming eruption.

Earthquakes

Scientists know where earthquakes will strike – along the active plate margins (see Figure 3.4 on page 67). They find it much more difficult to say when they will happen. Before some earthquakes, the land may be seen to rise or tilt. Sometimes the water level in wells is seen to fall. If local people notice these changes they can alert everyone to reach places of safety, well away from buildings.

If these changes do not occur, or are not seen, there is very little chance of predicting an earthquake. There have been recent improvements in detecting changes in electrical signals and in registering radioactive emissions. In order to register such changes many more scientific stations or satellites capable of recording these indicators are needed.

Although hazard prediction may be a science, it is still very much in its infancy. Those who benefit most are probably people who live in the hazardous environments of HICs. It is these areas that have the technology and can afford the equipment that is needed.

Preparing for hazards

If scientists were able to predict when earthquakes are shortly to happen, many lives would be saved. Even if earthquakes could be predicted accurately, they would still damage buildings. Recent earthquakes in different parts of the world, together with laboratory testing, have allowed engineers and architects to develop buildings that can cope with all but the most powerful earthquakes.

Figure 3.29 shows how different building materials respond to shock waves:

- wooden houses may burn in the aftermath of an earthquake, as they did in Kobe

- bricks fall out of buildings, so they are not good building materials in earthquake zones

- concrete is much better as long as it is reinforced by strong, flexible steel bars

- high-rise buildings with flexible steel frames do survive, but falling glass and bricks can cause injury and death.

Earthquakes may be the most difficult hazard to predict, but at least they are a hazard that does allow some adjustment or preparation.

With volcanoes, a certain amount can be done on the day to control lava flows by erecting barriers and cooling lava fronts with water. An obvious adjustment is to ensure that all buildings have sloping roofs to prevent the accumulation of ash. With tropical storms, it is important that walls are built to protect coastal areas against storm surges. Buildings constructed of concrete reinforced by steel bars are most likely to withstand the very strong winds. Cyclone shelters built in this way are increasingly being provided in LICs.

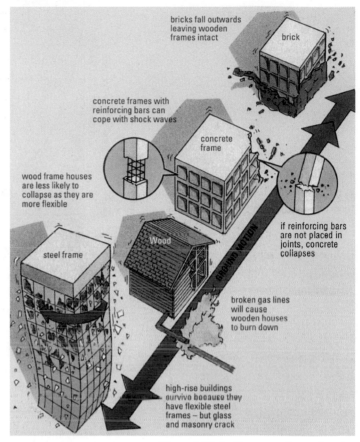

Figure 3.29: *Building to survive earthquakes*

What advantages do old wooden houses have in earthquake situations? What is their downside?

With two of the hazards – volcanoes and tropical storms – putting in place early warning systems gives people a chance to make sure they are ready to do what is necessary. With all hazards, education plays an important role in making people aware of emergency procedures – what to do during the actual event and in the immediate aftermath when panic and chaos often prevail.

3.7 Responding to hazards

Hazard response works on two time scales. There is the matter of what is done immediately after a natural hazard has struck – the **emergency response**. Later, there is a **review response** in which the whole natural hazard event is looked at. What happened this time? What needs to be done to restore the disaster area? What needs to be done so that next time the damage is less and death toll lower?

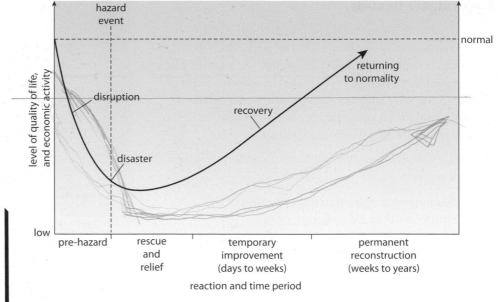

Figure 3.30 *Sequence of events following a hazard*

In your own words, briefly define these terms that appear in Figure 3.30:

- disruption
- disaster
- recovery.

Figure 3.30 shows the sequence of events immediately following a hazard. First of all, it is important that emergency services are able to identify quickly the worst hit areas and to access those areas. Time is critical if injured and trapped people are to be rescued. Different types of emergency services will be involved. There will be teams specialising in:

- releasing people and bodies trapped in collapsed buildings (Figure 3.31)
- using lifting gear and diggers to clear away rubble
- restoring basic services such as water, sewage, gas, electricity and communications
- providing medical help and counselling victims
- organising the distribution of emergency rations of food, water and clothing
- providing transport for emergency supplies – this is often done by the armed forces.

The important thing here is that all these services and others are well coordinated. This is often where emergency relief breaks down. If the disaster is a major one, it is likely to attract relief from international organisations, such as UN agencies, and voluntary organisations such as Oxfam and the Red Cross. A lack of coordination was one of the criticisms made following the Haiti earthquake (2010). However, the situation there was made more difficult by the damage done to the main airport and the seaport, by a weak government and by the great poverty of the people affected.

Explain how and why each of the following would hinder emergency aid:

- airport and seaport damage
- weak government
- widespread poverty
- little coordination.

After the emergency has been dealt with, the next stage of recovery (see Figure 3.22 on page 81) involves deciding what needs to be done to restore the disaster area back to normal – if it is decided that that is the right thing to do (Figure 3.32). It is possible that the area is believed to be too high risk and that it should be abandoned. This is where organisations such as the World Bank can play an important part in the recovery phase providing loans to rebuild infrastructure.

Figure 3.31: *Emergency services in operation*

Figure 3.32: *A restored disaster area that was badly hit by the 2004 tsunami*

The final stage is appraisal (see Figure 3.22 on page 81). This is the 'inquest', looking back at the disaster and first assessing how well or otherwise the emergency operations worked. Then the appraisal should consider whether there is anything more that could be done to reduce the impact if a similar event were to occur again. Attention will focus on the adjustments, by raising a range of questions. Can buildings in the area be made more hazard proof? Should areas be given greater protection, perhaps in the form of strengthened sea walls? Should settlements be relocated? Should the layout of urban areas be changed? This is where the United Nations International Strategy for Disaster Reduction (UNISDR) can help. It is able offer sound technical advice.

The human spirit is rather optimistic when it comes to natural hazards. First, there is often widespread feeling that the 'lightning will never strike here'. Secondly, there is the widespread belief that 'lightning never strikes the same place twice'. Without that optimism, people would find it difficult to live with the brutal truth that natural hazards can:

- strike at any time
- occur in virtually any place
- be more devastating than the one before.

Surprise is one of the nastier aspects of natural hazards!

If there was no such optimism, do you think people would still live in hazardous environments? Give your reasons.

End of chapter checkout

Checklists

Now you have read the chapter, you should know:

- ✓ what a hazard is
- ✓ the different types of hazard
- ✓ the global distribution, causes and characteristics of tropical revolving storms
- ✓ the global distribution, causes and characteristics of volcanic activity
- ✓ the global distribution, causes and characteristics of earthquakes
- ✓ how extreme weather conditions are measured
- ✓ the type and scale of damage caused by hazards
- ✓ the short-term impacts of natural disasters or hazards
- ✓ the long-term impacts of natural disasters or hazards
- ✓ the reasons why people continue to live in areas where there is a high hazard risk
- ✓ how hazards are managed
- ✓ how people predict and prepare for hazards
- ✓ how people respond to hazards immediately afterward an event and in the longer term
- ✓ how the risk of flooding is controlled

Make sure you understand these key terms:

Adjustment: changes designed to react to and cope with a situation, such as the threat posed by a hazard.

Earthquake: a violent shaking of the Earth's crust.

Emergency aid: help in the form of food, medical care and temporary housing provided immediately after a natural disaster.

Epicentre: the point on the Earth's surface that is directly above the focus of an earthquake.

Hazard: an event which threatens the well-being of people and their property.

Infrastructure: the transport networks and the water, sewage and communications systems that are vital to people and their settlements and businesses.

Lahar: a flow of wet material down the side of a volcano's ash cone which can become a serious hazard.

Natural disaster: a natural event or hazard causing damage and destruction to property, as well as personal injuries and death.

Natural event: something happening in the physical environment, such as a storm, volcanic eruption or earthquake.

Plate movement: mainly the coming together and the moving apart of tectonic plates.

Prediction: forecasting future events or changes.

Pyroclastic flow: a devastating eruption of extremely hot gas, ash and rocks during a period of explosive volcanic activity; the downslope flow to this mixture is capable of reaching speeds up to 200kph.

Risk assessment: judging the degree of damage and destruction that an area might experience as a result of a natural event.

Storm surge: a rapid rise in sea level in which water is piled up against the coastline to a level far exceeding the normal. It tends to happen when there is very low atmospheric pressure and where seawater is pushed into a narrow channel.

Subduction: the pushing down of one tectonic plate under another at a collison plate margin. Pressure and heat convert the plate into magma.

Tropical revolving storm: a weather system of very low-pressure formed over tropical seas and involving strong winds and heavy rainfall (also known as a cyclone, hurricane or typhoon).

Tsunami: a tidal wave caused by the shock waves originating from a submarine earthquake or volcanic eruption.

Volcanic activity: the eruption of molten rock, ash or gases from a volcano.

See the Glossary in the Active Book for more definitions

Questions

Try testing yourself with these questions:

1. a) What is a 'hazard'?
   b) Name the four main types of hazard.
   c) Give an example of each type.

2. In your own words and with the help of hazard examples, explain what is meant by 'risk' and 'adjustment'.

3. a) What is a 'tectonic plate'?
   b) With the help of labelled diagrams show the difference between a destructive and a collision plate margin.
   c) What are the outcomes at each type of plate margin?

4. Using Figures 3.4 and 3.5, identify those parts of the world where the most
   a) volcanoes, and
   b) earthquakes occur. Are the two locations the same?

5. a) What is the difference between the 'focus' and the 'epicentre' of an earthquake?
   b) Why is it that earthquakes pose a particular threat in coastal areas?

6. a) What are the hazards associated with volcanic eruptions?
   b) Do you think it is volcanic eruptions or earthquakes which pose the greater threat to human life? Give your reasons.

7. a) Tropical storms are known by different names in different parts of the world. Give three of these alternative names.
   b) What conditions are necessary for the development of a tropical storm?

8. Give two weather features as a tropical storm passes.

9. When are tropical storms most common in the Northern Hemisphere?
   - June and July when sea temperatures are warming
   - April and May when sea temperatures are cool
   - September and October when sea temperatures are warmest?

10. a) What is the 'Saffir-Simpson scale'?
    b) What are the three main types of damage caused by tropical storms?

11. Describe how tropical storms are tracked and their future paths predicted.

12. Describe the three main factors that affect the amount of damage and destruction caused by a particular hazard.

13. Do you agree that the impact of natural hazards is directly related to population densities? Give reasons for your answer.

14. Explain why tropical storms generally cause more damage in LICs. Use the case studies of Hurricanes Mitch and Floyd to support your answer.

15. Which do you think is the scarier natural hazard – an earthquake or a tropical storm? Give your reasons.

16. Give four reasons why people continue to live in high-risk locations.

17. a) What are the possible benefits of volcanic eruptions?
    b) Can you think of any other hazard that brings benefits?

18. a) Draw a labelled diagram showing the six steps involved in the management of a hazard.
    b) Describe in more detail what happens at one of those steps.

19. Describe the different ways in which the Japanese prepare for earthquakes.

20. What lessons were learnt from the Kobe earthquake?

21. Explain why the eruption of Mount Pinatubo was so devastating.

22. a) Describe the ways in which people try to predict earthquakes and volcanic eruptions.
    b) How successful do you think those ways are?

23. Choose two natural hazards and compare them in terms of how people prepare for them.

24. a) With the use of examples, explain what is meant by 'emergency aid'.
    b) Name some organisations that provide emergency aid.

25. Why are organisations like the World Bank and the United Nations important to long-term recovery from a hazard event?

Chapter 4: Economic activity and energy

4.1 Economic activities and sectors

The production of food (**farming**), the making of goods from raw materials (**manufacturing**) and the provision of **services** are essential to our lives. The term 'economic activity' is used to describe any type of undertaking within this broad range. Each and every economic activity does at least two things: it creates jobs (employment) and produces something for sale or **consumption**. Most economic activities are driven by the need for work and the desire to make a profit.

Introduction

This chapter is about a range of economic activities that provide people with work. They also help countries to develop and become more prosperous. A feature of many of them today is that they are changing their locations both within and between countries. The economic activities and lifestyles of the modern world are demanding more and more energy. The question is how to generate this energy – by using non-renewable or renewable resources?

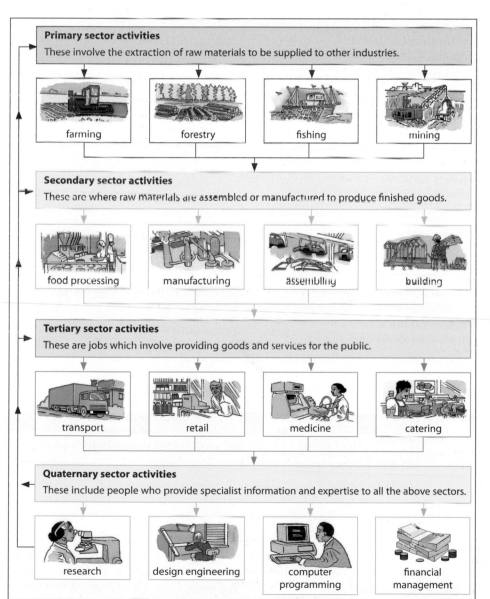

Primary sector activities
These involve the extraction of raw materials to be supplied to other industries.

farming   forestry   fishing   mining

Secondary sector activities
These are where raw materials are assembled or manufactured to produce finished goods.

food processing   manufacturing   assembling   building

Tertiary sector activities
These are jobs which involve providing goods and services for the public.

transport   retail   medicine   catering

Quaternary sector activities
These include people who provide specialist information and expertise to all the above sectors.

research   design engineering   computer programming   financial management

Figure 4.1: *Economic sectors and their activities*

Besides creating jobs and producing something for human use, economic activities involve capital – investing money and, in most cases, making some sort of profit.

Economic activities can be classified or grouped according to what they produce and the types of jobs they offer. Each group is known as an **economic sector** (Figure 4.1). Three are widely recognised throughout the world: **primary**, **secondary** and **tertiary**. A new, fourth sector – **quaternary** – has been added recently in more developed countries.

The four economic sectors

Let us look at each of these sectors and their typical economic activities:

- **primary sector** – working natural resources. The main activities are farming, forestry, fishing, mining and quarrying.

- **secondary sector** – processing things such as food or minerals (iron ore), making things by manufacturing (microchips), assembling (cars) or building (houses).

- **tertiary sector** – providing services. These include services that are commercial (retailing and banking), professional (solicitors and accountants), social (schools and doctors), entertainment (restaurants and cinemas) and personal (hairdressers and fitness trainers). Public and private transport is also included in this sector.

- **quaternary sector** – concerned with information and communications (ICT) and research and development (R & D). Universities are an important part of this sector.

As will be explained in Part **4.2**, the relative importance of the sectors in a country's economy is a good indicator of the level of economic development. Broadly speaking, the economy of a low-income country (LIC) relies heavily on the primary sector, whilst that of a high-income country (HIC) depends most on the tertiary sector. How do we measure the relative strength of the sectors? We need to use the same measure so that countries may be reliably compared. There are two different measures.

The first measure is employment. In other words, the sectors are compared in terms of the percentage of the total workforce that they employ. A pie chart is a good way of showing this information (see Figure 4.4 on page 95). However, not all labour is the same in the sense of the monetary value of what it does. For example, although what a farmer does is important in terms of feeding people, the monetary value of food is considerably less than perhaps the medical services of a doctor. The general level of pay also varies from sector to sector. Look at Table 4.1 which gives the average wage levels for some of the jobs in the different sectors.

> To which economic sector do each of the following belong:
> - a car ferry
> - a designer of computer software
> - a wind farm
> - a firm recycling plastic?

Primary		Secondary		Tertiary		Quaternary	
Farmworker	$19 280	Food operative	$26 290	Truck driver	$30 260	Computer programmer	$73 470
Fisherman	$28 460	Construction worker	$32 250	Travel agent	$32 470	Biochemist	$88 450
Miner	$41 360	Vehicle worker	$34 350	Nurse	$65 130	Design engineer	$89 080

Table 4.1: Average annual wage levels in the USA (2009)

It is because of these variations in the value of sector products and in sector pay that a second measure is used to assess the relative importance of the economic sectors. This is based on how much each sector contributes to the overall economic output of a country – their percentage of either **gross domestic product** (**GDP**) or **gross national income** (**GNI**). Again, the pie chart is a useful way of showing this measure.

4.2 Changes over time and space

The relative importance of economic sectors changes over time. As a country develops, the proportion employed in the primary sector decreases, and the proportion employed in the secondary and tertiary sectors increases. As the economy develops even further, numbers in the primary and secondary sectors fall further. After the tertiary sector becomes the largest employer, so a quaternary sector begins to emerge.

Reading Chapter 9.1 should help your understanding of development and sector shifts.

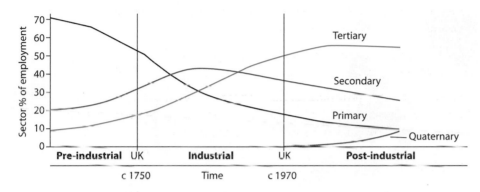

→ Tertiary grows

Figure 4.2: *Economic sector shifts in the UK*

Figure 4.2 shows how the sectors change with time over three phases. The critical phase is the industrial one. This occurs when manufacturing (the secondary sector) becomes more important than the primary sector, in terms of both employment and contribution to GDP. Cottage industries are replaced by mechanised industries housed in factories. This process of **industrialisation** is accompanied by important economic and social changes.

The three phases are the:

- **pre-industrial phase** – the primary sector leads the economy and may employ more than two-thirds of the working population. Agriculture is by far the most important activity

- **industrial phase** – the secondary and tertiary increase in productivity. As they do so, the primary sector declines in relative importance. The secondary sector peaks during this phase, but rarely provides jobs for more than half of the workforce

- **post-industrial phase** – the tertiary sector is clearly the most important sector. The primary and secondary sectors continue their relative decline. The quaternary sector begins to appear.

Mechanical
Commercial farming
(not subsistence)
Releases labour force
rural → urban migration
wages in factories
Disposable income → services

The important point here is that these **sectoral shifts** are part and parcel of the development process. The sequence or **development pathway** or **staircase** may be crudely explained as follows. The sequence starts as agriculture becomes mechanised, more commercial and shifts away from subsistence farming. This releases labour to take on other forms of work. People are free to move from the countryside and into urban settlements where traditional craft industries are replaced by factories making goods for expanding markets. The wages earned in the factories lead to there being more **disposable income** and much of this is spent on services. Gradually, the range of services available to people expands and the tertiary sector becomes dominant both in terms of employment and generating economic wealth.

Look at Chapter 9.3 for more information about the development staircase or pathway.

The increase in the amount of services provided by the government, and the people who work in public service provision, adds to this situation.

The quaternary sector appears when leading countries, and major cities within those countries, find that in order to keep ahead of the pack, they need to invest in higher education, research and development and new technologies. As countries move up the development staircase (see Figure 9.11 on page 248), not only are there these sector shifts, there is also a rise is the overall standard of living and in the level of **urbanisation**.

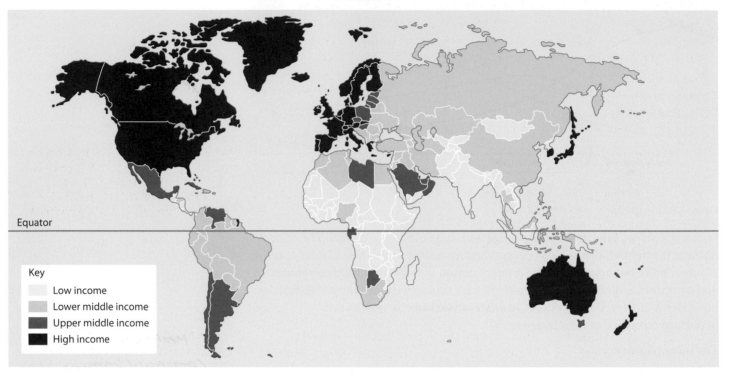

Equator

Key
- Low income
- Lower middle income
- Upper middle income
- High income

Figure 4.3: *The global distribution of economic development*

Referring to Figure 4.3, into which category do each of the following countries fall:

- India
- Egypt
- Japan
- Mexico?

You may need an atlas to help you.

Today, the world's countries are strung out up the development staircase. Some have made little progress up it, while others have gone a long way. Some are moving quickly, others hardly at all. As a result, it is possible to classify countries according to where they are on the development pathway. Figure 4.3 divides the countries of the world into four broad groups, based on **per capita GNI**:

- **low-income countries (LICs)** – occur largely in Central Africa and in South and Southeast Asia

- **lower** and **upper middle-income countries (MICs)** – these two groups are most common in South America, North and South Africa, parts of the Middle East, Eastern Europe and Asia

- **high-income countries (HICs)** – found mainly in North America, Western Europe and Australasia.

In each of these groups, the balance of the economic sectors is different. The primary sector is the most important one in LICs. The secondary sector is quite strong in most MICs. The tertiary sector is strongest in all HICs.

The following case study looks at the economies of three countries at different steps up the development staircase.

Case study: Sector shifts as seen in three countries

Ethiopia – a poor LIC

Ethiopia is ranked 170 out of 177 countries in terms of its level of development. This makes it one of the poorest and least developed countries in the world. It is located in the Sub-Saharan region of Africa. Figure 4.4 and Figure 9.2 on page 242 show that its economy is based on the primary sector – i.e. agriculture. The primary sector accounts for 75% of all employment but only 44% of GDP. This difference in percentage values reflects the fact that agriculture in Ethiopia is mainly subsistence farming (Figure 4.5). Few crops are grown for sale and possible export. The most important of these is coffee. However, recurrent droughts and a long-running war with its neighbour Eritrea have caused coffee production to vary greatly from one year to the next.

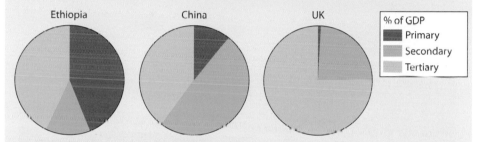

| % of GDP |
| Primary |
| Secondary |
| Tertiary |

Figure 4.4: *The economic sectors of Ethiopia, China and the UK (% of GDP)*

When reading this case, you should also refer to Figure 9.2 (page 242). Figure 4.4 compares the sectors of the three countries in terms of GDP. Figure 9.2 compares them in terms of employment.

Over 75% of Ethiopians live in rural areas. Cities and towns are few and far between. This explains why there is so little employment in the tertiary sector. A poor, largely rural population has little need of urban services, if only because it lacks money. However, since services are relatively more valuable than commercial crops, the small tertiary sector accounts for almost as much of the country's GDP as the primary sector.

Research possible reasons why Ethiopia is such a poor and undeveloped country.

Figure 4.5: *A farming landscape in Ethiopia*

The secondary sector (manufacturing) plays little part in Ethiopia's present economy. The country lacks mineral resources and the capital necessary for industrialisation, so at present manufacturing has largely to do with food processing. Ethiopia has yet to make much progress up the development staircase.

China – a rapidly emerging economy

China is a giant of a country in terms of its area and its population. Over the last 10 years, its economy has been taking giant strides. It is now the second largest economy in the world. In per capita terms, however, it is still a lower middle-income country. The secondary sector has been driving much of China's economic development (Figure 4.4). It now accounts for half the country's GDP, but only a quarter of the labour force. The industrial success is based mainly on cheap labour and **energy** (Figure 4.6). The wealth created by industry is already beginning to encourage growth in the tertiary sector.

Figure 4.6: *A modern industrial landscape in China*

Research the main types of goods being produced by Chinese manufacturers.

It is interesting to note that agriculture in the primary sector still employs large numbers of workers. However, this sector's contribution to GDP is shrinking fast.

UK – a post-industrial economy

The UK was the world's first industrial nation. It led the Industrial Revolution. Fifty years ago, manufacturing produced 40% of the country's economic wealth and employed one-third of the workforce. Today, however, it only produces 24% of the wealth and employs 18% of the workforce. As a result of the **global shift** in manufacturing, the country has experienced **de-industrialisation** (see also Part **4.5**). Many of the goods once manufactured in the UK are now made in China, India and other countries.

Figure 4.7: *A modern science park in the UK*

The UK's economy today is very much a service-based economy (Figure 4.7). Figure 4.4 shows that the tertiary sector provides jobs for 80% of UK workers; it creates 75% of the national economic wealth. However, we need to be aware that these figures for the tertiary sector also include those for the up-and-coming quaternary sector. Because it is often hard to distinguish between quaternary and tertiary sector work, we can only guess what the sector's contribution to the economy is – possibly 10–15%.

Finally, it is interesting to note the place of agriculture in the UK economy. UK farming produces about 60% of the country's food supply. The low labour percentage reflects the high level of mechanisation, while a low GDP percentage reflects the low price of farm products relative to manufactured goods and services.

For more information about science parks, see:

- Part 4.4 (page 101)
- Chapter 5.9 (page 139)
- Chapter 6.6 (page 161).

If you run your eye across the pie charts in Figure 4.4, you can begin to see what is meant by **sector shifts**. The relative importance of the three economic sectors changes as countries move up the development staircase.

4.3 Informal employment

So far we have recognised four different sectors. In some parts of the world, there is a fifth sector but it is not recognised in the official figures produced by governments. This so-called **informal sector** is also referred to as the 'black economy' in the sense that it is unofficial and unregulated. Yet this sector employs millions of people across the world, especially in LICs.

Causes of the informal sector

Check that you understand the difference between underemployment and unemployment.

It would be helpful first to look at the reasons why the informal sector develops. That should help us to understand its characteristics. In many LICs today large numbers of people are migrating from rural to urban areas. An important driving force behind that migration is the search for work and a regular wage, together with the belief that the quality of life is better in towns and cities. Whilst it is true that there are more job opportunities and higher wages, there are often more people of working age moving into urban areas than there are jobs available. Surplus labour means that there is **underemployment** and unemployment. In this situation, employers are able to pay their workers very low wages. The wages are so low they are not enough for the worker and his family to live on. Thus many people must find other ways of making a living outside the normal job market.

Characteristics

This informal activity might involve selling matches or shoelaces on the street, ice-cream vending, shoe-shining, rubbish collecting or scavenging bottles, cans and other types of waste for recycling. Some are so desperate as to resort to begging, petty crime or prostitution. Informal economic activities fall mainly within the tertiary sector. Informal employment is closely associated with another common feature of LIC urban areas – shanty towns (see Chapter **6.5**).

Figure 4.8: *Gridlocked traffic in Delhi*

An interesting group of informal activities falls under the heading of **paratransit**. These arise because of the inadequate official transport in LIC towns and cities. They usually take the form of minibuses, hand-drawn and motorised rickshaws, scooters and pedicabs (tricycles used as taxis). While these paratransit modes flourish because they are meeting the demand for cheap urban transport, they frequently add to the problems of congestion on already busy, overloaded roads (Figure 4.8).

These informal activities certainly have some benefits. For example, they provide a wide range of cheap goods and services that would otherwise be out of the reach of many people. They provide the poor with a means of survival. However, because earnings are so low, informal activities do nothing to break the **cycle of poverty** in LIC urban areas. Other costs associated with the informal sector include:

- no health care or unemployment benefits
- a high exposure to work-related risks
- an uncertain legal status.

Perhaps the worst aspect is the involvement of children in economic activity, rather than formal education. In Dhaka, the capital city of Bangladesh, it is estimated that there are half a million children in the informal sector. Most of them work from dawn to dusk, earning on average the equivalent of 50 cents (US) a day, to help support their families. The jobs range from begging and scavenging to domestic service and working as fare collectors for various forms of paratransit. These children work in vulnerable conditions, and are exposed to hazards such as street crime, violence, drugs, sexual abuse, toxic fumes and carrying excessive loads (Figure 4.9). The working conditions mean that the children often suffer extremely poor health and a range of development problems. There is little hope that these children will break out of the cycle of poverty particularly if they have no schooling.

For more information about the cycle of poverty, see:

- Chapter 6.8 (page 169)
- Chapter 9.7 (page 257)

Figure 4.9: *Children at work in the informal sector – brickmaking*

Make a two-column table and list:

- the benefits
- the costs

of informal employment. Which column do you think carries more weight?

4.4 The growth and location of tertiary and quaternary activities

Growth

Three important points that have already been made about the tertiary and quaternary sectors in this chapter:

- these two sectors involve the provision of a wide range of services
- the tertiary sector grows in importance with economic development – it generates much employment and economic wealth
- the quaternary sector is only found in the most economically-advanced countries – it is largely about information and communication and makes use of the latest technology.

As a country moves along the development pathway several things happen:

- it is able to afford more and better social services, such as schools, medical centres, hospitals and libraries

- people earn more money and have money to spend in the shops on 'basic' things, such as food and clothing

- after they have bought the 'basics', people have more money left (**disposable income**) to spend on 'luxuries', such as entertainment, holidays, eating out and recreation

- people's tastes change and this impacts on the tertiary sector. For example, cinemas have closed because many people now prefer to watch DVDs at home

- new technology creates and makes possible new services. Think of all those new services connected with ICT – broadband service providers, website designers, mobile phone networks, software programmers and the servicing of PCs and laptops.

Can you think of other ways in which people's changing tastes have affected tertiary services?

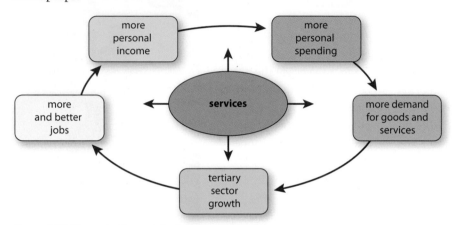

Figure 4.10: *The cycle of growth in the tertiary sector*

Figure 4.10 shows the cycle of growth within the tertiary sector. However, there are two other reasons for the 'rise' of the tertiary sector, particularly in the UK and other HICs. First, the tertiary sectors share of employment and GDP have been inflated by the decline in the primary and secondary sectors. Secondly, the population is becoming 'greyer'. Fifteen percent of the UK's population is over 64 years old. The rates of spending amongst retired people are rising faster than in any other age group. Far from staying at home in their cardigan and slippers, the 'SKI-ers' (so called because they are Spending the Kids' Inheritance) are keen shoppers and tourists. The 'grey pound' has a growing power and influence within the tertiary sector.

The key factors in the growth of tertiary activities are the rise in prosperity and personal wealth, together with the use of new technology.

Location

Nearly every economic activity – whether it is a quarry, a factory or a shop – is found in a particular place for good reasons. Those reasons are called **location factors**. They are, if you like, the 'needs' of the activity. For many services within the tertiary sector, a common 'need' is to be readily accessible to customers. After all, if there are no customers, there would be few services.

Look at the CBD of a town or city near you. Make of list of the main types of service present there.

The fact that accessibility is a key location factor explains why so many services are found concentrated in the central areas of towns and cities. These concentrations are known as **central business districts** (**CBDs**) and are to be found in LIC and HIC urban areas alike.

The CBDs are accessible because this is where the urban transport networks, both public and private, converge. Not only that, but the transport networks serving surrounding areas and linking to other urban settlements also converge here. Remember, that the customers of the services in the CBD are not just urban residents. They come from outside, from all those places lying within the town or city's **sphere of influence**.

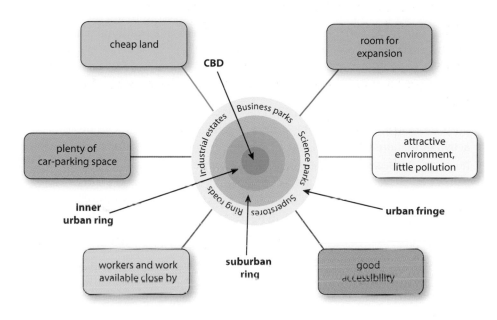

> Produce a diagram similar to Figure 4.11, but which shows the downside of these developments in the urban fringe. You might look at Chapter 6.8, especially page 165.

Figure 4.11: *The attractions of the urban fringe*

A feature of HIC cities over the last 25 years has been **decentralisation**. People and businesses, particularly tertiary activities, have been moving out from the CBD and inner city to the suburban ring and just beyond into the urban fringe. Figure 4.11 shows some of the attractions of the urban fringe to both tertiary and quaternary activities. Government policy in many HICs has been to contain suburbanisation and the outward spread of urban areas. However, the economic power of a whole range of businesses that wish to set up in the urban fringe has been very strong. So strong, in fact, that green belts and other planning controls have had to be relaxed. The signs of this happening in the urban fringe include the appearance of the following (Figure 4.12) (see also Chapter **6.6** on page 161):

- **superstores and retail parks** – large areas with adjacent car parks occupied by either one huge hypermarket or a number of retailing companies in separate buildings (Figure 4.12). These developments often serve customers drawn from more than one town or city

- **industrial estates** – areas of modern light and service industries with a planned layout and purpose-built road network

- **business parks** – areas created by property developers in order to attract firms needing office and retail accommodation rather than industrial units. They often include leisure activities such as bowling alleys, ice rinks and cinemas

Figure 4.12: *An urban fringe retail park*

- **science parks** – usually located close to a university or research centre with the aim of encouraging and developing **high-tech industries** and quaternary activities (see Figure 4.7 on page 97).

Finally, not all tertiary activities are confined to urban areas. One obvious exception is tourism, probably one of the most important tertiary sector activities today. It employs millions of people worldwide and creates huge amounts of economic wealth. In terms of tourist resorts, it is true that tourism has an urban 'face', but much tourism also takes place in rural areas – in national parks, for example, and in wilderness areas.

For more information about tourism, see Chapter 8.4, 8.5 and 8.6.

Case study: The global biotechnology industry

Biotechnology is one of the so-called high-tech industries, often located on purpose-built science parks. It is a large umbrella title to cover a range of activities that are broadly related to the modification of living organisms for human purposes. Its origins go back to the domestication of animals, the cultivation of plants and the 'improvement' of both animals and plants – i.e. making them more productive or disease resistant. Biotechnology involves applying sciences such as biology, in fields such as:

- healthcare – searching for plants with medicinal value, developing new drugs
- food production – the development of genetically modified (GM) crops and livestock
- industrial use of crops – vegetable oils and biofuels
- the environment – recycling, treating waste and cleaning up polluted sites
- warfare – the development of biological weapons.

Which countries shown in Figure 4.13 are not located in Europe or North America?

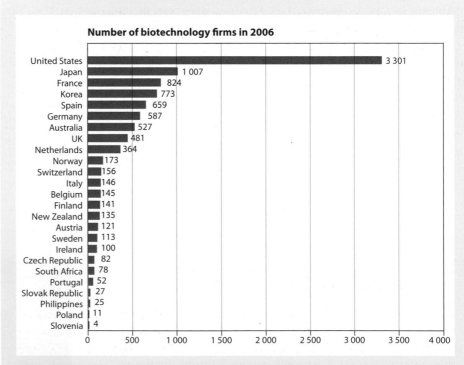

Figure 4.13: *The global distribution of biotechnology firms, 2006*

Biotechnology is primarily a quaternary activity since it is largely about research and development and serves all three of the other sectors. A basic location factor is a good supply of graduate scientists. It is this that perhaps explains why almost all of the world's biotechnology firms are located in HICs (Figure 4.13). Most of these firms have links with university research departments. Virtually half of all these firms are located in the USA.

Once these firms come up with a product, such as a new anti-malaria drug, that is believed to have a good market, then it will simply be a matter of setting up some form of factory-based mass-production. It is likely that such a factory could be set anywhere in the world where labour and land are cheap. It would not need to be located in an HIC, near the research centre or near to any particular market or raw material source.

4.5 The changing location of manufacturing

In Part **4.2** attention was drawn to the global shift in manufacturing. The global distribution of manufacturing is very uneven. The great majority of the world's manufacturing production is concentrated in a small number of countries (Table 4.2). In fact, over 50% is accounted for by three countries (USA, China and Japan).

Despite the fact that manufacturing today is highly concentrated, the distribution pattern is a changing one. If we were to compare the current situation with that of 50 years ago, significant **global shifts** would be apparent. Figure 4.14 shows that since 1970, the HICs' share of world manufacturing declined from 88 to 70%. Today, around 25% of manufacturing production occurs in MICs, particularly the so-called emergent economies of China, Brazil, Russia and India.

These three countries have become industrial leaders at different times – the USA at the beginning of the 20th century; Japan in the second half of the 20th century, and China at the beginning of the 21st century.

Country	Value of manufacturing production (2008) ($US billion)	Share of global production (%)
USA	1831	24
China	1399	18
Japan	1045	14
Germany	767	10
Italy	381	5
UK	323	4
France	306	4
Russia	256	3
Brazil	237	3
South Korea	231	3

Table 4.2: The top 10 manufacturing nations (2008)

How do you explain the fact that the UK has de-industrialised and yet, as Table 4.2 shows, it is still one of the world's leading manufacturers?

What is causing this gradual global shift in manufacturing from the HICs to the MICs? The location of manufacturing has always been influenced by factors such as raw materials, energy, labour, markets, transport and land. Those factors are still influential but their relative importance has changed and with it the location of today's manufacturing. There have been six particularly important developments:

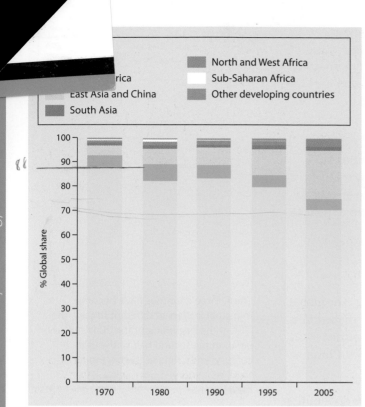

Figure 4.14: *The changing global distribution of manufacturing*

Legend:
- North and West Africa
- ...rica
- Sub-Saharan Africa
- East Asia and China
- Other developing countries
- South Asia

Y-axis: % Global share (0 to 100)
X-axis: 1970, 1980, 1990, 1995, 2005

For more information about the global shift in manufacturing, see Chapter 8.3 (page 215)

- **transnational corporations (TNCs)** – the emergence of huge companies that control much of the world's manufacturing. These companies are locating their factories in the cheapest and therefore most profitable locations

- **transport** – now much faster and cheaper. Therefore distance, say from raw materials or markets, is no longer as significant as it used to be

- **communications** – because of the speed and efficiency of modern communications, a manufacturing company can keep in immediate touch with factories scattered in different countries

- **energy** – much modern manufacturing relies on electricity as its main source of energy. Due to national grid systems, this form of energy can be made available almost anywhere

- **governments** – these are increasingly influencing the distribution of manufacturing. They are able to tempt industrialists to set up factories within their borders by various incentives, such as exemption from taxes or cheap ready-made factory buildings

- **new branches of manufacturing** – manufacturing is no longer just about making heavy goods such as steel, ships and chemicals. Manufacturing today is very much about making a widening range of consumer products such as electrical and electronic goods, clothes and furniture. Because of the four previous developments, the location of the production of these kinds of products is described as 'footloose'. In other words, their location is no longer tied by location factors such as the nearness of raw materials and markets.

The net effect of these developments has been to increase the importance of one location factor, labour. For many types of manufacturing, the costs of labour are critical. The TNCs, in particular, are constantly on the look-out for cheap labour. In the case of high-tech industries, it is not so much the cost of labour as their education levels and skills. It is because of the latter that the UK, despite losing many of its traditional industries, it is still the sixth leading manufacturing nation.

Case study: the M4 corridor in the UK

This corridor is a narrow belt of land that has become home to a growing number of services and high-tech industries. It is sometimes described as England's 'silicon valley'. Its spine is provided by the M4 motorway, which stretches westwards from London, along the main railway line to Bristol and Cardiff. It contains a number of well established cities and towns with significant manufacturing, such as Reading with its '3 Bs' industries (beer, biscuits and bulbs), Swindon with the railway workshops, Bristol with its port-related industries, and Cardiff – another port once famous for the export of coal, iron and steel, but now the home of the Welsh Assembly. There are parts of the corridor that have a long involvement in manufacturing. However, those old industries have now largely disappeared and been replaced by newcomers. Some of those that have disappeared have since 'resurfaced' in other countries.

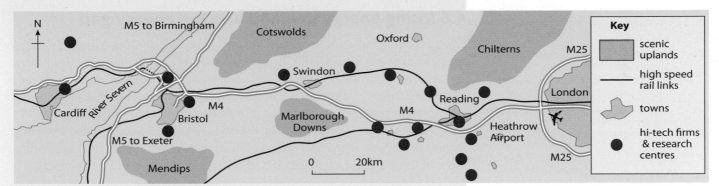

Figure 4.15: *The M4 corridor in southern England*

In the second half of the 20th century the character of the corridor began to change. There was a considerable growth in population because commuters and their families moved out of London in search of cheaper and better housing. The M4 motorway was opened and the main railway line was upgraded. New factories appeared, many of them associated with the food and drink industry. Others were involved in assembling cars, electrical and other household goods. However, most conspicuous among the new industrial enterprises were the so-called **high-tech industries**. Firms such as Compaq, NEC and Intel are here. All have business interests firmly in the quaternary sector. Reading, for example, has become home to a mix of businesses that include familiar names such as Microsoft, ING Direct, Prudential and Ericsson.

What factors have encouraged this quite remarkable concentration of high-tech industries (Figure 4.15)? The following have played a major part:

- **transport and accessibility** – mention has already been made of the M4 motorway and the high-speed railway link between London and South Wales. The presence of Heathrow Airport (Europe's major airline hub) is an important factor in the equation. The nature of much high-tech activity is essentially international. Both staff and products need to move around the globe quickly and often at short notice. The location close to London with its government offices and financial institutions is also an advantage

- **labour** – the need is mainly for graduate labour. Suitably qualified and experienced workers enjoy large salaries. They can afford to choose where they live. The corridor is able to offer many attractive residential locations, for example in the Chilterns and Cotswolds

- **universities** – many of the companies in the corridor are involved in research and development and for this reason 'feed off' links with universities and research establishments. The corridor contains at least three universities with high research rankings – Reading, Bristol and Cardiff. Not far outside the corridor to the north is Oxford University

- **incentives** – firms have been encouraged to set up here by various incentives offered by local government authorities, the UK government and also the EU. The incentives include earmarked greenfield sites at reduced prices and with tax exemptions.

Traditional location factors, such as raw materials and energy supply, are of little significance.

Research these four companies and find out more about their business interests.

4.6 Rising energy demand and the energy gap

Energy is one of the most important of all the world's resources. We need energy to keep us warm and to cook with. It gives us light and powers industrial machinery and transport. Fortunately, the natural environment provides us with a wide range of energy sources. A distinction is made between **primary energy** and **secondary energy**. Primary energy is fuels that provide energy without undergoing any conversion process, for example coal, natural gas and fuelwood. Secondary energy includes electricity, petrol and coke, which are made from the processing of primary fuels. In today's world, electricity is undoubtedly the leading source of energy.

There is another important distinction made in the world of energy. Energy sources such as fossil fuels (coal, oil and gas) are classed as **non-renewable**. Once used up, they cannot be replaced. Newer energy sources, such as solar, wind and tidal power are described as **renewable**. They can be used again and again. For this reason they are **sustainable**, and are likely to play an increasingly important role in the future.

Energy demand

The demand for energy across the world is constantly rising. This increase in demand is caused in part by the increase in population, and by economic development. The amount of energy a country uses is widely used as an indicator or measure of its level of development. As a country develops, energy-consuming activities, such as manufacturing, provision of services and transport increase in scale and importance. This rising demand for energy will be met by either the country using its own energy resources or importing from producer countries.

> Check that you understand the difference between:
> - primary energy and secondary energy
> - renewable and non-renewable energy.

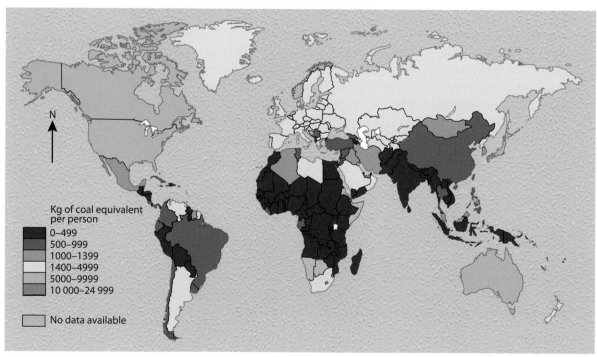

Figure 4.16: *Global energy consumption*

Kg of coal equivalent per person
- 0–499
- 500–999
- 1000–1399
- 1400–4999
- 5000–9999
- 10 000–24 999

No data available

Figure 4.16 shows the global distribution of **energy consumption**. It also shows energy demand. Europe and North America use 70% of the world's energy, although only 20% of the world's population lives there. These areas were the first to experience large-scale economic development. They used their own supplies of fossil fuels to provide the necessary energy for this development. Today, with many of their own reserves falling low or finished, they need to import energy, especially oil, to meet their ever-rising energy demand.

A noticeable feature of Figure 4.16 is the relatively low level of energy demand over much of South America, Africa and South and South-east Asia. This mainly reflects a relatively low level of economic development. However, remember that these regions enjoy warm climates and therefore little energy is needed for heating. Cooling is another matter and many HICs use much energy for cooling.

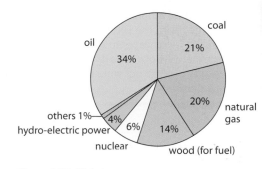

Figure 4.17: *Global energy sources*

Energy production

Figure 4.17 shows that three-quarters of the world's energy production comes from three sources: oil, natural gas and coal. All are non-renewable. The major producers of energy are the USA, Canada, Western Europe, Russia, parts of the Middle East, Australia and New Zealand (Figure 4.18). These areas are blessed with reserves of one or more of these main energy sources. By comparing Figures 4.16 and 4.18, we can see that the world's major consumers of energy are also the major producers. Put another way, levels of energy production are low in those countries with low levels of energy consumption and demand – i.e. the LICs. There are two different 'energy worlds'.

Describe the main features of the distribution of energy production shown in Figure 4.18.

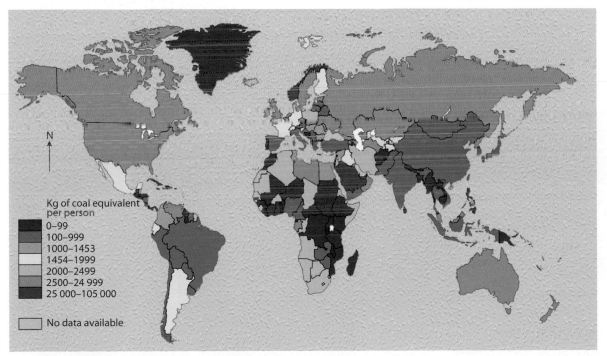

Figure 4.18: *Global energy production*

The UK's energy gap is being widened by the gradual exhaustion of North Sea oil and gas deposits. The UK still has plenty of coal, but it is cheaper to import foreign coal. Use of coal is however being reduced in order to cut emissions of carbon dioxide.

Energy gap

There is an increasing number of countries in the world facing what is referred to as an **energy gap**. Broadly speaking, this is the difference between a country's rising demand for energy and its ability to produce that energy from its own sources. This is well illustrated by the case of the UK (see page 109). Here and elsewhere, the gap is being widened by the deliberate phasing out of fossil fuels. The resulting loss of energy is greater than the amount of energy being developed from alternative renewable sources.

It is doubtful whether the world as a whole has yet reached the point of having an energy gap or crisis. It certainly has plenty of reserves of coal, oil and natural gas. However, these sources are non-renewable and their widespread use is being questioned and challenged by the need to reduce carbon emissions due to the possible link with global warming. If the world does have an energy problem today, it would be the growing mismatch between the distributions of energy consumption and production. This mismatch is creating not only national energy gaps, but also countries with energy surpluses. These surpluses give those countries huge geopolitical and economic power. They have the ability to hold other countries to ransom and many would question how that financial power is being used by some of those countries.

4.7 The need for energy efficiency

Two things are becoming very clear in today's world of energy, particularly as global demand increases and an increasing strain is placed on global energy resources:

- energy MUST be used sparingly and with the utmost efficiency

- the non-renewable sources of energy are finite and MUST be conserved. We simply cannot afford to be wasteful; energy is a precious resource. Neither do we want the pollution caused by burning them.

Figure 4.19: *Two simple energy-saving actions – insulating roof spaces and walking to school*

In terms of improving the efficiency with which energy is used, we have to recognise that all of us as individuals have responsibilities. It is easy to say we will leave it to our government to do what is necessary. There are many simple things that we can do in our everyday lives that will help save energy. The following are a few examples:

- walk or cycle to and from school rather than rely on your parents to drive you there and pick you up

- homes in temperate latitudes lose an average of 50% of their heat through the walls and loft spaces. Insulation to necessary to stop this. It may seem costly but in the long run it is more energy efficient. Curtains and blinds on all windows also provide insulation in summer from letting the heat in (reducing the need for air conditioning) and in winter from letting the heat out (reducing the need for heating)

- pack the empty spaces in the freezer and the refrigerator either with ice trays or polystyrene. The more space that is taken up, the less energy it takes to cool or freeze. Do not run the dishwasher or the washing machine unless they are full.

- many of us have more electronic and electrical gadgets than ever. Computers, mobile phones televisions and DVD players – all use energy. Putting your computer to 'hibernate' and even unplugging it for the night can save precious electricity. Instead of charging your mobile phone overnight, do so when you are still awake and unplug it as soon as it is done.

> Can you think of any more ways you might reduce your own energy consumption?

Case study: The changing energy situation in the UK

During the last 20 years there have been great changes in the UK's energy situation. The most important of these is that the demand for electricity increased by one-third. Another vital change is in the sources of energy used to generate this electricity. No longer is the UK heavily dependent on electricity generated in coal-fired power stations. Table 4.3 shows how much the pattern of energy sources used to generate electricity in the UK changed in 18 years. Coal has suffered a great decline, whereas natural gas has seen a massive increase in its importance. This has been called the 'dash for gas.' The attraction is that electricity can be generated more cheaply by burning gas rather than coal. Natural gas also burns more cleanly. Up until 2000, the UK relied entirely on its own gas fields, mainly in the North Sea, but as these fields are becoming exhausted so increasing amounts of gas are having to be imported from Belgium, Norway, Russia and the Middle East.

Energy source	% of electricity generated (1990)	% of electricity generated (2008)
Coal	64.2	36.9
Oil	11	1.3
Gas	1	34.5
Nuclear	21.5	21.4
Renewables	3.3	5.9

Table 4.3: Changes in the generation of electricity in the UK (1990–2008)

> Draw two piecharts to illustrate the data given in Table 4.3.

Nuclear power has changed little as a generator of electricity. Included in the 'renewables' category are energy sources such as hydroelectric power (HEP) and wind power. As you can see from Table 4.3, these still contribute only a small amount to the total electricity output of the UK, although in the future, contributions are expected to be greater.

Concerns over global warming, plus the increasing demand for energy, is forcing the UK government to reduce their reliance on non-renewable fossil fuels. The country is facing a growing energy gap. Closing this gap will require more dependence on nuclear power, as well as an increase in hydro-electric power possibly and the use of waste to produce biogas. This is when the gases produced in the decay of waste (including domestic and animal waste) is used to produce energy.

4.8 Renewable versus non-renewable sources of energy

Non-renewable sources

The world's energy resources can be divided into non-renewable and renewable resources. Non-renewable resources are finite – once they are used up they cannot be replaced because they take too long to form or regrow. They include the major fossil fuels formed over tens of thousands of years – coal, oil and natural gas.

Fact file: Coal

Status – non-renewable fossil fuel

Description – formed underground from decaying plant and animal matter

Lifespan – over 200 years

% share of world energy use – 23

Main producers – USA, China, Australia, India, South Africa, Russian Federation

Energy uses – electricity, heating, coke

✔ **advantages** – high world reserves; newer mines are highly mechanised

✘ **disadvantages** – pollution CO_2, the major greenhouse gas responsible for global warming; SO_2, the main gas responsible for acid rain; mining can be difficult and dangerous; opencast pits destroy land; heavy/bulky to transport

Fact file: Oil

Status – non-renewable fossil fuel

Description – formed underground from decaying animal and plant matter

Lifespan – about c 50 years

% share of world energy use – about 37

Main producers – Saudi Arabia, USA, Russian Federation, Iran, Mexico, Venezuela, China

Energy uses – electricity, petroleum, diesel, fuel oils, liquid petroleum gas, coke and many non-energy uses, e.g. plastics, medicines, fertilisers

✔ **advantages** – variety of uses; fairly easy to transport; efficient; less pollution than coal

✘ **disadvantages** – low reserves; some air pollution; danger of spills (especially at sea) and explosions

Fact file: Natural gas

Status – non-renewable fossil fuel

Description – formed underground from decaying animal and plant matter; often found with oil

Lifespan – 60 years

% share of world energy – 23

Main producers – Russian Federation, USA, Canada, UK, Algeria

Energy uses – electricity, cooking, heating

✔ **advantages** – efficient; clean – least polluting of the fossil fuels; easy to transport

✘ **disadvantages** – explosions; some air pollution

Which of the non-renewable sources of energy is best? Give you reasons.

There are two sources of energy that can be viewed as both non-renewable and renewable. In the case of fuel wood, if trees are planted for that specific purpose, then clearly the source is renewable. If, however, fuel wood is extracted by the felling of natural forests, then it is non-renewable. Nuclear energy involves the mining of non-renewable deposits of uranium to provide the necessary radioactivity. However, that radioactive material can be recycled and for this reason nuclear energy is renewable.

Fact file: Fuel wood

Status – non-renewable/renewable

Description – trees, usually in natural environment, but can be grown specifically for fuel

Lifespan – variable within each country, but declining except where there is large-scale reafforestation

% share of world energy use – about c 10

Main producers of energy – LICs, especially in Africa and Asia

Energy uses – heating, cooking (also used for building homes and fences)

✔ **advantages** – easily available, collected daily by local people; free; replanting possible

✘ **disadvantages** – trees used up quickly; time-consuming – wood must be collected daily; deforestation leads to other problems (soil erosion, desertification); replanting cannot keep pace with consumption

Fact file: Nuclear energy

Status – classified by some as non-renewable because of reliance on uranium as a fuel; others regard it as renewable in that the nuclear fuel may be re-used

Description – heavy metal (uranium) element found naturally in rock deposits

Lifespan – unknown

% share of world energy consumption – 6

Main producers of energy – USA, France, Japan, Germany, Russian Federation

Energy uses – used in a chain reaction to produce heat for electricity

✔ **advantages** – clean; fewer greenhouse gases; efficient; uses very small amounts of raw materials; small amounts of waste

✔ **disadvantages** – dangers of radiation; high cost of building and decommissioning power stations; problems over disposal of waste; nuclear accidents like Chernobyl raised public fears

It is absolutely clear that the world needs to look to renewable sources of energy. It is not just that the global stocks of three fossil fuels will run out one day. Using them, and also fuel wood, has an adverse impact on the environment. Burning them certainly contributes to global warming. Nuclear energy too has environmental impacts, but of a rather different kind, the most notable being the risk of nuclear explosions and the safe disposal of nuclear waste. Despite the risks, there are many think that much greater use will need to be made of nuclear energy in the future.

Which of the renewable energy sources is likely to be most exploited in your home country?

Renewable sources

There are number of energy sources which can be classed as renewable. These include:

- water (hydro-electric, tidal and wave power)
- wind
- the Sun
- geothermal energy
- biomass.

Renewable resources are generally cleaner than non-renewable sources, but as yet produce less than 10% of the world's energy needs. They are often referred to as **alternative sources of energy**.

Fact file: Hydro-electric power

Status – renewable

Description – good, regular supply of water needed; water held in a reservoir, channelled through pipes to a turbine

% share of world energy use – 3

Main producers – Canada, USA, Brazil, China, Russian Federation

Energy uses – electricity

✔ **advantages** – very clean; reservoirs/dams can also control flooding/provide water in times of shortage; often in remote, mountainous, sparsely populated areas

✘ **disadvantages** – large areas of land flooded; silt trapped behind dam; lake silts up; visual pollution from pylons and dam

Fact file: Geothermal

Status – renewable

Description – boreholes can be drilled below ground to use the earth's natural heat; cold water is pumped down, hot water or steam channeled back

% share of world energy consumption – < 1

Main producers – Japan, New Zealand, Russian Federation, Iceland, Hungary

Energy uses – electricity, direct heating

✔ **advantages** – many potential sites, but most are in volcanic areas at the moment

✘ **disadvantages** – sulphuric gases; expensive to develop; very high temperature can create maintenance problems

Fact file: Wind

Status – renewable

Description – wind drives blades to turn turbines

% share of world energy – < 1

Main producers – Denmark, California USA

Energy uses – electricity

✔ **advantages** – very clean; no air pollution; small-scale and large-scale schemes possible; cheap to run

✘ **disadvantages** – winds are unpredictable and not constant; visual and noise pollution in quiet, rural areas; many turbines needed to produce sufficient energy.

Fact file: Tidal

Status – renewable

Description – tidal water drives turbines

% share of world energy consumption – insignificant

Main producers – France, Russian Federation

Energy uses – electricity

✔ **advantages** – large schemes could produce a lot of electricity; clean; barrage can protect coasts from erosion

✘ **disadvantages** – very expensive to build; few suitable sites; disrupts coastal ecosystems and shipping.

Fact file: Solar

Status – renewable

Description – solar panels or photovoltaic cells using sunlight

% share of world energy – < 1

Main producers – USA, India

Energy uses – direct heating, electricity

✔ **advantages** – could be used in most parts of the world; unlimited supplies; clean; can be built into new buildings; efficient

✘ **disadvantages** – expensive; needs sunlight, cloud/night means solar energy is reduced; large amounts of energy require technological development and reduction in costs of PVs (photovoltaic cells)

Fact file: Biofuel

Status – renewable

Description – fermented animal or plant waste or crops (e.g. sugar cane); refuse incineration

% share of world energy consumption – < 1

Main producers – Argentina, Brazil, Japan, Germany, Denmark, India

Energy uses – ethanol, methane, electricity, heating

✔ **advantages** – widely available, especially in LICs; uses waste products; can be used at a local level

✘ **disadvantages** – can be expensive to set up; waste cannot be recycled; some pollution.

Most sources of renewable energy seem attractive options. They directly exploit aspects of the environment that are inexhaustible. Most do so without any serious adverse impact on the environment. However, their big downside is that they cannot produce energy in the same huge quantities as the fossil fuels. Maybe one day new technologies will enable renewable sources to increase their contribution to the global energy supply. Bearing in mind the link between burning fossil fuels and global warming, the only option at the present time is to make greater use of nuclear energy. There will be risks associated with this, but the world has no other choice – at least until the alternative renewable sources of energy are able to contribute much more to the energy budget.

Checklists

**Now you have read the chapter,
you should know:**

- ✓ the activities that are typical of each of the four economic sectors
- ✓ how the relative importance of these economic sectors changes over time
- ✓ why the relative importance of these sectors varies from place to place
- ✓ the features of informal employment
- ✓ the reasons for the growth of informal employment in LICs
- ✓ the factors causing the growth of tertiary and quaternary activities
- ✓ the factors affecting the location of tertiary and quaternary activities
- ✓ the reasons for the shift in the global location of manufacturing
- ✓ the part played by TNCs in this global shift
- ✓ the importance of energy
- ✓ the reasons for the growing gap between energy consumption and energy production
- ✓ why there is a need for energy efficiency
- ✓ the relative merits of using renewable and non-renewable sources of energy

Make sure you understand these key terms:

Economic sector: a major division of the economy based the type of economic activity. The economies of all countries are made up of three sectors; most HICs have a fourth sector.

Energy: heat and motive power. The former provided by the Sun and by burning coal, oil and timber; the latter provided by electricity, gas, steam and nuclear power.

Energy consumption: the amount of energy used by individuals, groups or countries.

Energy efficiency: making the most of energy sources in order to cut down on waste and reduce consumption.

Energy gap: a gap created because the loss of energy caused by phasing out the use of fossil fuels is greater than the amount of energy that is being developed from new, low-carbon sources.

Fossil fuel: carbon fuels such as coal, oil and natural gas that cannot be 'remade', because it will take tens of millions of years for them to form again.

Global shift: the movement of manufacturing from HICs to cheaper production locations in LICs.

High-tech industry: economic activities that rely on advanced scientific research and produce new, innovative and technologically advanced products, such as microchips, new medical drugs and new materials.

Informal employment: types of work that are not officially recognised and are taken up by people working for themselves on the streets of LIC cities.

Non-renewable energy: energy produced from resources that cannot be replaced once they are used. Examples include the fossil fuels of coal, oil and natural gas.

Primary sector: economic activities concerned with the working of natural resources – agriculture, fishing, mining and quarrying.

Quaternary sector: economic activities that provide highly skilled services such as collecting and processing information, research and development.

Secondary sector: economic activities concerned with making things, such as cars, buildings, and electricity.

Renewable energy: sources of energy which cannot be exhausted, such the Sun, wind and running water.

Tertiary sector: activities that provide a wide range of services and enable goods to be traded.

Transnational company (TNC): a large company operating in a number of countries and often involved in a variety of economic activities.

See the Glossary in the Active Book for more definitions

Questions

Try testing yourself with these questions:

1. a) How do the primary and secondary sectors differ?
   b) What distinguishes the tertiary sector from the other three sectors?
2. What do you think is the best way of measuring the relative importance of the economic sectors?
3. To which sector does research and development belong?
   - Primary
   - Secondary
   - Tertiary
   - Quaternary
4. a) What is the 'development pathway'?
   b) Using Figure 4.2, describe how the relative importance of the economic sectors changes with development.
5. Compare and discuss the pie charts of the three countries shown in Figure 4.4.
6. Suggest reasons why the tertiary sector is relatively insignificant in LICs.
7. What are the distinctive features of a post-industrial country?
8. a) What is 'informal employment'?
   b) Why is it so important in many LICs?
9. What do you think are the disadvantages of informal employment?
10. What are the reasons for the expansion of the tertiary sector in HICs?
11. Why are tertiary services concentrated in the centres of towns and cities?
12. a) Name four developments that are increasingly found in the urban fringes of HIC cities.
    b) What attracts these developments to the urban fringe?
13. a) What is meant by high-tech industries?
    b) Illustrate the kinds of activity that are involved in biotechnology.

14. a) Explain what is meant by the 'global shift in manufacturing'.
    b) Name a country that has:
       - lost manufacturing *UK*
       - become a new centre of manufacturing. *China*   *communication TNC*
15. a) Why has the global shift in manufacturing occurred? *Energy cheaper labour*
    b) What factors have made the shift possible?
16. a) Which countries listed in Table 4.2 are emergent economies?
    b) Name two emergent economies you would expect to appear if the list in Table 4.2 was extended to the top 15 manufacturing nations.
17. Make a list of the attractions of the M4 corridor as a location for high-tech industries.
18. What is the difference between:
    - primary and secondary energy
    - renewable and non-renewable energy?
19. a) What is the energy gap?
    b) Using Figures 4.16 and 4.18, identify some countries that have an energy gap.
20. What are the arguments in favour of using energy more efficiently?
21. Suggest some ways in which you might reduce your consumption of energy.
22. Examine the costs and benefits of using coal as a source of energy.
23. Is nuclear power a non-renewable or renewable source of energy? Justify your viewpoint.
24. What will happen when the world runs out of oil?
25. Write a short report either supporting or disagreeing with the statement: 'Most renewable sources of energy are clean and environmentally friendly'.

Chapter 5: Ecosystems and rural environments

Introduction

This chapter starts by looking at the most important part of the natural environment – its ecosystems. Even in the countryside, they are exploited and changed by human activities, particularly by farming. It is this exploitation, together with the presence of people and their settlements that convert natural into rural environments. Rural environments worldwide cannot escape the pressures of the modern world and as a result are undergoing great changes.

5.1 Biomes and their global distributions

The **biosphere** contains all the world's plant and animal life. That life or **biodiversity** may be broken down into major divisions known as **biomes**. There are 11 of them altogether. You may be familiar with the names of some of them. Perhaps the best known is the tropical rainforest that occurs on either side of the Equator (Figure 5.1). Perhaps less well known is the tundra found in the high latitudes near to the poles. The remaining nine biomes occur between these two global extremes.

The distributions of these 11 biomes are controlled by climate. Compare Figure 5.1 with Figure 5.2. Notice how both roughly change with latitude. Figure 5.3 shows how the two key factors of temperature and moisture affect biome distribution. Let us take a closer look at the nine largest biomes.

- **Tropical rainforest** – As the name clearly indicates, this biome occurs where the climate is warm and humid, along, and close to, the Equator. Because of the constantly high temperatures and rainfall, the vegetation grows more quickly than anywhere else on Earth. These conditions produce the greatest amount of living matter, referred to as **primary productivity**. The largest area of tropical rainforest occurs in the Amazon basin of South America.

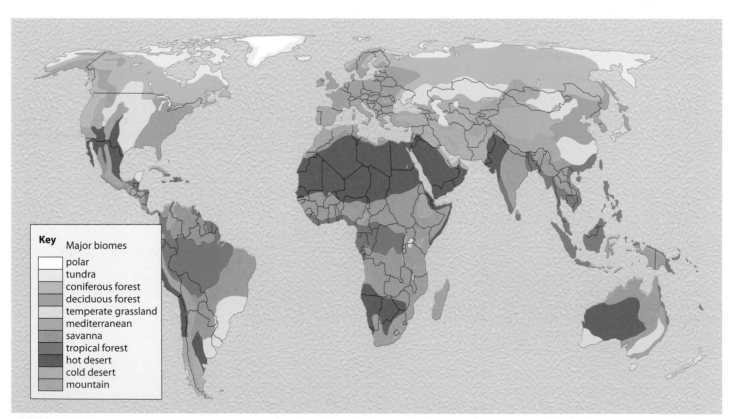

Key Major biomes
- polar
- tundra
- coniferous forest
- deciduous forest
- temperate grassland
- mediterranean
- savanna
- tropical forest
- hot desert
- cold desert
- mountain

Figure 5.1: *The biomes of the world*

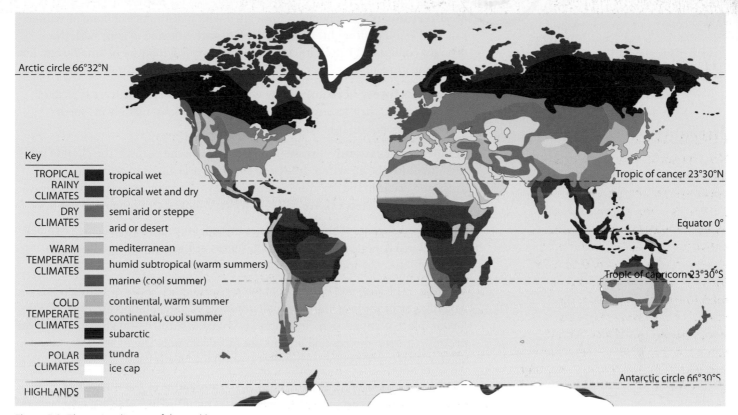

Figure 5.2: *The major climates of the world*

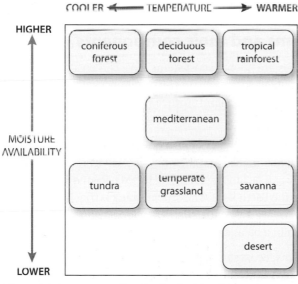

Figure 5.3: *Factors controlling the distribution of biomes*

Is it possible to locate the mountain biome on Figure 5.3?

- **Savanna** – This biome is also found along and close to the Equator but where the climate is much drier. As a result, the primary productivity is lower. Instead of tall trees, there are scattered bushes and grasses. This biome is most extensive in Africa.

- **Desert** – The distinguishing feature of this biome is the general lack of vegetation due to the lack of rainfall. As you will see in Figure 5.2, the biome extends over a wide range of latitude. Some of it occurs within the tropics, as in the Sahara Desert of Africa. Other parts of it are located outside the tropics, as in Asia. Because of this, the biome experiences a range of different temperature conditions.

- **Mediterranean** – This biome is associated with a distinctive climate of winter rain and summer drought. The typical plants are adjusted to cope with the drought conditions. The characteristic vegetation is a mixture of small trees, low scrub and grassland.

- **Deciduous forest** – Because of low winter temperatures, the trees typical of this biome shed their leaves. There are three main areas, namely in North America, Europe and East Asia.

- **Temperate grassland** – Grasses dominate this biome because the climate is unsuitable for the growth of trees and shrubs. Large areas of temperate grassland occur in the dry continental interiors of North America (the Prairies) and Eurasia (the Steppes). We will take a closer look at this biome in Part **5.3**.

- **Coniferous forest** – This biome occurs in high latitudes and stretches as a belt across North America and Eurasia. The leaves of the trees are needle-like to withstand the cold and loss of moisture.

- **Tundra** – The long and bitterly cold winters, the short hours of winter sunshine, strong winds and the small amounts of precipitation are not favourable to plant growth. Vegetation is typically stunted and grows close to the ground. Grasses, mosses and lichens are most common. Dwarf trees are found in sheltered places. This biome stretches around the North Pole.

- **Mountain** – This biome occurs in the high mountains of the world. The climatic conditions are similar to those in the tundra. They are very cold because temperatures decrease with altitude. This cold, plus strong winds, means that much of the precipitation falls as snow.

5.2 Ecosystems and their components

It is said that biomes are 'global ecosystems'. We can easily understand why they are described as 'global'. As we saw in the previous parts, each one occupies a significant area of the Earth's land surface (see Figure 5.1 on page 114). What is meant by the term 'ecosystem'?

Check that you understand the difference between a biome and an ecosystem.

An **ecosystem** is a basic working unit or **system** of nature. It consists of living organisms (plants and animals) and their physical environment (sunlight, air, water, rock and soil). They can be any size, ranging in scale from a small pond to one of the 11 biomes, even to the Earth itself. The crucial thing is that the living organisms and physical environment are linked together. They are often reliant on each other for survival and maintain a balance that ensures each of them continues to exist.

Like all open systems, ecosystems involve **inputs** and **outputs** as well as **internal flows of energy** (see also Figure 1.3 on page 3). Let us look at each of those three components.

An ecosystem does not exist in isolation. It is open and receives **inputs** from outside (Figure 5.4). Perhaps the most important of these is sunlight which is vital to both plant and animal life. The ecosystem also receives water, either from rain or streams. Other inputs include gases (e.g. oxygen and nitrogen) from the atmosphere and nutrients (e.g. calcium and magnesium) brought mainly by rain and streams.

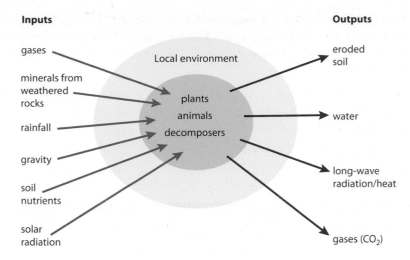

Inputs

- gases
- minerals from weathered rocks
- rainfall
- gravity
- soil nutrients
- solar radiation

Local environment

plants
animals
decomposers

Outputs

- eroded soil
- water
- long-wave radiation/heat
- gases (CO$_2$)

Figure 5.4: *The inputs, stores and outputs of an ecosystem*

For more information about other open systems, see:

- Part 5.5 (page 124)
- Chapter 1.2 (page 3)
- Chapter 2.6 (page 54)

Within the ecosystem, energy received from the Sun interacts with the soil and climate and leads to the growth of plants. This energy is then transferred to plant-eating animals, and then to animals that eat other animals. This sequence is known as the **food chain**. Plants are the **primary producers** of an ecosystem. The animals that feed on them are known as **primary consumers**. The animals that prey on other animals are **secondary consumers**. At the top of the some food chains are people – we might refer to them as **tertiary consumers**.

The ecosystem and its food chain might be thought of as a pyramid made up of layers or levels of producers and consumers (Figure 5.5). The layers become narrower up the pyramid. This tapering occurs because each successive level involves less **biomass** (weight of living material) and fewer species.

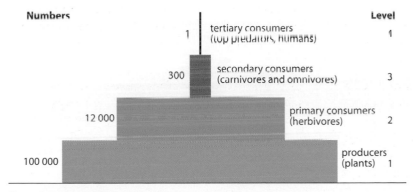

Numbers

- 1 — tertiary consumers (top predators, humans) — Level 1
- 300 — secondary consumers (carnivores and omnivores) — 3
- 12 000 — primary consumers (herbivores) — 2
- 100 000 — producers (plants) — 1

Figure 5.5: *The ecosystem pyramid*

Referring to Figure 5.5, give an example of:

- a primary producer
- a primary consumer (carnivore)
- a secondary consumer (omnivore)

Plants and animals that escape being eaten eventually die. Their remains gradually decompose. This decomposition releases carbon dioxide back into the atmosphere. It also releases vital nutrients back into the soil. The soil is also enriched by waste discharged by living animals. The enriched soil is thus able to support more plant growth. The character of the soil is determined not just by this enrichment but also by the geology (rocks) and the climate (temperature and precipitation).

This recycling of nutrients between the three **stores** – the plants, the animals and the soil – is what keeps an ecosystem going. However, the balance or harmony of an ecosystem can easily be changed. It only needs a small change to one of the inputs (for example, a slight change in climate) or some interruption of the nutrient flows (for example, by the arrival of some air-borne plant pest) to disrupt the equilibrium of the whole ecosystem. A minor change can lead eventually to a serious disruption of the ecosystem. Some examples were described in Chapter 2 (Parts **2.4** and **2.5**).

The greatest threat to the well-being and harmony of ecosystems comes from the top consumer, the human race. The most obvious example has been the long history of clearing ecosystems to create farmland. Many of the ecosystems offer resources and opportunities which people exploit. Today, these things are referred to as the **goods and services** of ecosystems (Table 5.1). They are among the outputs of an ecosystem, along with the other outputs shown in Figure 5.4.

You might compare the goods and services of forest ecosystems with those of coastal ecosystems (see Table 2.2, page 48).

Forest goods	Forest services
timber	removal of air pollutants
fuel wood	emission of oxygen
fodder	recycling of nutrients
food (honey, fungi, fruit)	maintenance of biodiversity
medicinal plants	recreational space

Table 5.1: Goods and services of forest ecosystems

Goods are material things or products that can be taken directly from the ecosystem and put to use. Examples include timber and food. Services are long-term benefits that people can gain from ecosystems. For example, mangroves provide coastal protection in tropical areas. Trees can remove carbon dioxide from the air we breathe. Table 5.1 above illustrates some of the more important benefits.

5.3 The temperate grassland biome

Figure 5.6: *A temperate grassland landscape*

Large areas of the temperate grassland biome are found in the continental interiors of Europe, Asia and North America (see Figure 5.1 on page 114). The biome also occurs on the Canterbury Plains of New Zealand, the plains of the Murray-Darling Basin in Australia and the pampas of the eastern coastal areas of South America.

The grasses of the biome seldom exceed a metre in height (Figure 5.6). Because of the dry climate and the cold winters, the grasses grow slowly. The grassland plants are physically adapted to cope with the dry conditions. For example, many have narrow, spine-like leaves with a downy surface to slow the loss of moisture through transpiration. They also have long roots to tap water deep in the soil.

The animal life of the temperate grasslands is rather limited because of the cold winters and because the vegetation grows so slowly. Slow-growing vegetation means a limited food supply. The Great Plains of North America were once roamed by herds of bison (buffalo). Because these animals were a good source of meat, they were hunted by the early European settlers almost to the point of extinction.

Whilst large animals may be in short supply, the grasslands hold good insect populations. These, together with grass seeds, provide food for many interesting species of bird. The grasslands also act as temporary feeding stations as birds migrate between their wintering grounds in warmer parts of the world and their breeding areas in high latitudes.

The soils are a vital part of the temperate grassland ecosystem and are quite distinctive. They are known as **chernozems**. They are black in colour, rich in calcium and remarkably fertile (Figure 5.7). They are enriched by the minerals released from the vegetation that dies during the cold winters.

Figure 5.7: *Digging in a dark and fertile chernozem*

Case study: The Midwest of USA

Refer to an atlas map of North America and locate the Great Plains of the Midwest.

When European explorers first visited the Great Plains of the American Midwest, they found the rather arid prairie grasslands grazed by herds of bison (or buffalo). These animals provided food for the sparse population of Native Americans. This vast ecosystem between the Mississippi River and the Rocky Mountains began to change, however, after 1862 when an Act allowed people from Europe to settle here. Each family was allowed to stake out a claim of 65 hectares of land. Most of those families set about turning their claims into farms. The herds of bison became virtually extinct. At first, the crop yields of wheat, maize (corn) and cotton from the newly-ploughed grassland were good. Manure from animals used to pull farm machinery was used to help maintain soil fertility. However, not enough was done to fertilise the soil and soon fertility began to drop under the pressure of continuous crop growing.

The settlers were soon to learn that frequent droughts were a feature of the climate. In the 1930s, a succession of severe droughts, high winds, soil exhaustion and a lack of ground cover saw the soil swept away from large areas. The Great Plains literally became a 'dust bowl'. Thousands of families were deprived of their livelihood and were forced to migrate westwards to California. There they hoped to find food and employment.

Since then, particularly after the end of the Second World War in 1945, methods of soil **conservation** have been successfully applied to the eastern and slightly more humid parts of the Great Plains. These methods include:

- improving the nitrogen content of soils by crop rotation and strip cropping

- planting tree belts to provide protection from wind erosion (Figure 5.8)

- retaining straw and crop litter after the harvest protects the soil from both the wind and occasional rain showers

- terracing and contour ploughing sloping areas to prevent soil being washed away

- the increasing use of **irrigation** by pumping water from the underlying **aquifer**.

Figure 5.8: *Soil conservation through the use of tree belts*

In your own words, explain the two concerns:

- over exploitation of the aquifer

- the growing of GM crops.

The agricultural situation today is much improved but there are still concerns. These include the overexploitation of the aquifer and the growing of genetically-modified crops (see Part **5.6**). In parts of the the drier western Great Plains, farming has been abandoned altogether. Some land is being restored to its original prairie grassland and herds of buffalo are being re-introduced.

5.4 Characteristics of rural environments

All countries today show the same major division between rural and urban environments, each with their distinctive ways of life. The process of **urbanisation** (i.e. becoming more urban) is now affecting all parts of the world. As a result, rural areas are becoming less populated. They are being 'eroded' by the spread of urban areas. Overall, the world's urban population is growing more rapidly than the rural population (Figure 5.9).

See Chapter 6.1 (page 145) for more information about urbanisation.

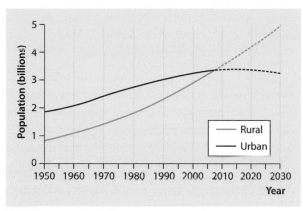

Figure 5.9: *The changing global balance of rural and urban populations, 1950–2030*

So what are the characteristics of rural environments? What makes them attractive to some people and unattractive to others? The main distinguishing components are shown in Figure 5.10.

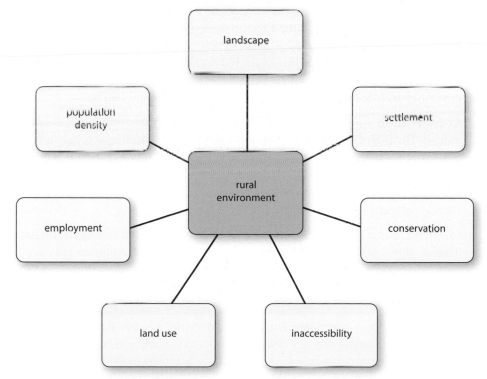

Figure 5.10: *The distinctive components of rural environments*

- **Landscape** – For many people, the term rural environment conjures up an image of a landscape with scattered settlements separated by open spaces – mainly green spaces given over to farming.

- **Population density** – Rural areas have relatively low population densities compared with the high densities of urban environments. Having said that, in some parts of the world rural settlements can be both large and very compact. Population densities within them can be as high as in many towns and cities. High mean densities in rural areas can also occur in rural countries such as Bangladesh.

- **Settlement** – The settlement pattern is typically made up of villages, hamlets and farmsteads. Settlements are separated from each other by unsettled tracts that are either farmed or left in a fairly natural state.

- **Employment** – Most jobs in rural areas belong to the primary sector. By far the most important employer is farming and the production of food. Other forms of rural employment include fishing, forestry and sometimes the working of minerals. In general, these jobs are poorly paid. It is because of this that so many people leave the countryside in search of better paid jobs in towns and cities.

- **Land use** – Whilst in many parts of the world, farming is the biggest use of land, there are parts of the rural environment where other activities become important. Traditionally, forestry was one such activity in areas with wooded ecosystems. Much mining and quarrying continue to take place in largely rural environments. However, there are two significant newcomers to the list of rural land uses – leisure and tourism. The urban populations of the world look increasingly to rural environments, not just for food, but also as places in which to relax and take a break from the routine of work.

- **Inaccessibility** – It is claimed that one of the reasons for the lack of development in rural areas is their lack of accessibility. Certainly there are many remote rural areas in the world. This is particularly the case in the more mountainous, more arid and more forested regions. However, the situation is changing. The improvement of rural roads, in particular, is allowing the rural environment to feature more in the provision of leisure and tourism.

- **Conservation** – A change is taking place in the way rural environments are valued. The rise of leisure and tourism is one example. Another is people are realising that the conservation of rural environments and their wildlife is important. This is vital in order to maintain the world's biodiversity. It is also beginning to seem vital in terms of helping to reduce global warming as trees recycle carbon dioxide into oxygen.

Think about a rural area that you know well. Which of the seven components contributes most to its rural character?

Rural environments are valuable and have much to offer modern society. In this day and age of global urbanisation, it is all too easy to think of such environments as being in some way 'second class' to the booming urban areas of the world.

Case study: Lake District National Park (England)

The Lake District in north-west England was declared a national park in 1951. Famed for its dramatic scenery (the lakes, mountain pools and craggy mountains) (Figure 5.11), its wildlife, its outdoor activities (walking, climbing, water sports) and its cultural traditions, this largely rural area was under threat. The threats were mainly commercial tourist developments and excessive visitor numbers to popular locations within it. The construction of the M6 motorway meant that the Lake District was accessible to day-trippers from the huge urban areas of Manchester, Merseyside and Glasgow. The whole area was in need of both protection and effective management.

Figure 5.11: *The Lake District's magnificent scenery*

After nearly 60 years of careful planning and management, the character of the Lake District remains relatively unchanged. Its traditional agriculture, its villages built of local stone, its recreational opportunities and its cultural traditions remain. This is remarkable, bearing in mind that over 15 million people visit the national park every year.

5.5 The farm as a system

In this book, you have been introduced to a variety of systems. The ecosystem (Part **5.2**) was shown to involve three key components – inputs, internal flows and outputs. The farm and farming, the biggest employer and use of land in rural environments, may also be looked at as systems involving the same three components.

Figure 5.12 shows that there are two main categories of input. There are the obvious **inputs** from the physical environment – the key ones are soil and climate. They are particularly important in influencing what sort of crops can be grown in an area. This is particularly the case with **subsistence farming**. In this system, the food that is produced is mainly consumed by those who produce it. With **commercial farming**, the system produces food that is sold to consumers. In this system, because of the money and technology that are available, it is possible to change or improve the soil with fertilisers. The climate can never be changed, but it is possible to

For more examples of systems, see

- Part 5.2 (page 116)
- Chapter 1.1 (page 1)
- Chapter 1.2 (page 3)
- Chapter 2.6 (page 54).

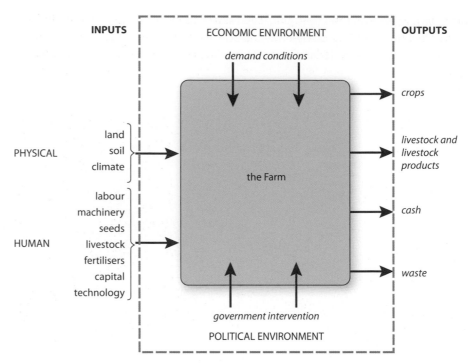

Figure 5.12: *The farm as a system*

overcome some of its challenges. The classic example here is irrigation which helps to supplement the amount of water provided by the climate. However, there are other actions that can be taken. For example, farmers can protect their crops from cold and wind by growing them in **glasshouses** and polytunnels (Figure 5.13). A lack of sunlight and of warmth can be met by lighting and heating the air spaces within these structures.

Glasshouses and polytunnels help 'improve' the climate, but do they have a downside?

Figure 5.13: *One way in which farmers can 'change' the climate*

Mention of possible ways of 'changing' the climate input of farming is a reminder that that the farm system needs human inputs such as labour (and machinery to do the work of people), capital and technology. The last two of these human inputs become more important as subsistence farming gives way to commercial farming (see Part **5.6**).

Figure 5.14: *A farm with its buildings and equipment – the stores of the farm system*

The **stores** of farming are more in number than those in the ecosystem. They include the farmland, farm buildings, equipment and labour, as well as stocks of seed and livestock (Figure 5.14).

The **outputs** of farming are mainly food (crops and livestock). If the farming is of a commercial nature, then profits in the form of cash will be another output. Less welcome outputs are some of the impacts of farming on the environment. These include the effects of disposing of farm waste, as well as the use of fertilisers and pesticides. More recently, there is concern about the possible impact of genetically-modified (GM) crops on wildlife – plants and animals.

Finally, since farming is an open system, it is also affected by conditions outside the farm. This applies particularly to commercial farming. This is greatly influenced by economic factors such as the level of demand and market prices. If both levels are low for a particular farm commodity, then the farmer will shift production to some more profitable product. Equally, commercial farming in many HICs is 'directed' by governments. By means of taxes and subsidies, farmers are encouraged to focus on the production of certain farm products. Within the European Union, agriculture is quite strictly controlled by the Common Agricultural Policy.

Look back at Figure 5.12 (page 124). What are:

- capital

- government intervention

- livestock products?

Figure 5.15: *Some different ways of raising a farm's income*

The Common Agricultural Policy (CAP) was introduced in 1963 with the aim of trying to increase food production within the EU. It was so successful that farmers began to produce surpluses. There were 'butter mountains' and 'wine lakes' to name but two examples. These surpluses could not be sold and as a result food was being stored and going to waste. The CAP had to be changed. So as from 1992 farmers were paid to take up to 20% of their cropland out of production. This **set-aside scheme** was one of a number of schemes designed to make farming more environmentally friendly.

Since 2003 the CAP has undergone more changes. Financial help to farmers has virtually disappeared. As a result, they have to look to other ways of making money (Figure 5.15). Many now run farm shops to sell their produce directly to passing customers. They have also had to diversify into non-farming activities as such as leisure and tourism. Thus the character of the farm system in the EU is changing from being only concerned with food production to providing a widening range of services. In short, the outputs of the farm system are changing in order to make more income.

5.6 Different types of farming

There are many different types of farming system. They may be distinguished on the basis of a range of criteria. We have already been made aware of one of these distinctions, namely between **subsistence farming** and **commercial farming**. This is the most important of all the distinctions. Actually, the titles represent two extremes. In the real world, there are many so-called subsistence farmers who sell or trade any food that is surplus to their needs. Equally, there are many commercial farmers who consume some of the food they produce.

Another distinction to be made in farming is based on what the farm system produces. **Arable farming** is concerned with the growing of crops, whilst the rearing of animals is known as **pastoral farming**. Again, in the real world, there are many farms involved in both types of farming – often referred to as **mixed farming**. Indeed, mixed farming has significant advantages, particularly if livestock are fed on the farm's own crops – a relatively cheap and efficient practice. The situation is even better if animal manure is used to fertilise the fields before crops are sown.

Figure 5.16: *Two examples of intensive farming – market gardening and rice cultivation*

A third common distinction is made between **intensive farming** and **extensive farming**. Intensive farming uses a small amount of land to produce a high yield. An example of this in HICs is horticulture (cultivating plants) or market gardening; an example in LICs is rice growing (Figure 5.16). Extensive farming uses large areas of land from which lower yields are obtained. An example in an HIC is shown in Figure 5.17 where highly advanced machinery is reaping vast areas of wheat, with hardly a worker in sight (wheat is a lower yield crop). In LICs, extensive farming is restricted mainly to animal herding (which usually takes place in less arable parts of the country).

Figure 5.17: *Two examples of extensive farming – mechanised wheat farming and nomadic herding*

Of the ways of increasing food production in Table 5.2, which do you think is best. Give your reasons.

extending the farmed area	applying herbicides and pesticides
crop rotation	mechanisation
irrigation	plant and animal breeding
application of fertilisers	genetic modification of crops and livestock

Table 5.2: Some ways of increasing agricultural production

A common goal of virtually all types of farming is to increase output. This is driven by the basic need to feed the world's growing population. Remember too that farming is not only about producing food. It also produces commodities that are used in industry (such as oilseed rape) and increasingly as a source of energy (such as biofuels). Table 5.2 shows a number of different ways in which agricultural production is raised. The most obvious way is simply to increase the amount of farmland, for example by draining marshes or clearing forests. However, here we are more interested in possible ways of raising the amount of food produced per unit area of farmland. In other words, how to intensify agricultural production. Of the various ways shown in Table 5.2, we will focus on two of them. One of them, irrigation, has been used throughout much of history. The other, genetic modification of crops and livestock, is a very new way.

Irrigation

Almost from the beginnings of agriculture in prehistoric times, people have irrigated their farmlands. They have done so in order to overcome the shortcomings of the climate, to provide sufficient water at critical times in the growth cycle of crops. Over the centuries, the scale of irrigation projects has greatly increased and so has their efficiency. The methods of irrigation have also changed. It is also noticeable that so-called irrigation schemes serve other purposes, such as the generation of hydroelectric power. There can be no doubt that irrigation has a proven track record of raising agricultural productivity. However, irrigation also has disadvantages.

See the following for more information about Bangladesh:

- Chapter 1.5 (page 14)
- Chapter 1.8 (page 30)
- Chapter 2.5 (page 51)
- Chapter 4.2 (page 99)
- Chapter 7.8 (page 205).

Case study: Irrigation in Bangladesh

That farmers in Bangladesh have to irrigate their crops may seem strange to us. After all, the country mainly occupies a huge delta and is often flooded during the monsoon season. How is it, then, that irrigation is necessary? The reasons lie mainly in the climate. Farming in Bangladesh was traditionally confined to the wet or monsoon season between June and September. Over the last 30 years, however, the demand for food (especially rice) has grown due to the fast rate of population growth. Demand for food has outstripped supply.

The only solution to increasing food shortages has been to grow crops, particularly rice, throughout the year. This has meant making water available (irrigating) during the long dry season between October and April. As a result, nearly 5 million hectares are now irrigated and food production has been greatly increased. The irrigation water comes mainly from wells. Around 90% of irrigation is in the form of small, local schemes (Figure 5.18).

Irrigation is not all good news:

- too much irrigation can easily lead to the ground becoming waterlogged. This is not good for plant life (i.e. crops)

Figure 5.18: *An irrigation well in Bangladesh*

- water used to irrigate the soil evaporates during the dry season. This causes salts to form a pan or hard layer within the upper layers of the soil. The salt is poisonous to plants

- in many places irrigation water is being pumped at too fast a rate. As a result, the water table is falling and wells have to be sunk to ever greater depths. Deep wells are expensive to drill.

Genetically modified (GM) crops

Genetically modified (GM) crops have been developed and are now grown mainly to reduce possible losses in production caused by diseases and pests. By cutting these losses, GM crops effectively raise agricultural productivity

The growth and use of GM crops has provoked widespread debate since the first GM crops were sold in 1995 (Table 5.3). Yet growing 'improved' varieties of plants (and animals) has been happening since farming began, with varied success. People have selectively bred the strongest of their plants and animals. In the 1950s, scientists discovered that **DNA** carried the genetic detail of living things. By the 1980s, it was possible to identify individual **genes** and transfer them and their specific qualities, for example the gene that may cause a plant to resist a certain pest. This laid the foundation for the world's **biotechnology** companies to develop today's GM industry.

To which economic sector does biotechnology belong?

Arguments for	Arguments against
higher crop yields	possible contamination of other plants
cheaper food	possible human health impacts unknown
better quality food	seedstock too expensive for LICs
less use of herbicides and pesticides	some plants do not produce seeds

Table 5.3: The GM debate

GM crops are designed to be resistant to competition from other plants, animals and insects. Genes containing this resistance are bred into the new GM crop. Some are resistant to herbicides, so competing weeds can be killed with a general spray which will not kill the crop. Others produce toxins which kill pests which try to feed off them, reducing the need for pesticides. Some have been modified to not produce pips or to look more attractive. Animals can also be genetically modified, although there are not yet any GM meat products on sale. Research is taking place into the possible genetic modification of cattle, sheep, pigs and fish.

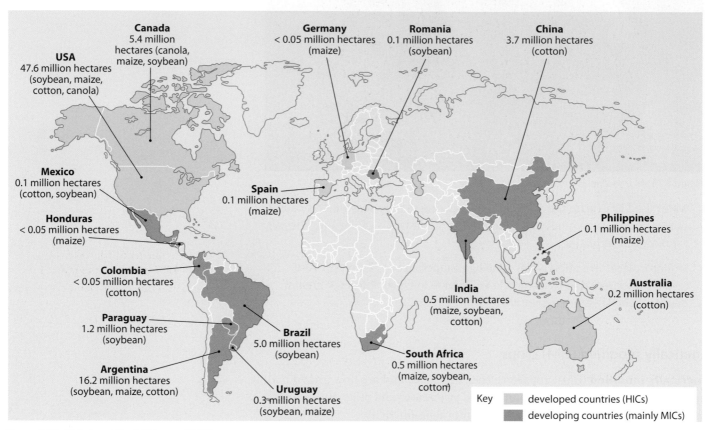

Figure 5.19: *Global growth of GM crops (2004)*

See Chapter 4.8 and the Fact file on biofuels (page 112).

Soybeans, oilseed rape and maize (corn) account for the majority of GM food crops, some of which are used for animal fodder. However, these three crops are also being grown for use as **biofuels**. Figure 5.19 shows the main producers of GM crops. The USA is the leading producer followed a long way behind by Argentina, Canada, Brazil and China. It is interesting to note that in China, production is focused on GM cotton rather than on food crops.

Case study: Genetically-modified (GM) crops in the USA

Roughly two-thirds of the world's GM crops are grown in the USA. Two-thirds of packaged food on sale in the USA contain GM ingredients. Unlike the fierce debate underway in the EU and other countries (Table 5.3), there has been little apparent opposition to GM food crops in the USA. This may be in part because such foods have been on sale for over ten years, with no measured effect on human health.

Figure 5.20: *Tins of GM tomatoes*

The USA saw the first ever GM food on sale in 1994. Flavr Savr tomatoes were designed to stay fresh longer and resist rotting without altering the taste. Unlike other tomatoes, they could be picked and transported when fully ripe. They were withdrawn from sale after two years because consumers were not prepared to pay higher prices for them.

The transnational corporation Monsanto is responsible for over 90% of the world's GM crops, and successfully grows soybeans, oilseed rape, maize and cotton. However, its attempts to promote GM wheat have had to be abandoned. This was largely because Japan and the EU, the main importers of US wheat, were worried about GM wheat cross-pollinating and contaminating the ordinary wheat crop.

There is no doubt that the GM debate (Table 5.3 on page 129) will continue for many years, both in the USA and across the world. Our knowledge of GM crops will need to be improved and backed by further research for sound decisions to be made as to whether they are or are not safe.

> Research Monsanto and find out more about this TNC. In which countries is it experimenting with GM crops

5.7 Food surpluses and shortages

Reference was made in Part **5.4** to our world being divided on the basis of where and how people live. This rural–urban division of the globe is a significant one, but there is another division of even greater importance. This is between those parts of the world where people have enough, even too much, to eat, and those parts where large numbers of people go hungry. Broadly speaking, this distinction based on food coincides with the distinction between HICs and LICs.

This division between a well-fed world and a hungry world reflects the critical balance between two key factors – population and food production (Figure 5.21). Let us look at this balance in the two 'worlds' of food supply. But before doing so, note that there is a third possible world (optimum population) in which population and food supply are in perfect balance.

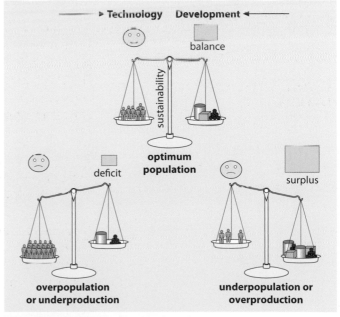

Figure 5.21 *The three worlds of food supply*

Food surpluses in HICs

Causes

While overproduction of food most commonly occurs in the developed part of the world, it does not occur in all HICs. There are two factors that together lead to overproduction (Figure 5.21).

The first is a stagnant or slowly growing population. This situation is found in countries where there is little difference between birth and death rates. The birth rate is low because the number of people of reproductive age is declining and because more couples are deciding not to have children. The death rate is also low because of good healthcare and generally healthier living conditions. The second force is agricultural productivity. This is rising because farmers in HICs are able to benefit from the latest farming technology.

The net outcome of these two forces – a stable number of mouths to feed and a rising production of food – is overproduction.

> Look at the piecharts in Figure 4.4 (page 95) and Figure 9.2 (page 242) to see what contribution farming makes to the UK economy.

Case study: Farming in the UK – overproduction?

Farming in the UK today is very different to what it was 200 years when it was a major part of the country's economy. Today, it accounts for around 1% of GDP and a similar percentage of all employment (Figure 5.22). Statistics show that agricultural productivity has increased considerably, thanks to mechanisation, making farms larger, specialising in particular lines of farm produce and taking advantage of many advances in farm technology. The last include using more effective fertilisers, pesticides and herbicides. Crop and livestock strains have been improved, thanks to breeding programmes and **genetic engineering**. Commercial pressures from the major food retailers, such as Tesco and Sainsburys, are also persuading farmers to become more efficient and productive. However, all this progress may be causing many UK farmers to wonder if there is a limit to how high agricultural productivity can be raised. This point is suggested because the rate of increase in agricultural productivity in the UK is definitely slowing down.

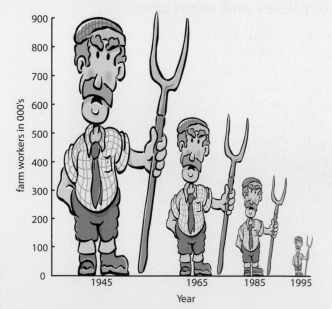

Figure 5.22: *The declining labour needs of UK farms*

Overproduction of food in the EU is causing farmers to find other ways of making a living. Farm diversification in the UK has occurred, as it has elsewhere within the EU. Farmland has also been taken out of production. However, is farming in the UK really overproducing? The reason for asking this question is quite simple. The UK now only produces 60% of its own food. It relies on other countries to provide the remaining percentage. Surely, that would not happen if UK farming was really overproducing?

This strange situation of the UK importing an increasing amount of its food is the result of two common beliefs of the public:

- that cheap food is a 'must'
- that 'seasonal' foods, such as strawberries, beans and apples, should be on the supermarket shelves throughout the year.

There is also a growing market for produce that cannot easily be grown in the UK due to its climate.

As a result, the UK's imports of food are made up mainly of:

- food that can be grown more cheaply outside the UK
- food that can only be grown in the UK during the summer months.

Look back at page 126 for more information about the EU's Common Agricultural Policy (CAP).

We will look at the consequences of the UK's food imports in the next part which is about food shortages in LICs.

Consequences

Figure 5.23: *Two consequences of overproduction, obesity and food wastage*

Research the Body Mass Index (BMI) and how it is used to distinguish between 'overweight' and 'obese'. You might just check out your own BMI.

One direct consequence of overproduction is that food becomes cheap relative to the general level of wages. The knock-on effect of this is to encourage people to eat more than they need to. It is estimated that on average an adult needs a balanced diet providing between 2000 and 2300 calories per day. Daily calory intake in the UK has now risen to an average of 3190 calories per person per day. As a result, in the UK, and in other HICs, the number of overweight and obese people is rising (Figure 5.23). Higher levels of certain cancers, diabetes, heart disease and strokes are occurring because people are eating too much food and too much of the wrong food (such as fast food and soft drinks).

Another consequence of overproduction is the wastage of food. Surplus food is stored away by farmers in the hope that prices might rise, but often it only rots. People buy too much food and much ends up in household waste-bins (Figure 5.23).

Reference has already been made in Part **5.5** to the fact that overproduction results in farmers being paid low prices for their food products. Low prices mean little or no profit. As a result, HIC farmers are being forced to diversify into activities unrelated to food production (see Figure 5.15 on page 126). Leisure and recreation are two such activities.

Food shortages in LICs

Causes

In LICs the situation is one of a high rate of population growth outstripping agricultural productivity (Figure 5.21). The net result is a shortage of food – more mouths have to be fed by roughly the same amount of food. Two changes are increasing this shortage of food:

- rural-urban migration – huge numbers of farmers are leaving rural areas in search of a better life in towns and cities. So there are fewer farmers
- a switch from subsistence to commercial farming means that more and more farmland is being used by agri-businesses to grow food for export rather than local consumption as it is more profitable for farmers.

The following case study gives some more detail.

Case study: Fresh vegetables, fruit and flowers from Kenya

Horticulture (the growing of vegetables, fruit and flowers) in Kenya has become one of the country's most important export industries. It accounts for two-thirds of total agricultural exports. Half a million people depend on the activity and the 135 000 workers who grow, cut and package fruit, vegetables and flowers for export. Kenya now supplies more flowers to the world market than any other LIC except Colombia.

Seventy-five per cent of the flowers are grown on 30 large farms around Lake Naivasha and transported by air to markets in Europe. Soils around the lake are fertile and the lake provides water for irrigation. With intermittent droughts over the past 10 years, pressure on the lake has increased. The population of the area has risen from 50 000 to over 350 000 in 25 years, but services have not kept pace with this, resulting in untreated sewage being discharged into the lake. Fertilisers and pesticides also run off and pollute the lake. Water levels have dropped and local fisherman have seen a decrease in catches. With flowers very much a luxury, can their cultivation and their environmental costs really be justified (Figure 5.24)?

Figure 5.24: *Kenya's thriving flower industry*

Much of this flower growing, as well as the production of fruit and vegetables, is taking place on land previously used for subsistence farming. Large agribusinesses based in HICs have bought the land. The promise of regular work and wages in the horticultural industry has easily persuaded many subsistence farmers to sell up. However, those farmers are beginning to see that the shift has a big downside. With more and more land being used to grow crops for export, there is less land being used to grow food for the horticultural workers themselves and for the growing urban population. This is leading to food shortages. Food shortages mean higher food prices. Higher food prices mean that wages are literally 'eaten up' by the cost of food.

Another minus of Kenyan commercial horticulture is the 'food miles' involved in transporting the commodities to the major markets in Europe. Think of the huge carbon footprint of the aircraft used to fly this fresh food and flowers to HIC supermarkets.

Although there is a downside to this shift to growing vegetables and flowers for the European market, some argue that it should not be stopped. To do this would deprive Kenya of the foreign currency it needs to finance its economic development.

Consequences

The consequences of food shortages are largely to do with health and poverty. In many African countries people only manage to consume 80% of the minimum recommended daily calorie intake (which is 2000–2300 calories). A lack of calories and a diet lacking in vitamins can quickly lead to **malnutrition**, making people weak and prone to disease. All too quickly people become too weak to work. They become trapped in a 'cycle of hunger' (Figure 5.25).

The present global food situation is absurd. Although they are able to, the rich countries no longer produce all the food they need. They look instead to the poorer countries to provide them with more food than they really need. Whilst one 'half' of the world's population grows fat, the other 'half' goes hungry.

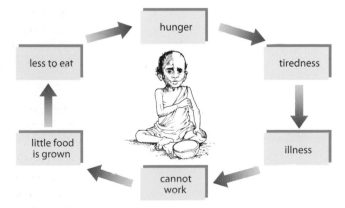

Figure 5.25: *The cycle of hunger*

5.8 Rural changes in LICs

Changes in LIC rural areas are largely linked to three processes – population growth, rural-urban migration and economic development. The changes are not all working in the same general direction. Some are benefiting rural areas; others are causing problems. As a result, the situation today in rural areas of LICs is not entirely clear-cut.

Population growth

Rates of population growth are generally high in LICs. These high rates of natural increase are the result of high birth rates and falling death rates. Due to big rural-urban migration, rates of population growth are much higher in urban areas. However, these growing urban populations need to be fed. They no longer have a link to subsistence farming. Feeding them is putting pressure on the countryside. Because of inefficient methods, farming is unable to cope and farmland is in danger of being overexploited. On top of this, farming is losing many of its workers as they join the movement to towns and cities. Since rural-urban migrants are typically young male adults, farming is being left to the women and older people who remain behind in the countryside. They can barely grow enough food to feed themselves, let alone feed others.

Figure 5.26: *Habitat destruction by fuel-wood collection*

For more information about fuel wood, look at Chapter 4.8 (page 111) and the Fact file on fuel wood.

It is not only farmland that is being pressured by the growing population. People, no matter whether they live in rural or urban areas need fuel for cooking. The collection of fuel wood for sale in urban areas is a profitable rural activity (Figure 5.26). However, it is having a devastating impact on the environment. It is now recognised as a major contributor to **desertification** (see Chapter 7.2 on page 180).

Rural-urban migration

Rural poverty is what persuades so many people to become rural-urban migrants. There is often little work in rural areas except in farming. Farming is often vulnerable to natural hazards such as drought and floods. Many rural areas are often remote and isolated with few facilities such as schools or clinics. Basic services such as electricity, clean water and sanitation are often lacking. At the same time, towns and cities seem to offer jobs and a regular wage, better housing and services and a range of facilities including schools, hospitals, shops and entertainment. However, many of these urban attractions are often just wishful thinking of what urban life might be like. The reality may be very different – few decent jobs, housing in shanty towns (Figure 5.27) and access to services and facilities barred by poverty. Sadly, many rural-urban migrants end up being very disillusioned.

There is more on shanty towns to be found in Chapter 6.5 (page 159).

Figure 5.27: *The reality of the rural dream – life in a shanty town*

Economic development

If rural-urban migration does have any benefit, it must be that it is helping to reduce the population pressure on rural areas. Some might argue that it is also helping economic development. Labour for the growth of activities in the secondary and tertiary sectors is made available. For example, workers for factories or staff to run transport services.

However, poverty is deeply rooted in rural areas (Figure 5.28). For example, more than half of Kenya's 31 million people are poor. About 75% of the poor people live in rural areas. The trebling of Kenya's population over the past 30 years is one of the basic causes of the rising rural poverty. Another cause is a low agricultural productivity. This is made worse by land degradation, insecure land tenure, poor farming methods and the loss of male labour due to rural-urban migration. HIV/AIDS, which is particularly prevalent among the population of working age, is also worsening the labour situation.

Figure 5.28: *Rural poverty*

The recent introduction of commercial farming in some LICs has been hailed by some as a significant step forward in terms of rural economic development. However, the Kenyan case study in Part **5.7** cautions us to think otherwise. Perhaps a better option would be tourism. Many LICs have the natural resources (scenery, wildlife and wilderness) which could be exploited for tourism. The HICs have huge numbers of tourists with leisure time and money who are looking for new locations, new attractions and new tourist experiences.

Eco-tourism promises most benefits because:

- it is based on natural resources
- it minimises the use of non-renewable resources and damage to the environment
- its profits stay in the local community
- it is sustainable and it contributes to the conservation of areas.

Not all rural areas have eco-tourism potential, but there are already some good projects for others to copy.

For more information about ecotourism, see Chapter 8.6 (page 227).

5.9 Rural changes in HICs

The main changes in the rural areas of HICs are related to the later phases of the urbanisation process. The changes vary from place to place, mainly depending on the distance and accessibility from large cities. Four broad types of rural area may be recognised (Figure 5.29):

- the urban fringe
- the commuter belt

- accessible countryside
- remote countryside.

We will now look at the changes associated with each of these.

Urban fringe

This is the rural space literally on the edge of the built-up area of towns and cities. It is rural space that is being 'eroded' by the outward spread of the built-up area. The main process of change here is **suburbanisation**. This involves the building of new homes most often in the form of large housing estates. These estates become occupied by either rural-urban migrants or people who choose move out of the older parts of the built-up area. The latter are attracted by the new housing and nearness to the open countryside. However, the occupiers of these new homes will need more than just a house. They will require services, such as shops, schools and medical centres.

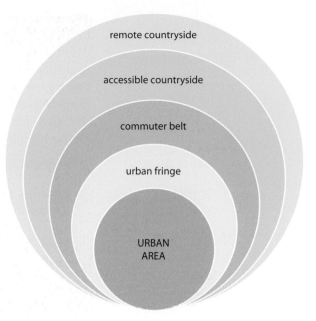

Figure 5.29: *Four types of rural area*

The four types of rural area in Figure 5.29 are being affected, in various ways, by the spread of urban influences. This spread is leading to a number of other changes:

- in population and the way of life
- in economic activities
- in the environment.

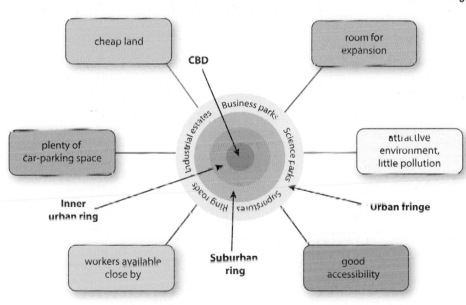

Figure 5.30: *The attractions of the urban fringe*

Other activities will also be attracted by the increasing number of people living in the new suburbs (Figure 5.30). Industrial estates, business and science parks will be drawn not just by the availability of labour nearby, but also by better accessibility (provided by ring roads and bypasses), cheaper land and the attractive setting provided by the remaining countryside. Large retailing complexes and superstores will be attracted by the relatively wealthy suburban customers living nearby. Given modern roads, those retailers will also be able to attract customers from other nearby urban areas.

There is less space in the urban fringe than the amount of land needed for the building of new homes and various kinds of 'park'. This rapid 'erosion' of the countryside just beyond the fringe of the built-up area has caused planners in some countries to act to protect the remaining greenfield sites (greenfield sites are sites that have never been used before). The most common action has been to create green belts around cities (Figure 5.31). Within these belts, there are strict controls that allow few, if any, new developments. London's green belt, first set up in 1947, has been a fairly successful example.

Figure 5.31: *Urban green belts in England and Wales*

What do you think are the consequences of creating a green belt around a town or city?

The commuter belt

The commuter belt lies just outside the urban fringe (Figure 5.29 on page 139). Change here is largely due to the arrival of commuters. These are mainly people who work in the nearby city and use its services. They are tempted to move here by:

- the attraction of cheaper and more spacious housing

- the availability of fast transport to the place of work. Most jobs are located either in a city centre or in new industrial estates and business parks in the urban fringe

- the opinion that the commuter belt offers a better quality of life; that it provides a better environment in which to bring up a family.

In short, people feel that the time and money spent on commuting are worth it. Figure 5.32 shows how far commuters in south-east England are prepared to travel each working day.

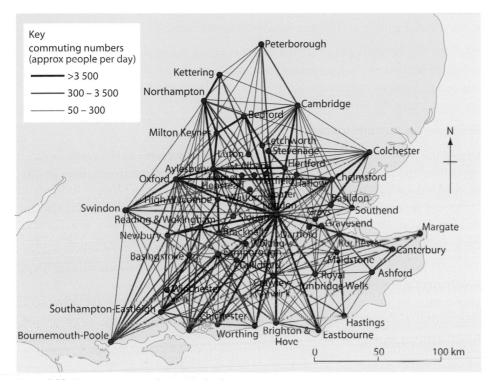

Figure 5.32: *Commuting in south-east England*

On Figure 5.32 measure the straight-line distances being covered by some of London's long-distance commuters.

The impact of commuting has changed the character of rural villages and hamlets. They are converted into 'dormitories' or detached suburbs (see **Urbanisation processes** on page 147). New housing estates are built on their edges. Older housing is modernised and often extended. The old village shops are replaced by small supermarkets. Rural crafts and the links with farming disappear. Communities often become divided into two with the 'urban newcomers' gradually overwhelming the 'rural natives'.

Accessible countryside

Accessible countryside lies beyond the commuter belt, but it is within day trip reach from the city. It is still very much a rural area. Three important changes are taking place in these areas.

Farming

Although farming remains a significant land use in the accessible countryside, its character is changing. Because of mechanisation and the amalgamation of farms into agri-businesses, it is no longer a major employer. Small farms can no longer support the large number of families they once did. Many farmers are finding it difficult to make a profit from traditional food production alone. If they want to stay in business, hard-pressed farmers have no choice but to diversify – by doing one of two things:

- find other ways of making money out of the farm, while continuing to farm
- turn their farms into completely different businesses.

With the first option, farms have moved into organic farming and, rather than selling to supermarkets, have set up their own farm shops. Examples of the second option are training racehorses or converting the farm into a golf course. More often the farm is used for recreation, leisure and tourism.

Look back at page 126 which gives more information about farm diversification.

Recreation, leisure and tourism

One of the features of 21st-century living is that many people in HICs have both spare time and disposable income. Both are being spent on leisure activities. In the accessible countryside, the leisure facilities are geared to the fact that in order to use them, city people will have to think in terms of a day trip rather than just a short drive in the car. Maybe the day will be spent on a farm visit, a fun day at a theme park, some birdwatching around a nature reserve or pony trekking (Figure 5.33).

The growth of recreation, leisure and tourism in the accessible countryside is not evenly spread. It tends to be focused on what are called **honeypots** – places that offer something that attracts large numbers of visitors. It might be especially attractive scenery, picturesque settlements or some well-known historic connection.

Retirement migration

People in HICs are living longer. Most people can expect to enjoy 10 or more years of retirement. As a result, more and more people are moving home once they have retired. They are doing this for a number of reasons:

- it is no longer necessary for them to live close to what was their place of work
- to downsize to a smaller home
- to sell their home for something cheaper and to use the difference in price as a sort of pension
- to move into a quieter, calmer and more attractive environment

As a result of the last point, quite a lot of this retirement migration is ending up in the accessible countryside.

Figure 5.33: *Using the countryside for recreation and leisure*

Remote countryside

This takes the best part of a day to reach from a city. It is almost totally rural. Probably the two most significant changes are **depopulation** and the dramatic decline in farming. The two are closely linked. Remoteness from markets and the costs of transport are two factors making farming in these parts uneconomic. The abandonment of farms has meant a serious loss of jobs.

For this reason, several generations of young people have been forced to leave the remote countryside in search of work in towns and cities. They have also been persuaded to move because of the declining quality of life. This decline in farming and loss of population has started a spiral of decline (Figure 5.34).

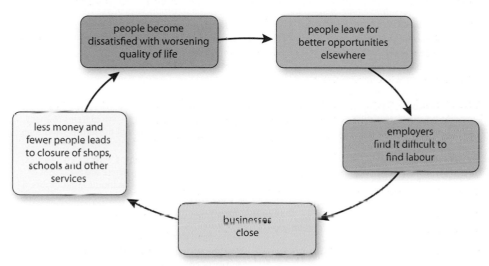

Figure 5.34: The spiral of decline in remote rural areas

However, it is not all bad news in the remote countryside. There are two positive changes. Fortunately there are, within the remote countryside, tracts of country that have been designated national parks. This has occurred in recognition that they offer something special. It may be spectacular scenery, wilderness or biodiversity. National parks and other protected areas attract holidaymakers and as a consequence tourism is now offering all sorts of employment opportunities – from jobs in hotels and restaurants to jobs as guides and park rangers.

The downward spiral is also being checked by the process of **counterurbanisation**. The loss of population from remote countryside is now being compensated by an inward movement of newcomers. Thanks to the broadband revolution, people tired of urban living and tempted by a rural setting are able to work from home in these remote parts. Some farmhouses have become **telecentres** or premises for **telecottaging**. Abandoned farm buildings are being turned into micro-businesses or cottage industries, such as making greetings cards, knitwear and beauty preparations. Even abandoned barns are being turned into upmarket offices or homes. Distance from the big cities is no longer the problem it used to be.

Make sure you understand the terms:

· counterurbanisation

· telecottaging.

End of chapter checkout

Checklists

Now you have read the chapter, you should know:

- ✓ what a biome is
- ✓ the global distributions of biomes
- ✓ about the temperate grassland biome and its agricultural use
- ✓ what an ecosystem is
- ✓ the main components of an ecosystem
- ✓ the distinguishing features of a rural environment
- ✓ how farming is seen as a system
- ✓ the different types of farming
- ✓ ways in which agricultural production is being raised
- ✓ the causes and consequences of food surpluses
- ✓ the causes and consequences of food shortages
- ✓ the changes taking place in the rural environments of LICs
- ✓ the changes taking place in the rural environments of HICs

Make sure you understand these key terms:

Accessibility: the ease with which one location is reached from another.

Arable farming: a type of agriculture which concentrates on the growing of plant crops, such as cereals and vegetables.

Biome: a plant and animal community covering a large area of the Earth's surface.

Cash cropping: the growing crops for sale as distinct from crops grown for consumption by the farmer and his family.

Commercial farming: a type of agriculture in which production is intended for sale in markets.

Conservation: the protection of aspects of the environment for the future benefit of people.

Counterurbanisation: the movement of people and employment from major cities to smaller cities and towns as well as to rural areas.

Depopulation: a decline in the number of people living in a particular area.

Ecosystem: a community and plants that interact with each other and their physical environment.

Fauna: animals.

Genetic engineering: changing the genetic material of a plant or animal to produce such things as a greater resistance to disease and a higher yield.

Glasshouses: structures of glass or polythene under which crops and flowers are grown. Such structures protect the crops from wind and heavy rain, as well as make the most of available sunlight.

High-yielding varieties (HYVs): grain crops where advances in plant breeding produced seeds that could more than double the yields over existing varieties.

Irrigation: the addition of water to farmland by artificial means, such as by pipelines and sprays.

Out-migration: the movement of people away from an area.

Pastoral farming: the rearing of livestock for meat or other products such as milk and wool.

Rural environment: areas of countryside largely concerned with farming and often with relatively low population densities.

Service provision: making available a range of commercial and social services, from shops to schools.

Subsistence farming: a type of agriculture concerned with the production of items to meet the food and living needs of the farmers and their families.

System: a set of interrelated components (stores) and processes (transfers). There are two types of system; an open system has inputs and outputs; a closed system has none.

Temperate grassland: a biome found in the dry interiors of continents and involving grasses rather than trees or shrubs.

See the Glossary in the ActiveBook for more definitions

Questions

Try testing yourself with these questions:

1. a) What are the names of the nine largest biomes?
   b) What two climatic factors most influence the global distribution of biomes?
2. Research the main characteristics of the tropical rainforest.
3. a) What is the difference between a biome and an ecosystem?
   b) Explain why the ecosystem is shown as a pyramid, as in Figure 5.5.
4. Using Table 5.1 as a guide, suggest what the 'goods and services' of the savanna might be.
5. Describe the following features of the temperate grassland biome:
   - distribution
   - vegetation.
   - soils
6. a) Why did farming in the Mid-West of the USA experience a crisis in the early 20th century?
   b) What was done to restore agricultural productivity?
7. What characteristics distinguish a rural environment from an urban environment?
8. Why has it become necessary to protect and manage some rural environments?
9. Explain how and why farming is a system.
10. a) Why do some governments try to control farming?
    b) Give some examples of this government intervention.
11. What is the difference between:
    - subsistence farming and commercial farming?
    - arable farming and pastoral farming?
    - intensive farming and extensive farming?
12. Describe six ways to increase food production.
13. Explain why irrigation has a downside.
14. Why is there so much controversy over the growing of GM crops?
15. Describe some of the consequences of an overproduction of food in HICs.
16. Why does the UK import 40% of its food?
17. What are the main causes of food shortages in LICs?
18. Using Figure 5.25, describe the sequence involved in the 'cycle of hunger'.
19. What are the symptoms of rural poverty in LICs?
20. What are the costs and benefits of the shift in LICs from subsistence to commercial farming?
21. What is the case for preserving rural space in the urban fringe?
22. What are the attractions of the commuter belt?
23. How are farms in the accessible countryside diversifying?
24. What are the main changes taking place in the remote countryside?

Chapter 6: Urban environments

6.1 The nature of urbanisation

The growth of towns and cities which leads to an increasing percentage of a country's population living in urban settlements is called **urbanisation**. Urban settlements (towns and cities) differ from rural ones (hamlets and villages) in terms of (Figure 6.1):

- their economies – they make a living from manufacturing and services rather than agriculture

- their size – they are larger in population and extent

- their densities of people and buildings which are generally high

- their way of life.

Introduction

This chapter is about towns and cities. Worldwide, the process of urbanisation is changing where and how people live and work. For many, urbanisation brings benefits, but there are also serious costs such as congestion, discrimination, pollution and poor housing. Perhaps these costs are greatest in LIC cities. Despite their overall prosperity, HIC cities also have their challenges. These include reducing the amount of deprivation and reviving worn-out parts of the built-up area. At the same time, however, important new developments are taking place around the edges of HIC cities.

Figure 6.1: *A modern central city landscape*

Figure 6.2 shows how the level of urbanisation (the percentage of the population living in urban settlements) varies across the globe. In general terms, it is the middle-income countries (MICs) and higher-income countries (HICs) that show the highest levels of urbanisation. The lowest levels are found in Africa and South-East Asia.

Towns and cities are growing in number and size all over the world. While the world's population is increasing fast, the urban population is increasing even faster. Figure 6.3 shows that the world population more than doubled between 1950 and 2000 but that the urban population more than trebled. Today, the rate of urbanisation has been such that half the world's population is now living in urban areas.

See Figure 5.9 on page 121 which shows the changing balance in the world's population. Clearly we have now reached the point where just over half the world's population lives in urban areas.

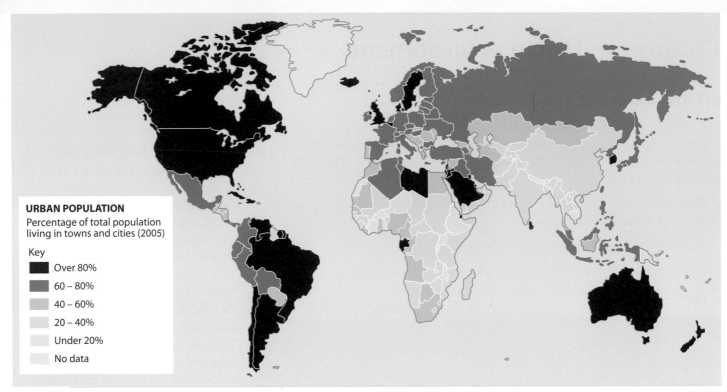

Figure 6.2: *Global distribution of urbanisation, 2005*

What is significant about present-day rates of urbanisation is the difference in the speed of growth between the cities in the higher-income countries (HICs) and those in the lower-income countries (LICs). The rate of city growth is much higher in the LICs (Figure 6.4). Present trends are expected to continue. However, the overall level of urbanisation remains higher in HICs.

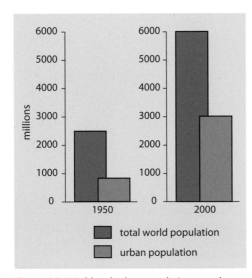

Figure 6.3: *World and urban population growth*

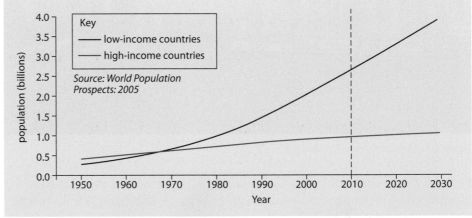

Figure 6.4: *Urbanisation in LICs and HICs, 1950 – 2030*

High rates of urbanisation are occurring in LICs because:

- most new economic developments in these countries are concentrated in the big cities

- push and pull factors are leading to high rates of rural-to-urban migration

- cities are experiencing high rates of natural increase in population.

In HICs, the rates of urbanisation are much slower for the simple reason that a large proportion of the population is already living in towns and cities. The built-up areas of towns and cities continue to grow. Because of modern transport and communication, the urban way of life is gradually spreading into rural areas. In fact, the countryside and its settlements are experiencing what is referred to as **rural dilution**.

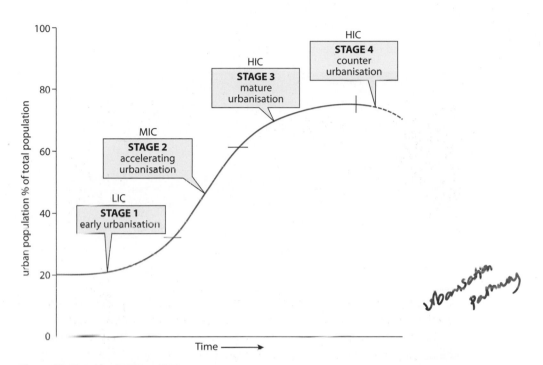

Figure 6.5: The urbanisation pathway

These differences between LICs and HICs encourage us to think of an urbanisation pathway. The pathway shows how the level of urbanisation changes over time (Figure 6.5). Countries become more urban as they develop economically. They gradually move from being an LIC towards becoming an HIC. A country starts at a very low level of urbanisation (Stage 1), but there comes a time when the rates of economic development and urbanisation speed up (Stage 2). Later, as the pace of economic development slows, so too does the rate of urbanisation (Stage 3). The level of urbanisation begins to flatten out, often when roughly two-thirds of an HIC's population is living in urban settlements. As shown by Figure 6.5, the pathway takes the form of an S-shaped curve. The curve may begin to drop as **counterurbanisation** gains in strength.

It is important to remember:

- that not all countries will progress very far along the pathway

- that countries will vary in terms of their speed along the pathway. The speed will be largely controlled by the pace of economic development.

Urbanisation processes

Urbanisation is a process of change that converts rural areas, regions and countries into urban ones. That change also involves a number of other processes that affect the built-up areas of towns and cities as they grow.

Urban settlements first appear as a result of **agglomeration**. That is the concentration of people and economic activities at favourable locations such as at river crossing points, estuary mouths or close to a mineral resource (coal, iron or oil). In early times, defence was an important locational consideration. As towns grow, so they expand outwards by a process known as **suburbanisation**. This adds to the built-up area, but the building densities are generally lower than in the older parts of the town (Figure 6.6). The creation of these new suburbs made up of houses, places of employment and services is encouraged by:

- improvements in transport that allow people to move easily between the new suburbs and the town centre

- overcrowding, congestion and rising land prices in the older parts of the town

- a generally decline in the quality of the residential environment near the centre

- the arrival of more people (mainly from rural areas) and new businesses.

What do you think it is that appeals to those people who choose to live in the suburbs?

Figure 6.6: *Suburban sprawl*

As a result of these two processes – agglomeration and suburbanisation – some towns grow into cities. Towns and cities located close to another sometimes join together into one vast continuous built-up area known as a **conurbation**. As we shall see on the next page, this scaling up in the size of urban settlements does not end there.

As urban settlements continue to prosper and grow, a new process sets in. People start to move out of the town or city altogether and to live instead in smaller, often mainly rural settlements. These are often called **dormitory settlements**, because many of the new residents only sleep there. They continue to have links with the town or city they have left. They **commute** to the same place of work and continue to make use of urban services, such as shops, colleges and hospitals.

As cities and conurbations continue to grow even bigger, a rather different process sets in. Rather than just moving out to suburbs and dormitory settlements, people and businesses move further out either to smaller towns and cities or to rural areas. This process is known as **counterurbanisation**.

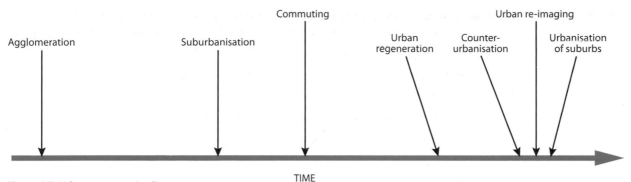

Figure 6.7: *Urban processes timeline*

In this section we have looked at a number of different processes. They can be put in a time sequence (Figure 6.7). This sequence can be married up with the urbanisation pathway (Figure 6.5 on page 147). In the early stages of the pathway, urbanisation mainly involves agglomeration and suburbanisation. In the later stages, although both agglomeration and suburbanisation continue, decentralisation and counterurbanisation become more important.

Two new processes have begun to appear in HIC cities. They are:

- **urban regeneration** – this involves re-using areas in the old parts of cities abandoned as people and businesses have moved out to the suburbs or beyond. This process has allowed the **re-imaging** not just of city centres but of whole cities (see Part **6.8**). A well known example of this is the regeneration of the deserted docklands and warehouses of London into upmarket offices and residential apartments.

- **urbanisation of suburbs** – suburbs are typically areas of low density development. Today, however, as rural space is being eroded by urbanisation, governments are keen that more use should be made of suburban areas. Vacant building plots and open spaces are being developed; large detached houses are being replaced by flats and maisonettes. No longer are suburbs being protected as just residential areas. Shops and other services are being located in the suburbs. In short, suburban densities are being raised to an urban level.

Other well-known urban regeneration schemes in the UK include:

- Salford Quays, Manchester
- Cardiff Bay, South Wales
- Bradford, Yorkshire.

The emergence of megacities

The maps for 1970 and 2000 show great changes in the world's 'top ten' cities (Figure 6.8). In 1970, half were in HICs and half in LICs. By the year 2000, only two of the ten were found in HICs. Not only has the global distribution changed dramatically, but so too has the total number of people living in our largest cities. In 1970, the figures ranged from 16.5 million (New York, then the biggest city in the world) to 6.5 million (Calcutta). By 2000, the most populous city was Tokyo with 26.7 million people. The population of New York, rated number ten in 2000, had fallen slightly to 16.3 million.

The size of big cities is another feature of world urbanisation. For many years the **millionaire city** (a city of more than one million people) was considered a big city, especially since in 1900 there were only two – London and Paris. Now there are about 400 (Figure 6.9).

Largest cities in 1970 (1 is largest)

Largest cities in 2000 (1 is largest)

Figure 6.8: *Global urban growth*

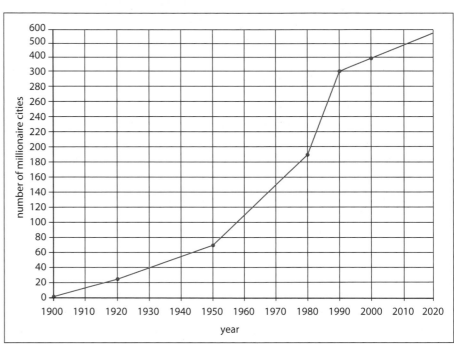

Study Figure 6.9. Describe the trends in the growth in the number of millionaire cities during the 20th century.

Figure 6.9: *Growth of millionaire cities (1900–2000)*

More recently, the term **megacity** has been used to describe cities with populations of over 10 million. In 1970 there were just four of these, but by 2010 there were 24 of them. The United Nations estimates that by the year 2015 there will be nearly 30 megacities, over half of which will be in Asia.

What are the reasons for the growth of these megacities? Figure 6.10 shows four main factors being involved:

- **economic development** – this is the driver of all economic growth and urbanisation. Presumably megacities are produced by a fast and sustained rate of economic growth.

- **population growth** – given the size of these cities, there must be high rates of population growth. Large volumes of rural-urban migration among young adults, plus high rates of natural increase are needed to explain the size of these cities. Young people will be drawn to live in these cities by the 'buzz' of feeling close to 'where it is all happening'. There is kudos and 'street cred' to be living and working in such 'cool' places

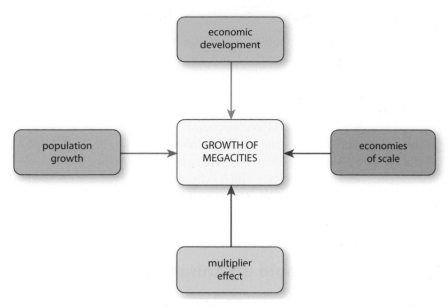

Figure 6.10: *Factors encouraging the growth of megacities*

- **economies of scale** – there are advantages to be gained from cramming as much as possible into one megacity rather than into a number of smaller cities. Since distances within a megacity are less than between smaller cities, there are financial savings (economies of scale) to be made in terms of transport. Communication between people and businesses will be easier (another economy)

- **multiplier effect** – with cities, success leads to more success. Once a large city is prospering, it gathers a momentum which will carry it forward. So it will lead to more prosperity and growth. There are more jobs so more people come which means there are more people who need goods and services, which creates more jobs and so the cycle goes on.

Being located in a megacity has a powerful attraction to both people and businesses. However, there is a downside. All of the problems described in Part **6.2** over the page are present in megacities and are probably even more acute. However, probably their worst aspect is to be seen at a national level. Megacities grow and prosper at the expense of towns, cities and regions elsewhere within the country. Megacities become powerful **cores** that create large **peripheries** around them.

Can you think of any other downside to the growth of megacities?

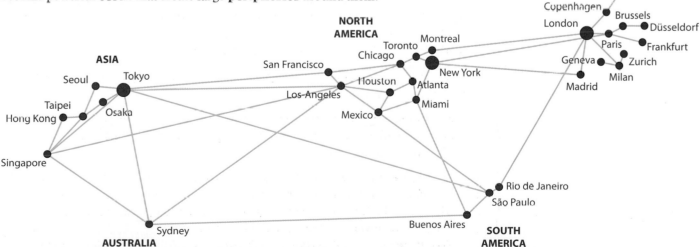

Figure 6.11: *Distribution of global cities*

Global or world cities

Megacities are urban areas with populations greater than 10 million. **Global** or **world cities**, on the other hand, can be of any size. At present there are 31 such cities (Figure 6.11). They all have populations over 1 million and seven of them are megacities (Buenos Aires, Hong Kong, Mexico City, New York, Rio de Janeiro, São Paulo, Seoul). What distinguishes a global city from a megacity? Global cities are recognised worldwide as places of great prestige, status, power and influence. All global cities are critical hubs in the growing global economy. There are three 'top dog' global cities. They are London, New York and Tokyo. These are the financial centres of the global economy and it is from this that they derive their power and influence. Each of these three cities is the hub of a network of smaller global cities. Four global cities are located outside these three networks – Rio de Janeiro, São Paulo, Buenos Aires and Sydney, all in the Southern Hemisphere.

> What is the difference, if any, between a megacity and a world city?

> Just check that you understand the main causes of rapid urbanisation, namely:
>
> - high volumes of rural-urban migration
> - high rates of natural population increase
> - a quickening rate of economic development.

6.2 The problems of rapid urbanisation

The world is rapidly becoming urbanised, and the pace of urbanisation is greatest in LICs. For example, the population of the city of São Paulo in Brazil grew from 7 million in 1970 to an estimated 20 million in 2010. Covering an area of 8000 km², it is now the second largest urban area in the Americas. Here, as elsewhere in the developing world, this rapid and often unplanned growth has created a range of problems, mainly because of the speed at which it has occurred.

- **Housing** – Much of the rapid growth of LIC cities has been caused by people moving in from rural areas or other parts of the country. When they arrive, there is nowhere for them to live, especially as many are looking for cheap, low-cost housing. Millions of people live in what were meant to be temporary **shanty towns** or **squatter settlements** (for more information see Part **6.5**). Even for those with money, the demand for housing exceeds supply. As a result, housing is expensive relative to people's wages and salary. In general, because of poor transport, the most sought-after housing is close to the city centre with its shops and places of work.

- **Access to water and electricity** – It is commonly the case that the provision of basic services does not keep up with the growth of population. As a consequence, not all parts of the built-up area are provided with running water, sanitation or electricity. Many people have no option but to rely on fires for cooking and lighting, and on polluted streams for water and sewage disposal.

- **Traffic congestion and transport** – The provision of proper roads and public transport is another aspect of city life that lags behind the growth in population. As a result the transport systems in the city are overloaded and overcrowded, and traffic congestion is a major problem for everyone – rich or poor. The high numbers of vehicles also causes high levels of atmospheric pollution in cities, many of which suffer regularly from smog (a mixture of smoke and fog).

Figure 6.12: *Traffic congestion*

- **Health** – There are not enough doctors, clinics or hospitals to deal with the rapid increase in population. With large parts of the mushrooming city having little or no access to clean water or sanitation, diseases and infections, such as typhoid and cholera, spread quickly. Atmospheric pollution leads to widespread respiratory problems.

- **Education** – Rapid population growth also means a lack of schools. Although most cities manage to provide some primary education, not all children go on to secondary school. This is because of the cost and because many children have to work to help support the family.

- **Employment** – Although people are attracted to cities for work, many are unable to find proper paid work. Instead they are either unemployed or become part of the massive **informal sector**, surviving as best as they can. This includes selling goods on the street (Figure 6.13), working as cleaners or shoe-shiners or cooking and selling food from home or by the roadside (see Chapter **4.3** on page 97 for more information on the informal sector). Even where there is paid work in new factories, these are often many kilometres away from the shanty areas where most newcomers live.

- **Social problems** – Given how close to each other people live and the poor conditions experienced by sometimes millions of city dwellers, it is not surprising that they also suffer from high crime rates, drug trafficking and theft. The poorest areas are often inhabited by violent street gangs.

Figure 6.13: *Informal street-side workers*

6.3 The segregation of urban land uses

Look at the built-up area of most towns and cities and you will see the same recurring features – a **central business district**, industrial areas, a variety of residential districts, small shopping centres and so on. Figure 6.14 shows the segregation that is typical of HIC cities. What causes this segregation of different urban land uses? Why are the different land uses not jumbled up together?

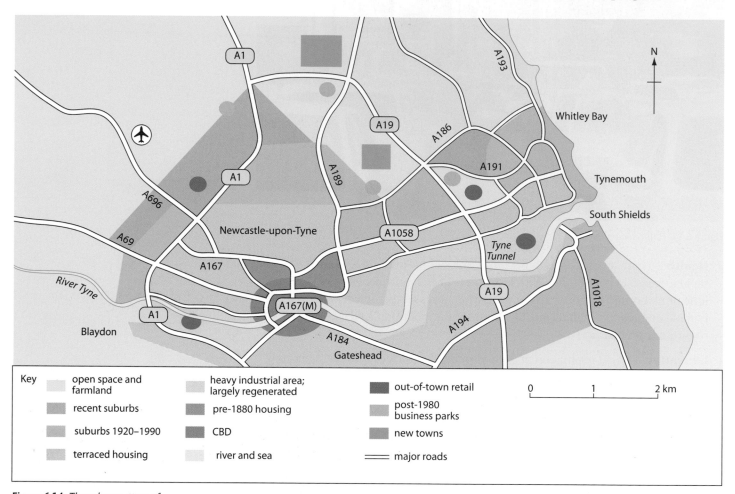

Figure 6.14: *The urban pattern of Newcastle-upon-Tyne, England*

Study Figure 6.14. In what ways has the River Tyne influenced the urban pattern?

The main cause of the segregation is the **urban land market**. As with the selling of any item, a particular site within the built-up area will normally be sold to the highest bidder. The highest bidder will be that activity that can make best use of a site. It is usually retail shops that can make the best financial use of land and property. To understand this, two related points need to be made clear.

First, land values vary within the urban area. Generally, they decline outwards from the centre, from the **peak land-value intersection** (Figure 6.15). However, relatively high land values are also found along major roads leading from the centre and around ring roads. Small land value peaks occur where radial and ring roads cross each other. Businesses will pay extra for sites in these locations, because they are locations enjoying good accessibility.

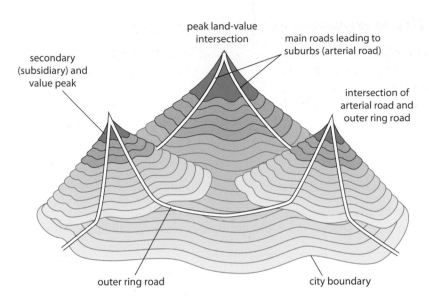

Figure 6.15: *Urban land values*

Describe the pattern of 'relief' created by urban land values, as shown in Figure 6.15.

Secondly, similar activities or land uses come together because:

- they have the same locational needs. These may be large amounts of space or being accessible to customers and employees

- they can afford the same general level of land values.

Thus retailing and other commercial businesses (particularly offices) will cluster in and around the centre. This is the most accessible part of the built-up area. As a result of the clustering, they help define a central business district (CBD). In contrast, manufacturing also needs accessible locations for the assembly of raw materials and the dispatch of finished goods. However, it is a less capital-intensive use of space than shops or offices. Therefore, it has less buying power. So manufacturing is found outside the CBD and most often along major roads that provide good accessibility and transport links. Housing is even less competitive on the urban land market. For this reason it tends to be pushed further away from the centre. As land becomes cheaper towards the urban fringe, so houses can become more spacious.

In which part of the industrial HIC city were most factories located?

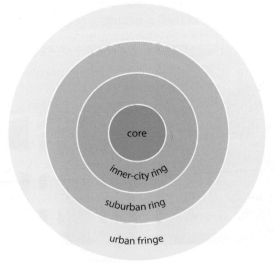

Figure 6.16: *The four zones of a city*

Because towns and cities grow outwards from a historic nucleus, they show concentric zoning – that is, a series of rings wrapping around the historic nucleus or core. Hence, it is possible to recognise in all towns in all cities, no matter where they are located in the world, the same four features (Figure 6.16):

- a **core** – the oldest part of the city which normally contains the central business district

- an **inner-city ring** – early suburbs, so old housing and often some non-residential land uses

- a **suburban ring** – present suburbs with housing as the dominant land use

- an **urban fringe** – countryside being 'eroded' by the outward spread of the built-up area to provide space for housing and some non-residential uses.

We may make three more generalisations about the structure of cities as one moves outwards from the core:

- the general age of the built-up area decreases

- the style of architecture and urban design change

- the overall density of development decreases.

This urban model of four zones applies to virtually all towns and cities. What varies in different parts of the world is the character of each zone – namely what goes on in them in terms of land use and the type of people living there.

6.4 The segregation of people in cities

People, like land uses, become sorted within the urban area by the same urban land market and the same process of bidding for sites. People become segregated into groups on the basis of their social class, type of occupation and ethnicity (Figure 6.17). People prefer to live close to those whom they think are of the same status. However, the reason for most of these differences is personal wealth. The wealthiest people are able to buy smart and large homes in the best locations. The poorest people have no option but to live in cramped or substandard housing in the worst residential areas. Many of them are unable to buy a home. Instead they have to rent. Due to their limited means, they are forced to occupy only a small amount of space, and therefore have to live at high densities.

Figure 6.17: *Different types of housing typically occupied by different socio-economic groups*

Globally, one of the most obvious signs of the sorting of different population groups into different spaces are the ghettos that are to be found in many cities. A **ghetto** is an area where an ethnic minority is concentrated and is the dominant population group. In the UK, there has been much immigration from Commonwealth countries in Africa, the Indian subcontinent and the Caribbean. The immigrants have settled and become concentrated in parts of the inner areas of towns and cities.

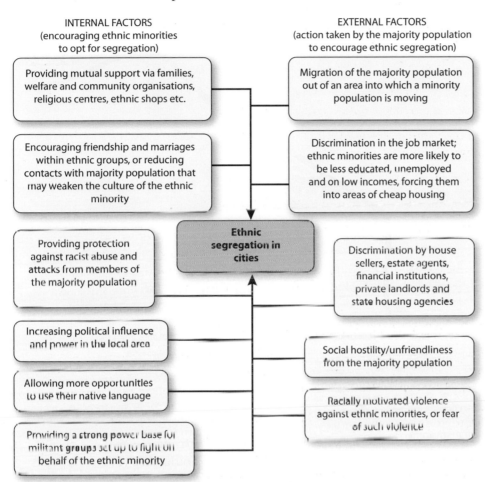

INTERNAL FACTORS
(encouraging ethnic minorities to opt for segregation)

EXTERNAL FACTORS
(action taken by the majority population to encourage ethnic segregation)

Providing mutual support via families, welfare and community organisations, religious centres, ethnic shops etc.

Migration of the majority population out of an area into which a minority population is moving

Encouraging friendship and marriages within ethnic groups, or reducing contacts with majority population that may weaken the culture of the ethnic minority

Discrimination in the job market; ethnic minorities are more likely to be less educated, unemployed and on low incomes, forcing them into areas of cheap housing

Ethnic segregation in cities

Providing protection against racist abuse and attacks from members of the majority population

Discrimination by house sellers, estate agents, financial institutions, private landlords and state housing agencies

Increasing political influence and power in the local area

Allowing more opportunities to use their native language

Social hostility/unfriendliness from the majority population

Providing a strong power base for militant groups set up to fight on behalf of the ethnic minority

Racially motivated violence against ethnic minorities, or fear of such violence

Figure 6.18: *Factors encouraging ethnic segregation in cities*

It is widely believed that the inner-city ghettos have come about because immigrants have been forced to live in areas of poor housing. The external factors shown in Figure 6.18 support the idea that the ghettos develop because of discrimination against some immigrants. However, the internal factors suggest that an ethnic minority gains some benefits from being concentrated in a particular area.

The interesting question associated with ethnic segregation is this – is the segregation more of a voluntary process than a forced one?

Case study: Zomba (Malawi)

Zomba is a city of just 100 000 people in the African state of Malawi in central Africa. For nearly 75 years, it served as the British colonial capital of what used to be called Nyasaland (now Malawi). In 1964 Malawi became an independent state and 10 years later Zomba was replaced by Lilongwe as the capital city. The city is best known for its British colonial architecture. Here in the centre of

Zomba was the Governor's residence, the army barracks and the Gymkana Club with its polo field and huge park. The Club was very popular with government officials and settlers from Britain and other European countries as a place for socialising.

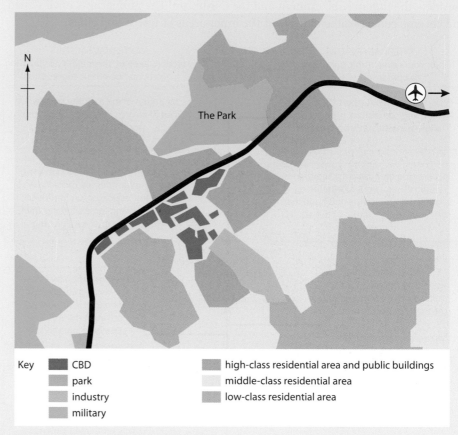

Key
- CBD
- park
- industry
- military
- high-class residential area and public buildings
- middle-class residential area
- low-class residential area

Figure 6.19: *The urban pattern of Zomba*

What similarities, if any, do you see in the urban patterns of Zomba (Figure 6.19) and Newcastle-upon-Tyne (Figure 6.14 on page 154)?

Because of its history, the centre of the city today is the Park that was once part of the Gymkana Club. The central business district (CBD) lies to the south (Figure 6.19). This is the most accessible part of the city where the main roads meet. It contains verandah-style shops built during the colonial period, as well as a large market. Factories are mainly concentrated in two locations – one along the main road leading to the airport and the other close to the CBD. The rest of the built-up area is occupied by housing. Overall, the pattern of land use is not dissimilar to that found in HIC cities.

Three classes of residential area may be distinguished:

- **high-class residential areas** lie mainly to the north of the CBD and close to the Park. These areas date mainly from the colonial times when they housed the colony's administrators and European settlers. Consequently, it has the infrastructure – water, sewerage and electricity – not found in other parts of the built-up area. The social pattern is the opposite to that found in HIC cities where the inner city tends to house the poor.

- **middle-class residential areas** surround the high-class residential areas. Many of these areas started out as low-class housing. They have since been upgraded and provided with some basic amenities.

- **low-class residential areas** are found on the lower land to the south-east of the where there is a risk of flooding. These areas are essentially shanty towns. There is one notable area close to the CBD on its south-western side – again this is an area prone to flooding.

Figure 6.20: *Part of Zomba's CBD*

6.5 Shanty towns

The speed of urbanisation in LICs is fast and continues to accelerate. Most people who migrate to LIC cities come from poor rural areas in search of work. There are no houses for them, so they build homes on the only land available which is usually in areas of no economic value, on the edge of town, along main roads or on steep slopes. These DIY housing areas are generally referred to as **shanty towns**. In many instance, people build on land that they do not own, or on which they do not have permission to build. As a result, such areas are also known as **squatter settlements**.

Many of the areas on which shanty towns are built are unsafe. They may be prone to flooding or landslides or are in heavily polluted locations. Usually they are not serviced with refuse disposal etc. The actual dwellings are made out of scrap materials such as packing boxes, metal and plastic sheeting. However, for many, even living in a shanty town and working in the informal economy can be better and offer greater opportunities than the life they have left behind in rural areas.

Shanty towns are known by different names around the world;

- favelas (Brazil)
- barriadas (Latin America)
- bidonville (North Africa)
- bustees (Indian subcontinent)
- squatter settlements (North America).

Case study: São Paulo's favelas

About 20 per cent of the residents of São Paulo, Brazil's largest city, live in shanty towns (known here as 'favelas') and scratch a living in the informal sector. São Paulo has approximately 2500 favelas. Some of the best known are Heliópolis (population around 60 000), Paraisópolis (30 000) and Jaguare (24 000). All are away from the city centre but close to new factories. Some of the biggest favelas are now up to 40 years old, and it is these which have seen the greatest level of improvement (Figure 6.22).

Figure 6.21: *A favela in São Paulo – note the city centre in the distance*

Figure 6.22: *A favela in São Paulo in the process of being redeveloped.*

When they were first built, few homes had even the most basic facilities, and there were no community facilities. Many people would illegally hook up to overhead electricity lines. Over time, communities developed and became organised. In Jaguare, a strong Neighbourhood Association has developed. By working together, people in this favela have persuaded the Brazilian government to help them reduce crime and offer people, especially children, a wide range of sport or other activities.

Community groups have actively campaigned in many favelas to improve housing conditions and have put pressure on city authorities to provide basic services such as water, sanitation and electricity. Some of these are via self-help or site-and-service schemes. The government or a non–governmental organisation (NGO) provides building materials which local people use to build better homes. The PROSANEAR programme is a partnership between the Brazilian Government and the World Bank. It has done much to deliver water and sanitation to a growing number of São Paulo's favelas.

In some favelas, help has been made available so residents can get legal rights over their homes and land. This means that they are more secure, and can sell (and buy) property. This stability has also encouraged further investment in favelas. There are also schemes to lend small sums of money to people running businesses in favelas via '**microlending**'. A microcredit scheme was launched in Heliópolis favela by a US non-profit-making organisation and a Brazilian bank working together. Local people with small businesses, such as bakers and grocery store owners, may apply for loans of between $100 and $1500 to develop their businesses.

No two favelas are exactly alike. Because of this, any improvement programme has to be tailored to suit the specific conditions in each favela. Hence the variety of actions just described. However, if any project is to succeed, it is vital that there is community approval and participation. A majority of residents (often set as high as 80% of them) must agree to the project for it to be accepted and to work. They also have to agree to pay some of the costs of installing and providing the services. Sadly, for many residents, this last requirement is too much.

As life improves in an increasing number of São Paulo's favelas (Figure 6.22), there is concern that this will merely encourage more newcomers to the city. In the long term, there needs to be other solutions. The best would probably be to improve the quality of life in the rural areas of Brazil, and so reduce the volume of rural-urban migration. São Paulo is seeing new **edge cities** like Berrini and Jardines develop on the city's outer limits. These may help by encouraging rural-urban migrants – and existing residents – to live away from the main city.

This is a very important point, that no two shanty towns are alike. The only thing they have in common is that they have arisen in order to provide poor people with some basic shelter in urban areas.

6.6 Changes at the edges of HIC cities

The areas where the green fields and open spaces of the countryside meet the built-up parts of the towns and cities is known as either the **rural-urban fringe** or the **urban fringe**. Here countryside is being lost by the outward growth of towns and cities, particularly their suburbs. The **greenfield sites** of the open land around the edge of a city are in great demand for housing, industry, shopping, recreation and the needs of the public utilities, such as reservoirs and sewerage works.

One reason for urban growth and change in the rural-urban fringe is a feeling of dissatisfaction with the city (Figure 6.23).

- Housing is old, congested and relatively expensive

- There are various forms of environmental pollution – air quality is poor, and noise levels are high

- Companies find that there is a shortage of land for building new shops, offices and factories. As a consequence, what unused land there is, is costly.

These are all **push factors**. There are also **pull factors** on the urban fringe.

For more information about changes in the urban fringe, see Chapter 5.9 (page 139).

- Land is cheaper so houses are larger.

- Factories can be more spacious and have plenty of room for workers to park their cars.

- Closeness to the main roads and motorways allows for quicker and easier customer contacts.

- New developments on the outskirts are favoured by the personal mobility allowed by the car.

What else is happening around the urban fringe? Besides the appearance of new housing estates, there are significant non-residential developments. We shall focus on four of these.

Retail parks

In HICs there has been a great increase in **out-of-town retailing**, with large purpose-built **superstores** and shopping centres located at or just beyond the urban fringe. The number of superstores has increased dramatically in the UK since 1980. It is easy to understand why. More people own their own cars. The large car parks are free. Access is easy because the shopping centres are located next to main roads and motorway junctions. In contrast, city centre shoppers face traffic congestion and expensive parking. The larger out-of-town centres have shopping malls which are bright and modern with everything under one roof. Other facilities, such as multi-screen cinemas or bowling alleys, are often included within the shopping centre, or are located close by, so that there is something there for all the family.

Often, due to good main roads, the big retailing developments are serving customers drawn from more than one town or city.

Industrial estates

These are areas of modern light and service industries with a planned layout and purpose-built road networks.

Business parks

These are areas created by property developers in order to attract firms needing office accommodation, rather than industrial units. These often include leisure activities such as bowling alleys, ice rinks and cinemas.

Science parks

These are usually located close to a university or research centre with the aim of encouraging and developing high-tech industries and quaternary activities.

An important point about all four developments is that they have been created to serve much wider areas than the town or city in which they are located.

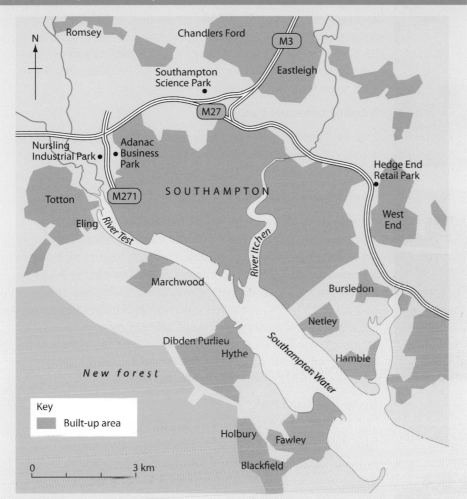

Figure 6.23: *The Southampton area*

Southampton is a city with a population of just over 200 000. For many centuries, the built up area within was confined to the peninsula between the Itchen and Test estuaries. Since the late 19th century, however, the built-up area has spilled over to the east of the River Itchen. For much of the time since the end of the Second World War in 1945, the growth of the built-up area has been held back by a green belt – a tract of countryside in which urban development was prohibited. In the postwar years, the city's economy prospered, largely due to its port. The economic growth attracted workers and their families to the Southampton area. However, because of the green belt there was no room to build the houses for the incoming workers. Instead, the housing had to be built on the other side of the green belt at Totton, Chandlers Ford, Eastleigh and West End. These places became Southampton's 'detached' suburbs or **commuter dormitories**.

Nursling Industrial Park

Southampton Science Park

Hedge End Retail Park

Adnac Business Park

Figure 6.24: *Four developments in Southampton's urban fringe*

The motorways that run through the green belt – parts of the M3, M27 and M271 – mean that there is very good accessibility. As a result of great pressure from developers, the green belt restrictions have been relaxed. Certain types of business have been allowed to take advantage of this accessibility and granted permission to build on a limited number of specified sites. There have been four major developments.

Nursling Industrial Park

The main businesses on this large estate located beside the M271 are so-called service industries, of which distribution and storage are the main ones.

Southampton Science Park

Southampton Science Park is a 17-hectare development in a prime location close to the M3 motorway to London. The Science Park provides high-quality office and laboratory space in attractive landscaped surroundings. Companies such as BskyB and Merck rub shoulders with young, fast-growing technology companies in fields such as nanotechnology. The result is a thriving business and research community of over 60 companies. All are attracted by the Park's strategic location, the quality of the environment and access to some of the UK's leading scientific expertise at the University of Southampton.

Hedge End Retail Park

This out-of-town shopping centre is one of the largest retail parks in the south of England. It is located just off the M27 and is home to Marks and Spencer, J Sainsbury, Homeworld, Currys, PC World, as well as stores selling ranges of bulky goods.

Adanac Business Park

This development was only approved in 2008. It is a 74-acre site and its first occupant will be the Ordnance Survey which produces all the maps of the UK. The park is earmarked for major office developments and 'large space' occupiers like the Ordnance Survey.

Imagine that you have been asked to promote one of Southampton's 'parks' described above. What points would you make in your sales pitch?

The greenfield versus brownfield debate

Not everyone is happy with the continued loss of countryside around the towns and cities of HICs. Many environmentalists believe that new developments should be built on **brownfield sites** – that is land within the built-up area that has been abandoned and is now lying idle – rather than on greenfield sites.

For more on the use of brownfield sites, see Part 6.8.

The question of where to build (on greenfield sites at the edge of the built-up area or on brownfield sites well inside the built-up area) arises in connection with a range of urban land uses – housing, retailing, industries and offices. With all land uses, there are arguments for and against each type of site. As Table 6.1 shows, each has its advantages and disadvantages.

Site	Advantages	Disadvantages
Brownfield site	• Reduces the loss of countryside and land that might be put to agricultural or recreational use • Helps to revive old and disused urban areas • Services, such as water, electricity, gas and sewerage already in place • Located nearer to main areas of employment, so commuting reduced	• Often more expensive because old buildings have to be cleared and land made free of pollution • Often surrounded by rundown areas so does not appeal to more wealthy people as residential locations • Higher levels of pollution; less healthy • May not have good access to modern roads
Greenfield site	• Relatively cheap and rates of house building faster • The layout is not hampered by previous development so can easily be made efficient and pleasant • Healthier environment	• Valuable farm or recreational space lost • Attractive scenery lost • Wildlife and their habitats lost or disturbed • Development causes noise and light pollution in the surrounding countryside • Encourages suburban sprawl

Table 6.1: The advantages and disadvantages of using brownfield and greenfield sites

There is no clear winner in this particular debate. It all depends on:

- the particular land use. Housing is fairly flexible in terms of where it might be built, but shops, offices and industries need more specific locations.

- the circumstances of the particular town or city. Is the green space really valuable? Are there serious problems and high costs involved in reusing the brown space?

- your own set of values. Do you think that the countryside should be protected at all costs or do you think that more should be released for urban growth?

6.7 Deprivation and poverty in HIC cities

It is easy to think that poverty is an LIC problem and that shanty towns only occur in LIC cities. The reality is that even within so-called wealthy countries there is poverty and that many HIC cities have their areas of poor housing, known as slums rather than shanty towns. HIC cities also contain people who are literally living and sleeping on the streets.

Figure 6.25: *A slum area in an HIC city*

In HIC cities, the term **deprivation** is widely used in connection with poverty. Deprivation is said to occur when a person's well-being falls below a level which is generally thought of as an acceptable minimum. This minimum standard applies not just to one, but a number of different aspects of daily life. In the UK, a **multiple deprivation index** (MDI) has been developed to assess the level of deprivation across the whole country. It is based on seven different quality of life indicators:

- income
- employment
- health
- education
- access to housing and services
- crime
- the living environment.

Calculating the index is quite complicated, but once it is done all the local authorities can be compared. From this comparison, it is possible to identify both the most deprived areas and the best areas.

Check that you understand what is meant by 'deprivation'. The indicators show that it is more than just a lack of money.

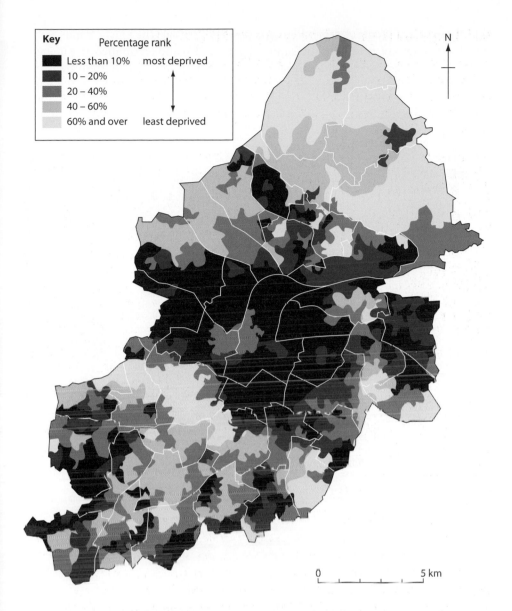

Key Percentage rank

Less than 10% most deprived
10 – 20%
20 – 40%
40 – 60%
60% and over least deprived

N

0   5 km

Figure 6.26. *Distribution of multiple deprivation in Birmingham, England*

Figure 6.26 shows the distribution of deprivation in Birmingham, once of the UK's largest cities. The areas of greatest deprivation occur in two main locations:

- the more central parts of the city – here deprivation coincides with areas of either old and substandard housing or high-rise apartment blocks that were built after the end of the Second World War to house people displaced by slum clearance schemes

- towards the city's edge – here deprivation mainly occurs in the estates of social housing built by the city for rent to poorer households.

The grey areas on Figure 6.26 are the areas with least deprivation (the best areas). They are therefore the parts of the city where wealthier people live, as in the northern part of the city and in a belt lying to the south-west of the city centre.

Look at the Case study of London (Chapter 9.6, page 253) which contains two more maps based on the MDI.

What are the symptoms of deprivation and poverty? Perhaps the most obvious are the physical signs of poor housing (slums) (Figure 2.26) and an unattractive living environment (noise, unsightliness, graffiti, etc.). Services, provided in these areas, such as schools, medical centres, sports facilities, park and shops, are often of a poor quality.

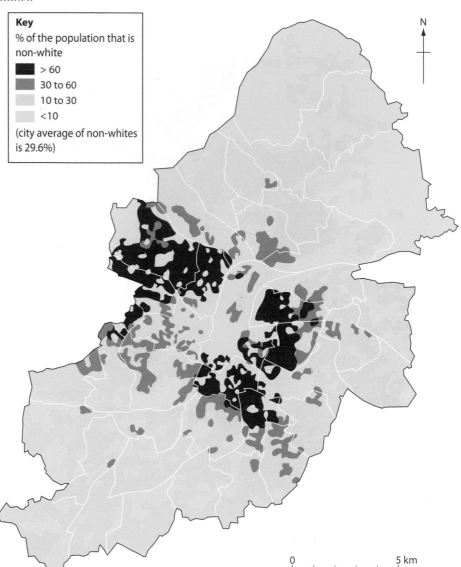

Figure 6.27: *Distribution of non-white people in Birmingham, England*

During the 1950s, when large numbers of immigrants from Commonwealth countries were encouraged to enter the UK, many settled in Birmingham. It had plenty of cheap, rundown housing. There were plenty of jobs to be had in the factories and in public transport.

The people who live in these areas of poor housing also feature characteristics that are part of the symptoms of deprivation. In general, there is a relatively high incidence of unemployment and single-parent families. Many of those of working age are able only to take on unskilled, manual work. Many have received only a minimal education. There is also a relatively high incidence of crime and what are called domestic disputes (troubles between partners), anti-social behaviour, etc. What is also noteworthy is the concentration of Birmingham's ethnic minorities from India, Bangladesh, Pakistan and the Caribbean in some of the most deprived parts of Birmingham (Figure 6.27). A comparison of Figures 6.26 and 6.27 shows that well. Ethnic minorities are often the 'victims' of high levels of deprivation.

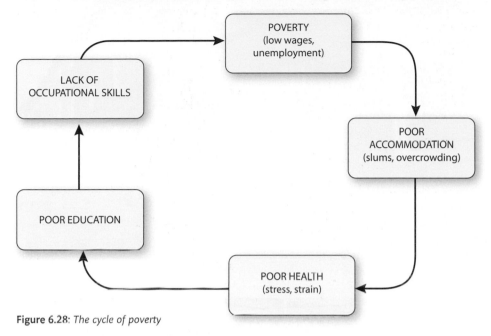

Figure 6.28: *The cycle of poverty*

In studying the occurrence of deprivation, we need to be aware of what is called the **cycle of poverty** (Figure 6.28). This is based on the idea that poverty and deprivation are passed on from one generation to the next. The children of poor parents may receive little parental support and may be forced to attend inadequate schools. As a result, they leave school at the earliest possible opportunity with few qualifications. This, in turn, means that they have difficulties finding work and can therefore only expect to earn low wages. The children they have are born into the same environment of deprivation. Thus families tend to remain 'trapped' in a cycle of poverty, being unable to improve their circumstances. The challenge to societies around the world is how to make it possible for people to break out of this cycle of poverty.

It is widely agreed that the best way of breaking the cycle of poverty is by education – i.e. providing good schools and colleges that put the emphasis on skills learning. The challenge – to break the mindset that truancy is better than training!

6.8 Urban rebranding

Many inner-city areas have the reputation of being depressing places in which change has usually meant decline and decay. While city authorities and businesses have invested in the CBD in the UK, much less has been spent in the inner city that wraps around the CBD – that is, until recently.

The inner city really started life as 19th century suburbs built around historic cores. Terraced houses were built, often close to factories where many residents found work (Figure 6.29). The first decline in the fortunes of the inner city started in the first half of the 20th century. Many people and businesses moved out to new homes and premises in the new suburbs. This outward movement left behind empty buildings and dwellings occupied by poor families who could not afford to move to the suburbs.

Figure 6.29: *Nineteenth century inner-city housing*

Figure 6.30: *A rundown estate of high-rise blocks*

As Figure 6.30 shows, those high-rise blocks of the 1960s have become the slums of today and now await redevelopment.

The inner city was left to decay until the 1960s when **redevelopment** began to take place. Many of the old terraced houses were bulldozed and replaced by high-rise tower blocks, with people rehoused in flats (Figure 6.30). This was thought to be a low-cost, high-density solution to the challenge of providing decent housing for all. Within 20 years, however, it was recognised that the attempts to renew the inner city in this way had been a big mistake. Figure 6.31 indicates some of the problems of living in high-rise flats.

Figure 6.31: *Experiences of living in high-rise flats*

Once again, as in the early 20th century, the wealthier people abandoned the inner city, leaving behind a residue of poor households – pensioners, one-parent families, students and people from ethnic minorities. In many cities, the tower blocks were eventually demolished. Adding to the decline was **deindustrialisation** (see Chapter **4.5** on page 103) – this had a particularly bad impact on the inner city. Factories were abandoned and large areas laid waste only to become dumping grounds for rubbish. The stock of brownfield sites became huge. The loss of jobs and the deterioration in services resulted in an increasing amount of social unrest and crime among those people unable to move out.

The turn of the millennium coincided with a turnaround in the fortunes of some inner-city areas. A key factor was the increasing difficulty of commuting from the suburbs and dormitory towns to workplaces in the CBD. Commuting was proving expensive and physically demanding on overloaded transport systems. People began to ask themselves why spend so much time and money travelling to work? What is wrong with living in the inner city closer to work?

Figure 6.32: *A gated community and a gentrified area*

Some of the inner-city's brownfield sites are now being used for the construction of expensive housing (often in **gated communities**) for young, upwardly-mobile people (Figure 6.32). Areas of the original 19th century housing that survived the bulldozer are undergoing **gentrification**. Old factory buildings that survived are being conserved and converted into flats, art galleries and museums.

Figure 6.33: *Canary Wharf, London and Salford Quays, Manchester*

Describe the changing fortunes of the HIC inner city. Are you able to draw a diagram to show what happened?

– deindustrialisation

Quite suddenly, the inner city is on the up. It is becoming the 'cool' place in which to live. Much money is being invested by developers to improve the services and environmental quality of quite large areas. Indeed, whole areas are being rebranded. Notable examples of this inner-city revival in the UK include Canary Wharf in East London and Salford Quays in Manchester. Interestingly, both these examples have involved regenerating and re-imaging old docklands (Figure 6.33).

HIC cities today are facing two major challenges:

- what to do with large areas of the central and inner parts of the city with their ageing and increasingly obsolete buildings, as well as premises vacated by businesses that have moved elsewhere

- how to find new ways of making a living following deindustrialisation (the closure of factories and loss of jobs in manufacturing in the cities) and the decline in the appeal of some central city areas (the CBD losing out to urban fringe developments).

The two challenges are related if only because the older areas of the city have been amongst the worst hit by deindustrialisation and the decline in the CBD. Two closely-related processes are used to deal with these two challenges:

- **regeneration** – transforming the economy of a city or part of it by encouraging new businesses to replace those that have closed and moved elsewhere. Another strategy is to upgrade the quality of the built environment by either finding new uses for old and often empty buildings or clearing them to make way for new ones.

- **re-imaging** – changing the standing and reputation of a whole city or part of it by focusing on some new identity or function and changing the quality and appearance of the built-up area (Figure 6.33).

Check that you understand the difference between urban regeneration and re-imaging.

Together these two processes are referred to as **rebranding** – to help sell an urban area to a new target market. The responsibility for doing this rests with a number of **urban managers**. These are people with particular interests in the whole rebranding process. Most often, the process will be started by local planners and politicians who want to improve their areas (Figure 6.34). It is they who decide that something needs to be done and ensure that there are no obstacles or opposition to the rebranding. The next stage involves setting up some sort of partnership between the local government authority, on the one hand, and developers and potential employers on the other. The property developers are crucial to the designing and funding of what needs to be done. Employers in such businesses as shops, offices and even manufacturing need to be brought in to the scheme since it is they who will provide the new work that hopefully changes the economy and the whole image of the area.

Figure 6.34: *A brownfield site awaiting re-use*

Successful rebranding relies critically on three things:

- a good partnership between public and private enterprise
- capital
- vision.

Case study: Re-imaging Bradford

Bradford in West Yorkshire, England with a population of around 500 000, is one of the 10 largest cities in the UK. Its growth was based on the textile industry, particularly wool, but this industry collapsed during the second half of the 20th century. This was largely due to the invention of new synthetic fabrics. Faced with deindustrialisation, Bradford City Council has been forced to do three things:

- find a new range of economic activities to support the city
- find new uses for land that was once occupied by the woollen industry
- shake off its old image of a rundown city of closed woollen mills – and create a new image for the city.

Bradford has done well in terms of building up a new economy. It now has some modern engineering, chemicals and ICT industries. It has also developed a leisure and tourism industry by turning its industrial heritage into tourist

Bradford, like Birmingham (see page 167), has a large immigrant population, mainly drawn from the Indian subcontinent. Many entered the UK during the 1950s and 1960s. They were attracted by jobs in the old textile mills that have since closed down.

attractions. Many of the mills still stand, and their exteriors have been smartened up. Inside, they have become museums, craft centres and galleries or been converted into small business units or flats. Other old buildings associated with the woollen industry have undergone a different form of regeneration. They have been demolished and the resulting brownfield sites filled with blocks of offices and flats, shopping centres and premises for Bradford's new industries.

From this urban regeneration, a re-imaged Bradford has emerged. New life has been breathed into the city. However, two challenges remain – to improve the quality of its inner-city housing and to create more harmony between Bradford's ethnic groups. Bradford has one of the largest non-white populations in the UK.

i

ii

Figure 6.35: *Above: Bradford at the height of the woollen industry; and Left: Putting old mills to new uses*

End of chapter checkout

Checklists

Now you have read the chapter, you should know:

- ✓ about the nature of the three processes: urbanisation, suburbanisation and counterurbanisation
- ✓ the factors that affect the rate of urbanisation
- ✓ what megacities are, and why they have developed
- ✓ the main problems caused by rapid urbanisation
- ✓ the reasons for similar land uses to concentrate in particular parts of urban areas
- ✓ the reasons for the segregation of different ethnic and socio-economic groups of people within urban areas
- ✓ the consequences of this segregation of different groups of people
- ✓ the characteristics and problems of shanty towns
- ✓ how attempts are being made to deal with challenges of shanty towns
- ✓ the types of change taking place on the edges of cities in HICs (high-income countries)
- ✓ the arguments used in the debate about whether it is better to use brownfield rather than greenfield site
- ✓ the symptoms and locations of areas of social deprivation and poverty in HIC cities
- ✓ about the changing fortunes of the inner areas of HIC cities
- ✓ the roles of different managers in regenerating and re-imaging cities

Make sure you understand these key terms:

Accessibility: the ease with which one location can be reached from another; the degree to which people are able to obtain goods and services, such as housing and healthcare.

Brownfield site: land that has been previously used, abandoned and now awaits a new use.

Congestion: acute overcrowding caused by high densities of traffic, business and people.

Counterurbanisation: the movement of people and employment from major cities to smaller cities and towns as well as to rural areas.

Environmental quality: the degree to which an area is free from air, water, noise and visual pollution.

Ethnic group: a group of people united by a common characteristic such as race, language or religion.

Greenfield site: land that has not been used for urban development

Land value: the market price of a piece of land; what people or businesses are prepared to pay for owning and occupying it.

Megacity: a city or urban area with a population larger than 10 million

Poverty: where people are seriously lacking in terms of income, food, housing, basic services (clean water and sewage disposal) and access to education and healthcare. See also Social deprivation.

Shanty town: an area of slum housing built of salvaged materials and located either on the city edge or within the city on hazardous ground previously avoided by urban development.

Social deprivation: when the well-being and quality of life of people falls below a minimum level

Social segregation: the clustering together of people with similar characteristics (class, ethnicity, wealth) into separate residential areas.

Socio-economic group: a group of people sharing the same characteristics, such as income level, type of employment and class.

Squatter community: see Shanty town.

Suburbanisation: the outward spread of the urban area, often at lower densities compared with the older parts of a town or city.

Urban regeneration: the investment of capital in the revival of old, urban areas by either improving what is there or clearing it away and rebuilding.

Urban re-imaging: changing the image of an urban area and the way people view it.

Urban managers: people who make important decisions affecting urban areas, such planners, politicians and developers.

Urbanisation: growth in the percentage of a population living and working in urban areas.

See the Glossary in the ActiveBook for more definitions.

Questions

Try testing yourself with these questions:

1 a) What is meant by urbanisation?
   b) State three causes of urbanisation.

2 Why are cities in LICs growing faster than those in HICs?

3 What are the distinguishing features of each of the following urbanisation processes:
   - suburbanisation
   - decentralisation
   - counterurbanisation
   - urban regeneration?

4 a) What is a 'dormitory settlement'?
   b) How are conurbations formed?

5 a) What is a megacity?
   b) Describe how the number and distribution of megacities are changing.

6 a) What are 'world cities'?
   b) Name three world cities.

7 What are the main causes of rapid urbanisation in LICs?

8 Describe four problems, other than the growth of shanty towns, created by rapid urbanisation.

9 a) Describe the pattern of urban land values shown in Figure 6.15.
   b) What other features of the city change with increasing distance from the centre?

10 a) Identify the four zones of a city.
    b) Why do similar activities tend to come together at particular locations within the city?

11 Give two typical features of a CBD

12 a) What are the features that distinguish different groups of people within the city?
    b) Why do those different groups live in different parts of the city?

13 a) What is a ghetto?
    b) What are the reasons given for their existence?

14 a) What are shanty towns?
    b) How and why do they develop?

15 Examine some of the ways of improving living conditions in shanty towns.

16 What are the push and pull factors responsible for people moving to the urban fringe?

17 Explain why retailing is moving out of the CBD to out-of-town retailing parks.

18 a) Name three other types of business development found on the edges of HIC cities.
    b) What do they find attractive about the urban fringe as a location?

19 a) Distinguish between brownfield sites and greenfield sites.
    b) What are the arguments that favour using brownfield sites?

20 a) What is meant by deprivation?
    b) What is the 'cycle of poverty'?

21 Using Figure 6.26, identify those parts of Birmingham with low levels of deprivation.

22 a) What were the reasons for the decline of the inner city in the 20th century?
    b) What are the reasons for its revival in the 21st century?

23 a) What is meant by:
   - gentrification
   - gated communities?
    b) Who has benefited most from these two developments? Give your reasons.

Chapter 7: Fragile environments

Introduction

This chapter is about environments that are 'fragile' for one of two reasons. They are either very sensitive to the basic presence of people. In the semi-arid areas of the world, for example, people are aggravating the problems of soil erosion and desertification. Or the environments are made fragile because they are suffering from large-scale exploitation. This is true of the tropical rainforest. What is happening in these fragile environments is among the causes of global warming and climate change, the final topic in this chapter.

7.1 Fragile environments and sustainability

The well-being of the Earth's physical environments is of vital importance to us all. Our living standards and our health depend on the quality of those environments. However, natural environments are very fragile. There is a delicate balance between non-living (climate, rocks, soils) and living (plants, animals) parts. Natural hazards, such as fires, high winds and volcanic eruptions, have always disturbed environments and made them more fragile (Figure 7.1). However, in most cases, they have recovered. For thousands of years, humans have been making use of environmental resources to provide food, fuel and building materials. They have done so without causing too much environmental damage. Early people lived in harmony with the environment.

Figure 7.1: *Fire – a natural environmental disturbance*

Many environments are 'fragile' because of the delicate nature of most ecosystems. You might look at Chapter 5.2 (page 116). This should help you to understand why.

However, it is the growth of the world's population that today most threatens to disturb the fragile balance of environments. Humans have disturbed 90% of the Earth to some degree or another. It is hard to find areas of truly natural wilderness untouched by human activity

In this chapter, the focus is on three processes that are responsible for making environments more fragile – soil erosion, desertification and deforestation. Besides damaging natural environments, these three processes are all also linked to the important issue of global warming and climate change. They are both causes and consequences of climate change. This will be discussed later in Parts **7.7**, **7.8** and **7.9**.

Figure 7.2: *The oil spill – a particularly damaging form of human disturbance*

It is important to understand that the three processes examined in this chapter are not the only ways in which natural environments are being upset and made more fragile. But all these practises that upset environments have to do with exploiting the land. Pollution of the air, land and water is a major culprit (Figure 7.2). So too are various forms of river and coastal management. They are well intentioned, but they often disturb the workings of sensitive natural systems.

In studies of fragile environments, two terms keep cropping up: **ecological footprint** and **sustainability**.

The **ecological footprint** is a measure of the mark we humans make on the natural world. It considers how much land and sea are required to provide us with the water, energy and food we need to support our lifestyles. If the Earth's resources were shared equally among everyone, it is believed that a 'fair share' for everyone would be a little less than 2 hectares of the globe. The UK has an ecological footprint of about 5.5 global hectares per person. This means that if everyone in the world consumed resources at the rate of people in the UK, we would need two more planets to sustain the world's present population. Figure 7.3 shows how the ecological footprint varies between the regions of the world. Just look how deep the 'footprint' of North America is.

Sustainability is certainly one of today's buzz words. What does it mean? This is not an easy question to answer because this one word can be defined in so many different ways! The best-known and widely-accepted definition of sustainability is roughly as follows:

'actions and forms of progress that meet the needs of the present without reducing the ability of future generations to meet their needs'.

Examples of river and coastal management are to be found in:

- Chapter 1.7 and 1.8
- Chapter 2.7.

Are you able to express the basic idea behind the term 'sustainability' in your own words? It is not easy!

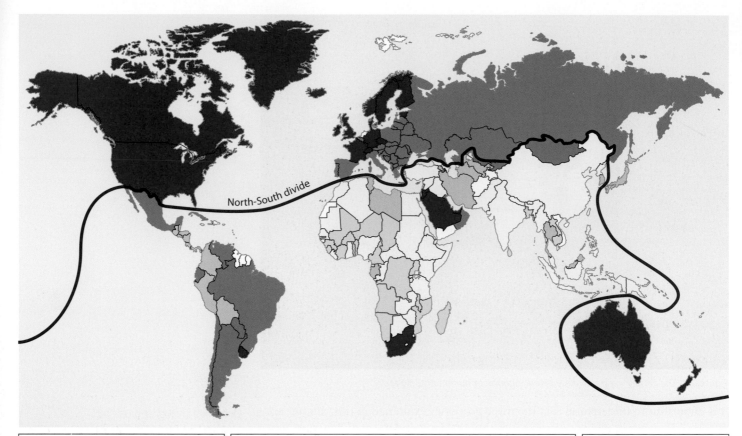

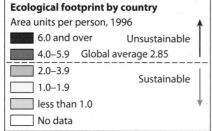

Ecological footprint by country

Area units per person, 1996

■	6.0 and over	Unsustainable
■	4.0–5.9	Global average 2.85
▨	2.0–3.9	
□	1.0–1.9	Sustainable
▨	less than 1.0	
□	No data	

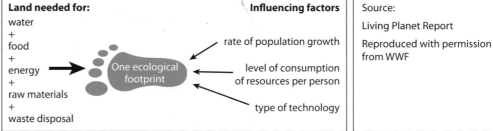

Land needed for:

water
+
food
+
energy
+
raw materials
+
waste disposal

→ One ecological footprint

Influencing factors

← rate of population growth

← level of consumption of resources per person

← type of technology

Source:

Living Planet Report

Reproduced with permission from WWF

Figure 7.3: *Global variations in the ecological footprint*

Describe the main features of the global footprint variations shown in Figure 7.3.

This means that if we are to continue to make use of the resources that nature has provided in the global range of different environments, we need:

- to do so with much more moderation
- to be aware of how easily the balances of those environments are upset
- to reduce our ecological footprint to a minimum.

This may mean that we will even have to say 'no' to economic development in some environments. This should be the case with the few remaining truly wilderness areas, such as Antarctica (Figure 7.4), the tundra of Siberia and the Amazon rainforest. It is vital that the biodiversity and pristine nature of such environments be protected for the general 'health' of the Earth and its people. Otherwise our present abuse of the planet promises an unsustainable future.

The link between the ecological footprint and sustainability is that the ecological footprint theory helps us to judge how sustainable our lives are now. It helps us to make judgements about the future too. We know that the global population will continue to grow for at least the next 50 years. It warns us of the extent to which the world's environments will become even more fragile (Figure 7.5). It advises us as to what is **sustainable**.

Figure 7.4: *Antarctica – one of the few remaining wilderness areas*

Figure 7.5: *Moving towards an unsustainable future!*

7.2 Soil erosion and desertification

Soil erosion

Soil erosion is the washing or blowing away of top soil. A result of erosion is that the fertility of the remaining soil is greatly reduced. Soil erosion is a natural process, but it is made worse by people. There are three main types of soil erosion:

- **sheet erosion** – this occurs in those parts of the world where there is moderate rainfall. When this falls on bare soil, the top of the soil will be removed down slope

- **gully erosion** – where there is intense rainfall, as during tropical storms, the force of the water can cut gullies in slopes (Figure 7.6). This is most likely to happen where there is little vegetation cover

- **wind erosion** – in dry parts of the world, loose dry soil is readily blown away by the wind.

Figure 7.6: *Gully erosion*

Soil erosion is made more rapid and severe where there is misuse of the land. Activities that cause problems include:

- removing vegetation by cutting down trees and bushes for fuel or to make way for more farmland. As a result, the soil is exposed to the wind and rain

- overgrazing by animals. The result is the same as above

- overcultivating the soil by failing to 'feed' it with fertilisers or by growing the same crop in the same field year after year. This **monoculture** weakens the soil structure and removes vital minerals from the soil. The net result is that crops will fail and the soil will be left exposed to the forces of erosion

Be sure that you understand why vegetation provides the best protection against soil erosion.

- compacting the soil by the use of heavy machinery. This reduces the rate at which rainwater is able to infiltrate the soil. So much of the rainwater flows across the soil surface and erodes the soil as it does so

- ploughing fields in the same direction as the slope. This readily encourages gullying.

In general, we may say that the threat of soil erosion increases with the sparseness of vegetation. It also does so where population numbers are so great that they put pressure on the land.

There is much more on soil erosion to be found in Part 7.3 (page 185).

Desertification

Desertification is the term used to describe how once productive land gradually changes into a desert-like landscape. The process is not necessarily irreversible and, as Figure 7.7 shows, it usually takes place in semi-arid land on the edges of existing hot deserts. As with soil erosion, there are both natural and human causes of desertification. Some of the causes are the same as for soil erosion.

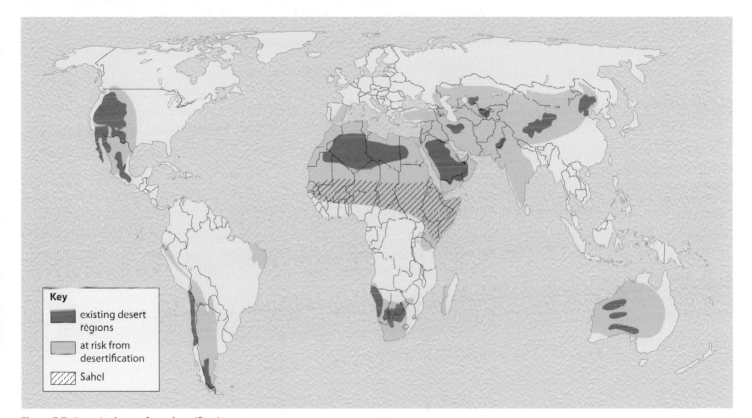

Key
- existing desert regions
- at risk from desertification
- Sahel

Figure 7.7: *Areas in danger from desertification*

Natural causes include (Figure 7.8):

- changing rainfall patterns – rainfall has become less predictable over the past 50 years and the occasional drought year has sometimes extended to several years. As a result, the vegetation cover begins to die and leaves bare soil

- soil erosion itself – the removal of soil means less support for the vegetation

- intensity of rainfall – when rain does fall it is often for very short, intense periods. This makes the rain difficult for the soil to capture and store – so water resources become less.

```
┌──────────┐      ┌──────────────┐      ┌──────────────┐
│  CLIMATE │ ───▶ │ less rainfall│ ───▶ │  bare soil   │
│  CHANGE  │      └──────────────┘      └──────────────┘
└──────────┘                                   │
                                               ▼
                                    ┌──────────────────┐
                                    │    increased     │
                                    │   water-flow     │
                                    │     overland     │
                                    └──────────────────┘
                          ┌──────────────┼──────────────┐
                          ▼              ▼              ▼
┌───────────────────────────┐  ┌──────────────┐  ┌──────────────┐
│ water drained from soil,  │  │ water table  │  │  water flow  │
│ so soil is dry and blown  │  │   lowered    │  │    washes    │
│ away more easily and so   │  └──────────────┘  │  soil away   │
│  creating a dust bowl     │         │          └──────────────┘
└───────────────────────────┘         │
                 └─────────────┐       │      ┌──────────────┘
                               ▼       ▼      ▼
                        ┌────────────────────────┐
                        │   few plants grow and  │
                        │  little farming possible│
                        └────────────────────────┘
                                    │
                                    ▼
                        ┌────────────────────────┐
                        │     DESERTIFICATION     │
                        └────────────────────────┘
```

Figure 7.8: *Natural causes of desertification*

The main human causes of desertification are (Figure 7.9):

- population growth – rapid population increase puts more pressure on the land to grow more food

- overgrazing – too many goats, sheep and cattle can destroy vegetation. Interestingly, this is often most common around water holes in desert fringe areas

- overcultivation – intensive use of marginal land exhausts the soil and crops will not grow

- deforestation – trees are cut down for fuel, fencing and housing. The roots no longer bind the soil, leading to soil erosion

These problems are exacerbated for people in any sub-Saharan countries because of years of civil war. Crops and animals have been deliberately destroyed resulting in famine and widespread deaths.

Of the four human causes of desertification which do you think is the most significant? Give your reasons.

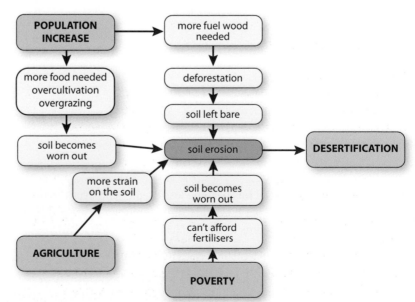

Figure 7.9: *Human causes of desertification*

As with many other fragile environments, it is usually a combination of different factors which results in damage to a specific area.

It is estimated that about 20% of the world's population have to cope with the effects of desertification in over 60 countries. One of the regions most at risk is in the Sahel region of Africa, an area south of the Sahara desert stretching the width of the continent. It makes up a large part of Sub-Saharan Africa, the poorest region of the world.

Case study: Desertification of the Sahel, Africa

The Sahel is a narrow belt of land in central Africa. It borders the southern edge of the Sahara Desert (Figure 7.10). The Sahel has a semi-arid climate as shown in Figure 7.11 over the page. Temperatures are always hot and there is a long dry season from June through to January. There is just enough rainfall for grasses to grow, as well as some shrubs and trees in this harsh environment.

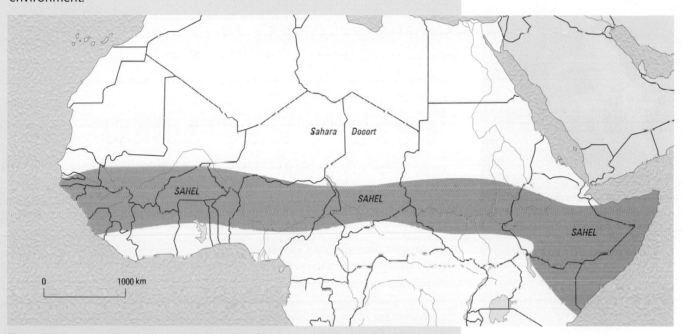

Figure 7.10: *Location and present extent of the Sahel, Africa*

The world biomes map (Figure 5.1 on page 114) shows that the Sahel region is in an area classified as savanna. The natural vegetation of savanna is a mixture of grassland, trees and shrubs. However, the mix of each of these three types of plant changes as one moves northwards from the tropical rainforest. The climate becomes drier, so that a rather wooded savanna gives way to grassland with occasional shrubs. Eventually, on the margins of the hot desert, the savanna is nothing more than thin grassland. It is these areas which are amongst those most at threat from desertification.

On the equatorial edges of savanna there are also more animals. As the trees thin out towards the middle of savanna regions, large herds of wild animals like wildebeest, antelope and zebra are found. On the drier desert edges like the Sahel region there is far less wildlife. Rainfall is seasonal and unpredictable and it is very dry for much of the year (Figure 7.11). Here you often find nomadic herders who move from place to place with goats and cattle in search of water and grazing.

Look at Figure 7.10. How many countries now find they are part of the Sahel?

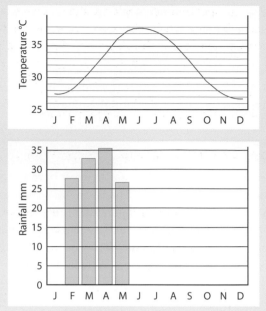

Figure 7.11: *The climate of the Sahel*

Figure 7.12: *The Sahel before and after desertification*

In the Sahel there have been some years when less rain has fallen. Fewer grasses have grown and trees have died. The landscape becomes much more like desert (Figure 7.12).

Climate change is one cause of desertification. Desertification is also speeded up by human activity. Until the 1960s, water was plentiful and crops and livestock did well. Then there was an increase in population. More and more trees were felled to provide fuel and building materials. It was possibly this that was responsible for the climate becoming drier.

As this was happening, people tried to grow the same crops and rear the same number of animals. This quickly led to overcultivation and overgrazing and much ground was laid bare. The absence of vegetation meant that no humus was being added to the soil. Without humus, the soil was able to hold little or no water. So, as the soil dried out, so it was quickly eroded by wind and occasional flash floods.

Since the 1970s, crop failures have become almost an annual event. Over 100 000 people have died of starvation. Even more people have migrated to less arid areas. Millions of animals have died.

A variety of techniques has been developed to prevent the further spread of desertification and also to rehabilitate the land that has already been damaged. One successful method of catching rain when it falls is a simple technique set up by Oxfam in Burkina Faso. Small stone walls are built following the slope of the land which then act as dams when the rain falls, stopping surface water run-off and allowing it to sink into the soil. This simple, inexpensive method can increase crop yields by up to 50 per cent.

Most scientists are of the opinion that people are the root cause of desertification. However, recent research using satellite images is showing that some areas that have suffered desertification are now showing signs of recovery. They are beginning to receive more rainfall. Could it be that natural changes in climate over short time periods are the root cause of desertification, and not people? Nobody can be sure at present. One thing that is certain though. The semi-arid lands are fragile environments and people must use them with great care.

7.3 Consequences and management of soil erosion

Consequences

The consequences of soil erosion are all negative. For most people, the more serious of these is the one illustrated in Part **7.2** – the fall in food production. From this, a number of unwanted consequences follow. By far the most important is the loss of farmland and the reduction in food production. Food shortages quickly lead to:

- **malnutrition** – the lack of a proper diet exposes people to all sorts of disease. The mortality rate is raised

- **famine and starvation** – if food shortages persist, then famine and starvation follow. The mortality rate is raised even higher

- **migration** – there comes a time when people are faced by two stark choices – either stay put and die, or migrate elsewhere (Figure 7.13). The latter is easier said than done. If they do move to somewhere that is free from soil erosion, there are few chances of finding farmland that they can legally cultivate. It is more likely that those who decide to move will head off to a town or city. Here they would hope to find work and use their wages to buy food and shelter

- **food aid** – if the famine affects a large enough area and population, there is a chance of receiving international food aid. For a while, this will help to reduce malnutrition and starvation. However, it will do nothing to 'cure' the soil erosion.

Many of the people who are forced to migrate as a result of soil erosion and desertification remain within the borders of their country. They make up what the UN calls 'internally-displaced people' (IDPs). See Chapter 8.8 (page 234)

Figure 7.13: *Malnourished people on the move*

Management of soil erosion

In general, the damage caused by soil erosion is extremely difficult to put right. This is particularly the case where gullying has taken place. The best thing that soil management can do is to stop the soil erosion happening in the first place.

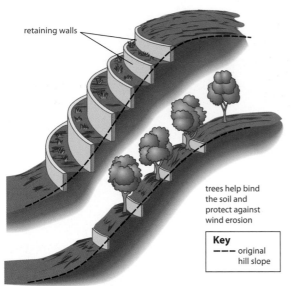

retaining walls

trees help bind the soil and protect against wind erosion

Key
- - - original hill slope

Figure 7.14: *Terracing and tree planting to limit soil erosion on a slope*

Removal of the vegetation cover is a widespread cause of soil erosion. Plant cover reduces the impact of raindrops and hailstones on the soil. Roots reduce surface run off by allowing water to filter down into the soil. Roots also bind the soil particles together. It is vital that the surface of the soil should be protected, especially at those times of the year when soil erosion is most likely to occur. This might be during the wet season when rains are particularly heavy. It might also be when strong winds are most likely to occur. The key need is to have the soil protected either by crops or by mulch.

The use of trees and hedges as wind breaks can certainly reduced the effects wind erosion (Figure 7.14). Steep slopes can be protected from sheet erosion and gullying by terracing. Another technique is to contour-plough slopes – that is, by ploughing along the line of the contour rather than up and down the slope. Strip cropping is rather similar – different types of crop are aligned along the contours. In some cases, rows of trees or shrubs might be interspersed with crops. This gives the soil double protection – wind breaks and contour cultivation.

Maintaining water in the soil is another way of reducing soil erosion. More water in the soil means a better chance of maintaining the vegetation cover. There are quite simple ways of doing this:

- building small dams across streams
- building earth walls along contours
- planting tress and protecting them from grazing animals.

All these techniques have proved effective in reducing run off and allowing time for infiltration. The outcome is retaining water where it falls.

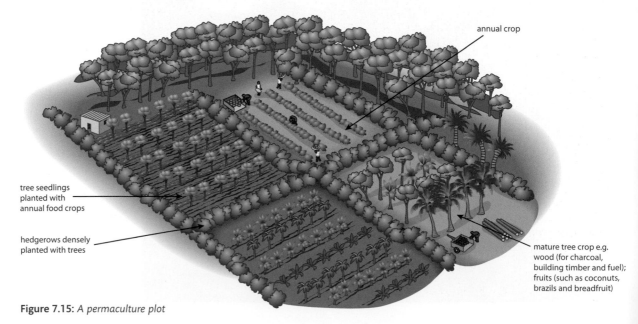

annual crop

tree seedlings planted with annual food crops

hedgerows densely planted with trees

mature tree crop e.g. wood (for charcoal, building timber and fuel); fruits (such as coconuts, brazils and breadfruit)

Figure 7.15: *A permaculture plot*

Organic farming is an effective way of avoiding soil erosion. Organic farming does not use artificial fertilisers. It relies instead on crop rotation. This involves growing manure crops, such as clover, which are ploughed back into the soil. This ensures that there is plenty of water-retaining humus in the soil. Animal waste is also used to maintain the good health of the soil.

Permaculture is a type of organic farming that is particularly suited to the needs of LICs. In permaculture farmers use no inputs such as chemicals or pesticides from outside the area where they farm. They grow a mix of food and tree crops, and often keep a small number of livestock (Figure 7.15). Trees are planted around the fields and these soon produce mulch and protect the soil from the wind. The soil is never left exposed to the sun and wind. Livestock, particularly chickens, are allowed to forage after crops have been harvested, and in return provide manure.

Research those areas of the world where permaculture is catching on as a way of producing food.

7.4 Causes of deforestation

Deforestation is the cutting down of trees. Many primary forests in temperate countries have almost disappeared after centuries of logging (cutting down trees for timber) and land clearance (usually to plant crops). However, it is only fairly recently that large-scale deforestation has started to take place in the world's tropical rainforests (Figure 7.16). The speed of deforestation has alarmed scientists and conservationists. The future welfare of tropical rainforests is an important environmental issue.

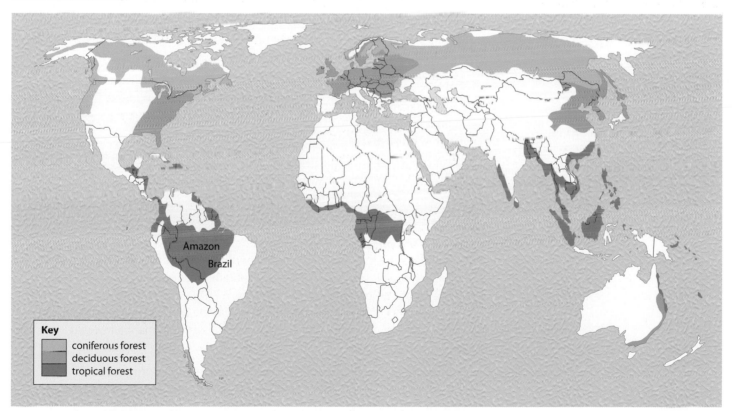

Key
- coniferous forest
- deciduous forest
- tropical forest

Figure 7.16: *The world's forests*

Why are rainforests being cut down?

Commercial logging/timber extraction (globally 26%)
only valuable trees are chopped down (selective logging) but as they fall, they damage other trees. Even more damage is caused by 'clear-felling', where other trees are also chopped down and chipped for pulp.

Agriculture (globally 32%)
areas of tropical rain forest have been cleared for plantations growing a single crop such as rubber or coffee. Plants and grassland are grown which huge herds of cattle graze on for a few years before another area is cleared for seeding with grass.

Road building
roads have been built through rain forests to enable minerals, timber, cattle and crops to be moved easily. Roads also bring in new settlers who clear areas for farming.

Mining
large areas of forest are cleared for the open-cast mining of minerals such as iron, gold and copper.

Land for peasants
land allows peasants to grow their own food and the wood that is cut down provides them with fuel. It stops overcrowding in other parts of the country.

HEP (hydroelectric power)
rivers are dammed and huge areas of forest are flooded as a result.

Figure 7.17: *The reasons why rainforests are being cut down*

Areas of tropical rainforest are cleared for a variety of reasons (Figure 7.17). Most obviously, trees are felled for their timber and sometimes their medicinal drugs. Large areas have been deforested in order to make land for farming, housing and industry. Mining and hydroelectric power (HEP) schemes have also led to land clearance. In a worrying number of cases, the logging and land clearance have been illegal or without any sort of control. Some LIC governments have encouraged the clearance of forests because:

- the revenue earned from selling timber, the sources of medicinal drugs and minerals helps to pay off debts and to fund economic development
- more land is needed to house and feed the fast-growing populations in countries such as Brazil and Malaysia.

The following case study illustrates in a little more detail the causes of deforestation.

Case study: The Amazon rainforest, Brazil – part 1

Brazil is the largest country in South America. In the north, the climate is equatorial. The hot, wet greenhouse conditions produce a very rapid growth of vegetation all year round. The tropical rainforest of Brazil's Amazon region is the largest of its kind in the world (Figure 7.18). Study Figure 7.19 and notice the five layers of vegetation and the large variety of different trees and plants. There are over 1000 different tree species, for example mahogany, teak and rosewood.

For centuries the Amazon rainforest has been inhabited by groups of Amerindians. They hunt for animals, collect fruits and clear small patches of the forest to grow crops. This type of farming is called **slash and burn**. The clearing is small and after two or three years it is abandoned and the forest once again develops. The Amerindians do no long-term damage to the forest and their use of the forest's resources is sustainable.

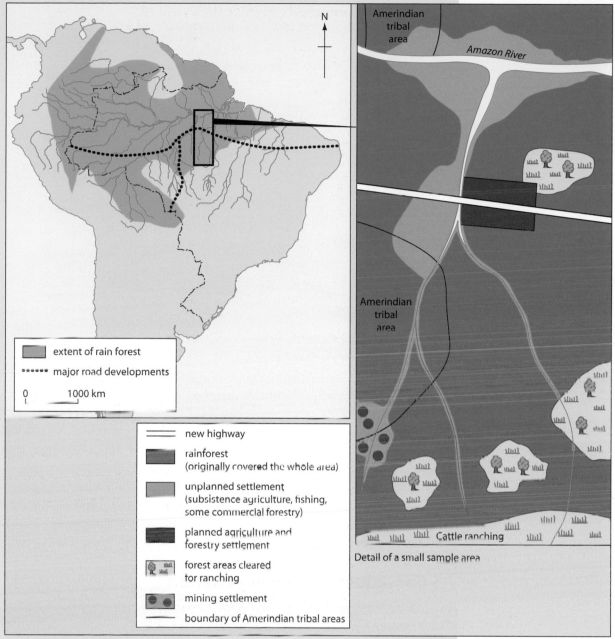

Figure 7.18: *The Amazon rainforest*

Recent human activity in the rainforest has been much more devastating (Figure 7.18). Large-scale deforestation has taken place for a variety of reasons:

- mining, for example the iron ore mine at Carajas in the Amazon Basin

- road building, for example the Trans-Amazonian Highway in Brazil

- new settlements and small farms to house migrants from the cities

- logging for timber exports, for example teak and mahogany in the Amazon Basin

- huge cattle ranches

- other types of farming, particularly palm plantations producing biofuel

- extracting plants for their medicinal value

- reservoirs and dams for a number of hydroelectric power schemes, for example Itaipu, Tucurui and the Xingu complex.

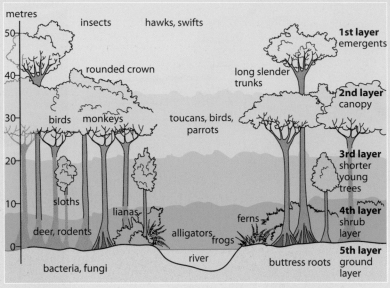

Figure 7.19: *A vertical section of the tropical rainforest*

The list above of the damaging uses made of the land occupied by the tropical rainforest clearly illustrates that this land is more than useful – it is valuable. So you might ask – why not exploit the resources of the forest? The short answer is that this would have unwanted global consequences. In the next part, we will look to this same area to illustrate some of these consequences.

Whilst the Amazon basin contains the largest area of tropical rainforest in the world, deforestation is also occurring in other locations. This is true for central Africa and south-east Asia (Figure 7.16). Equally, the deciduous and coniferous forests of temperate latitudes are also suffering. In short, deforestation is a global problem – not just a tropical problem.

7.5 Consequences of deforestation

Case study: The Amazon rainforest, Brazil – part 2

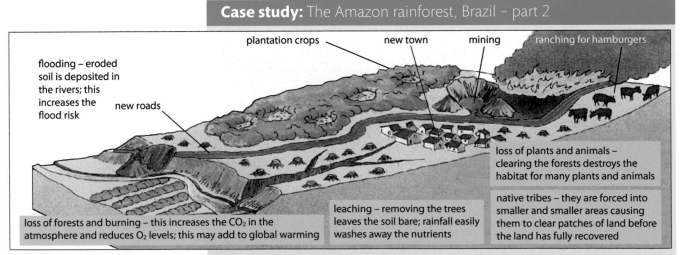

Figure 7.20: *Some problems caused by deforestation*

Figure 7.20 illustrates some of the physical consequences of deforestation. This process has had an adverse impact on drainage, soils and wildlife in the Amazon basin.

In addition, there are other unwanted consequences.

● Mining is typically open-cast, and destroys large areas of vegetation and pollutes rivers (Figure 7.21). Mercury is especially toxic

Figure 7.21: *The scars of mining*

● Roads have opened up the Amazon, allowing easier access and encouraging uncontrolled development in addition to planned, new settlements (Figure 7.22).

What sort of uncontrolled developments are the new roads likely to encourage?

Figure 7.22: *The Trans-Amazonian highway*

- When loggers fell the more profitable hardwood trees like teak, ebony and mahogany, they also unnecessarily destroy large areas of the forest (Figure 7.23)

Figure 7.23: *Logging in action*

- Clearing land for cattle grazing not only releases carbon dioxide as trees are burned, but leads to nutrient loss and soil erosion. It is the rainforest vegetation which provides the fertility for these otherwise poor soils

- Large areas have been flooded and indigenous tribes moved from their lands to create HEP schemes

- Biodiversity has been lost as habitats for animals, birds and insects are destroyed, alongside a wide variety of medicinal plants.

Today, there is great concern about the rate of deforestation for a number of reasons. Table 7.1 gives some information about rates of deforestation in nine tropical countries. The first concern is the loss of **biodiversity**. Biodiversity is itself a natural resource. It is a vital part of the Earth's life-support system. Humans are dependent on biodiversity for so many things that are part of everyday life. Biodiversity provides us with a whole range of goods and services. Some of these have already been mentioned in Part **7.4**. They range from the food we eat (both animal and vegetable) to timber, from drugs and medicines to fibres for clothing and resins for glues. Without biodiversity, we would soon perish. Maintaining it is vital to the health of our living planet, and us who occupy it.

Country	Original extent of forest cover (km²)	Present extent of forest cover (km²)	Present rate of deforestation (% per year)
Brazil	2 860 000	1 800 000	2.3
Colombia	700 000	180 000	2.3
Ecuador	132 000	44 000	4.0
Indonesia	1 220 000	530 000	1.4
Ivory Coast	160 000	4000	15.6
Madagascar	62 000	10 000	8.3
Mexico	400 000	110 000	4.2
Philippines	250 000	8000	5.4
Thailand	435 000	22 000	8.4

Table 7.1: Deforestation of rainforests in selected countries

Study Table 7.1. Which country lost the most forest cover in:

- absolute terms

- percentage terms?

The second and perhaps even greater concern is that deforestation is contributing to the build up of greenhouse gases. This, in turn, is generally thought to be a cause of global warming. The world's forests absorb the carbon dioxide that is in the atmosphere. Deforestation means that levels of carbon dioxide build up in the atmosphere (Figure 7.24). Carbon dioxide is not only a major greenhouse gas. It is a potential killer of humans.

Figure 7.24: *Wholesale deforestation in Madagascar – this area was once covered by forest*

The two consequences of deforestation just looked at are both highly negative. They are definitely costs. However, deforestation is not necessarily all bad news. For a number of LICs, deforestation can stimulate much-needed economic development. There is no doubt that the Brazilian economy has benefited from exploiting and selling the resources of its vast area of rainforest. Its small neighbour Guyana is just beginning to do so. Asian countries like Indonesia,

Thailand and the Philippines have been doing so for longer. In the Ivory Coast, deforestation of this small West African country is almost complete (Table 7.1). Madagascar is clearing its forests at a swift rate, largely in order to pay off the country's debts. Are today's Ivory Coast and Madagascar the shape of things to come for all those countries that have rainforests?

It is interesting to note that protests about deforestation come strongest from the governments and people of HICs. In reply, LICs ask why should they be denied this chance to develop their economies? How else will they ever be able to catch up with the HICs? The answer may lie in the sustainable management of the tropical rainforest.

7.6 Managing rainforests in a sustainable way

The loss of forests, not only in the tropics, but all over the world is causing concern. Many governments and international organisations recognise the need to manage forests to ensure the resources are there for future generations. This is called **sustainable management** (Figure 7.25). The key to sustainability is using resources now in such a way that future generations will still be able to use the same resources. Sustainability is the ability of one generation to hand over to the next at least the same amount of resources it started with.

Sustainable management of any resource should:

- respect the environment and cultures of local peoples

- use traditional skills and knowledge

- give people control over their land and lives

- use appropriate technology – machines and equipment that are cheap, easy to use and do not harm the environment

- generate income for local communities – not transnational companies

- protect biodiversity.

However, it is difficult for some governments, especially of LICs, because they need the money that exploitation of the forests brings.

The sustainable management of forests can be achieved by:

- protection of forests – in some countries areas of forest are conserved and protected as national parks where none or very little development is allowed to take place

- carefully planned and controlled logging in forests

- selective logging of only those trees that are valuable, leaving the rest of the forest untouched, for example in parts of Indonesia only 7 to 12 trees per hectare are allowed to be felled

- replanting of forested areas that have been felled

- restrictions on the number of logging licences given to reduce the amount of forest loss

- heli-logging, for example in Sarawak where helicopters are used to remove the logs because less damage is done to the remaining forest

- developing alternative energy supplies, for example biogas, solar and wind power to reduce the amount of wood needed for fuel.

Another possible consequence of deforestation is global warming. See Parts 7.7, 7.8 and 7.9.

For more information about alternative energy sources, see Chapter 4.8 (page 111).

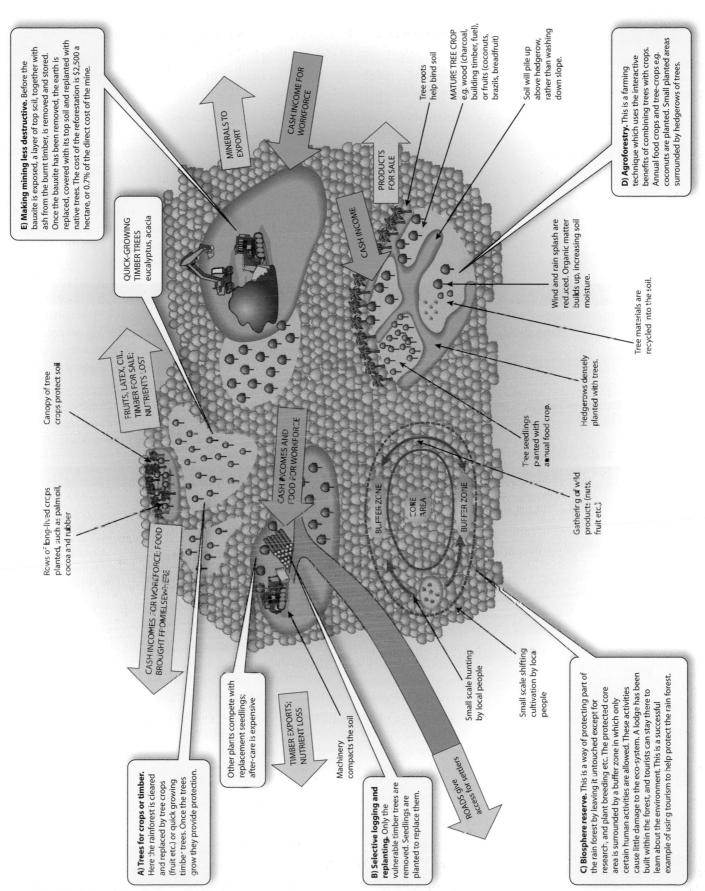

E) Making mining less destructive. Before the bauxite is exposed, a layer of top soil, together with ash from the burnt timber, is removed and stored. Once the bauxite has been removed, the earth is replaced, covered with its top soil and replanted with native trees. The cost of the reforestation is $2,500 a hectare, or 0.7% of the direct cost of the mine.

MINERALS TO EXPORT

CASH INCOME FOR WORKFORCE

QUICK-GROWING TIMBER TREES eucalyptus, acacia

Tree roots help bind soil

MATURE TREE CROP e.g. wood (charcoal, building timber, fuel), or fruits (coconuts, brazils, breadfruit)

Soil will pile up above hedgerow, rather than washing down slope.

PRODUCTS FOR SALE

CASH INCOME

D) Agroforestry. This is a farming technique which uses the interactive benefits of combining trees with crops. Annual food crops and tree-crops e.g. coconuts are planted. Small planted areas surrounded by hedgerows of trees.

Canopy of tree crops protect soil

FRUITS, LATEX, OIL, TIMBER FOR SALE; NUTRIENTS LOST

Wind and rain splash are reduced. Organic matter builds up, increasing soil moisture.

Tree materials are recycled into the soil.

Hedgerows densely planted with trees.

Rows of long-lived crops planted, such as palm oil, cocoa and rubber

CASH INCOMES FOR WORKFORCE; FOOD BROUGHT FROM ELSEWHERE

CASH INCOMES AND FOOD FOR WORKFORCE

Tree seedlings planted with annual food crop.

BUFFER ZONE

CORE AREA

BUFFER ZONE

Gathering of wild products (nuts, fruit etc.)

Other plants compete with replacement seedlings; after-care is expensive

TIMBER EXPORTS; NUTRIENT LOSS

Machinery compacts the soil

Small scale hunting by local people

Small scale shifting cultivation by local people

A) Trees for crops or timber. Here the rainforest is cleared and replaced by tree crops (fruit etc.) or quick growing timber trees. Once the trees grow they provide protection.

B) Selective logging and replanting. Only the vulnerable timber trees are removed. Seedlings are planted to replace them.

ROADS give access for settlers

C) Biosphere reserve. This is a way of protecting part of the rain forest by leaving it untouched except for research, and plant breeding etc. The protected core area is surrounded by a buffer zone in which only certain human activities are allowed. These activities cause little damage to the eco-system. A lodge has been built within the forest, and tourists can stay there to learn about the environment. This is a successful example of using tourism to help protect the rain forest.

Figure 7.25: *Using the rainforest in a sustainable way*

Two rather different but related ways of conserving the rainforest are:

Very similar to agroforestry is permaculture. See Part 7.3 (page 186).

Agroforestry – combining crops and trees i) by allowing crops to be grown in carefully controlled areas within the forest or ii) by growing trees on farms outside of the rain forest.

Substitution – finding alternative sources for the resources being taken from the rainforest. The second form of agroforestry would be one example – i.e. grow the timber and fuel on plantations elsewhere, using faster-growing trees. Making better use of savanna areas for livestock grazing would be another example.

More and more countries are realising that, if the tropical rainforest is to have a future, it needs concerted international action. The United Nations has a number of international programmes. There are also some important international treaties. Some examples of both are given in Table 7.2. Some more will be examined in Parts **7.7**, **7.8** and **7.9**.

International programmes	Aims
United Nations Programme on Reducing Emissions from Deforestation and Forest Degradation (UN-REDD)	This programme deals with a wide range of pressing issues, including how best to counter the forces driving deforestation and how best to ensure that the needs of local and indigenous peoples are met. It also includes making payments if forested areas are left untouched.
United Nations Forum on Forests (UNFF)	The main objective is to promote the management, conservation and sustainable development of all types of forests and to strengthen the long-term commitment of governments to this end.
International treaties	
Convention on International Trade in Endangered Species of Wild Fauna and Flora (CITES) (1973)	This is an international agreement between governments. Its aim is to ensure that international trade in specimens of wild animals and plants does not threaten their survival.
International Tropical Timber Agreement (ITTA) (2006)	This aims i) to promote the expansion and diversification of international trade in tropical timber from sustainably managed and legally harvested forests and ii) to promote the sustainable management of tropical timber-producing forests.

Table 7.2: International action on deforestation

One of the biggest challenges for the international community is to stop the huge amount of illegal logging that is still going on in the rainforests. Given the remoteness of rainforest areas, illegal logging can easily go on unnoticed. Spotting where it is happening can be difficult. However, satellites are now helping to monitor this. Non-government organisations such as Greenpeace and the Worldwide Fund for Nature (WWF) are also playing a part in tracking down illegal loggers as are education and lobbying organisations running websites such as *www.Illegal-logging.info*.

Greenhouse gases occur naturally in the atmosphere. However, they can also be produced and released by a range of activities (Figure 7.28). Carbon dioxide is the main cause for concern as it accounts for nearly three-quarters of all greenhouse gas emissions. Factory emissions; burning fossil fuels like oil, coal and gas in power stations, and exhaust emissions from motor vehicles are the major sources of such emissions. The main producers are HICs, with the USA alone responsible for 36% of all greenhouse gas emissions. However, the effects are felt by everyone.

In a greenhouse, the Sun shines through the glass and warms up the plants inside. When the Sun stops shining, the heat does not disperse; it is trapped inside the greenhouse. In the same way, heat is trapped inside the Earth's atmosphere. During the day, radiation from the Sun heats the Earth (Figure 7.29). At night, clouds often trap this heat as it radiates back out. Gases in the atmosphere also trap this heat. This is the **greenhouse effect**. In recent years, the amount of these greenhouse gases has greatly increased. Greenhouse gases build up in the atmosphere, preventing heat from radiating back out. This build-up is thought to be the main cause of the gradual increase in world temperatures known as **global warming**.

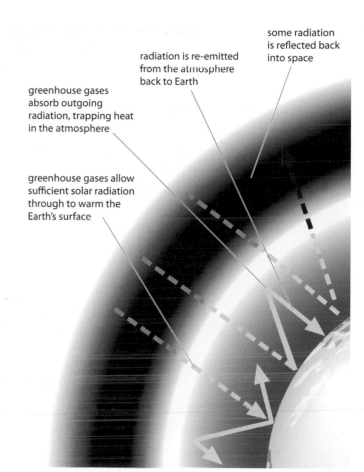

greenhouse gases absorb outgoing radiation, trapping heat in the atmosphere

radiation is re-emitted from the atmosphere back to Earth

some radiation is reflected back into space

greenhouse gases allow sufficient solar radiation through to warm the Earth's surface

Figure 7.29: *The greenhouse effect*

It is important to note, however, that some scientists are not convinced that people and their activities are the cause of today's global warming. They argue that the recent changes in global temperatures are simply part of natural climate change. The Earth's climate has changed a great deal over geological time. Even in historic times, there have been quite sudden changes in temperature – alternations of hot and cold periods. Some scientists believe that the present global warming could be connected with changes in the activity of the Sun (Figure 7.30).

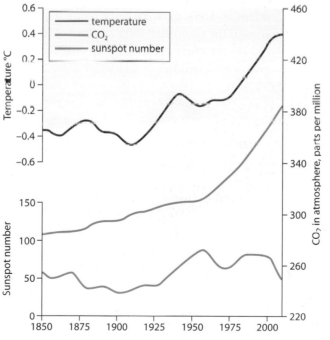

Figure 7.30: *Causal relationships?*

So having looked at Figure 7.30, which do you think is a more likely cause of rising temperatures—CO$_2$ emissions or sunspot activity?

7.8 Consequences of global warming and climate change

Although opinion may be divided about the causes of global warming, everyone is agreed that it is taking place. The global pattern of climate is certainly changing. Figure 7.31 shows some of the possible effects of global warming and where they are most likely to occur on the Earth's surface. Let us take a closer look at some of them.

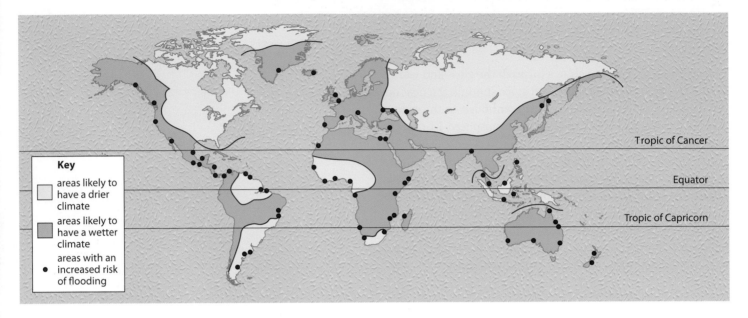

Key

☐ areas likely to have a drier climate

☐ areas likely to have a wetter climate

• areas with an increased risk of flooding

Figure 7.31: *Possible effects of global warming*

Rising sea levels

Higher temperatures have already led to the shrinking of many of the world's major glaciers. In Greenland and the Arctic, ice is melting at a rapid rate and the extent of Arctic pack-ice is shrinking (Figure 7.32). In Antarctica, especially around the peninsula, large sections of ice sheet are breaking off as temperatures rise. As the **stores** of ice in polar and high mountain regions are unlocked and melt, vast quantities of meltwater will cause the global sea level to rise.

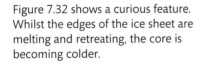
Figure 7.32 shows a curious feature. Whilst the edges of the ice sheet are melting and retreating, the core is becoming colder.

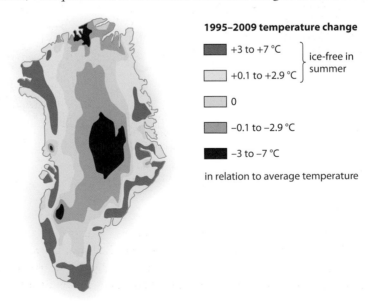

1995–2009 temperature change

☐ +3 to +7 °C ⎫ ice-free in
☐ +0.1 to +2.9 °C ⎭ summer

☐ 0

☐ −0.1 to −2.9 °C

☐ −3 to −7 °C

in relation to average temperature

Figure 7.32: *Melting of the Greenland ice sheet*

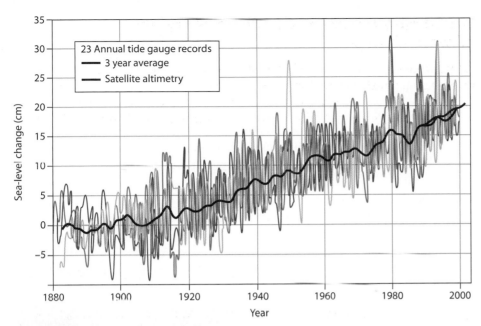

Figure 7.33: *Recent sea-level rise, 1880–2005*

Figure 7.33 shows that the global sea level has risen by 20 cm since 1880.
Although there is general agreement that sea levels will continue to rise, there is
less agreement about by how much. Most predictions about future sea level rises lie
in the range of 1 to 2 metres by the year 2100.

Compare Figure 7.33 with Figure 7.30
(page 199). Do you think that all the
graph lines are 'telling the same story'?

Figure 7.34: *Miami – an endangered city*

The rise in sea level poses a serious threat. It cannot be ignored. The threat is
greatest in the world's major coastal cities. Miami (USA) tops the list of the most
endangered cities in the world, as measured by the value of property that would be
threatened by a one-metre rise in sea level. This would flood all of Miami Beach and

leave downtown Miami on an island of water, disconnected from the rest of Florida (Figure 7.34). Other threatened US cities include New York, New Orleans, Boston, Washington, Philadelphia, Tampa and San Francisco. Osaka, Kobe, Tokyo, Rotterdam, Amsterdam, and Nagoya are among the most threatened major cities outside North America.

With such a threat in the future, the continued development of low-lying areas around the world has to stop. It would be irresponsible to continue. However, the threat of a rising sea level does not end with the drowning of coastal areas and low-lying islands. What would happen to the people who had to be evacuated? Where would they be resettled? There would be massive volumes of migration. What would happen to all the economic activities and wealth that once occupied the drowned coastal space? Could they be relocated as easily as people? Coastal submergence would have a devastating impact on the economies of many countries, and none more so than on that of the USA. The retreat from the coast would cause a major global upheaval. The human settlement pattern would be changed almost beyond recognition.

Figure 7.35: *A future with more severe tropical storms*

More hazards

It is generally recognised that one key effect of global warming will be to increase extreme weather. More extreme weather will mean more frequent and more intense natural hazards such as tropical storms, tornadoes, heatwaves, droughts and cold snaps (Figure 7.35). Warmer seas mean more intense storms; tropical storms have increased in frequency, intensity and power since 1980. Three-day continuous rainfall events in the Northern Hemisphere, a principal cause of flooding, have also increased significantly since 1980. Global warming is thought to be causing the

For more on the tropical storm hazard, see Chapter 3.3 (page 70).

cyclical ocean current and temperature changes in the Pacific known as El Nino and La Nina to become more frequent. These fluctuations in the Pacific seem to be having unpredictable global weather effects. With frequent and longer droughts, desertification is increasing and the Sahel region is expanding at an alarming rate. Heatwaves are also on the increase. The persistence of temperatures above 40°C over a period of weeks is thought to have killed 13 000 people in France during August 2003.

Ecosystem changes

The change in climate resulting from global warming will change the distribution of ecosystems. The general warming will push the world's biomes polewards (see Figure 5.1 on page 114). In the Northern Hemisphere, for example, the coniferous forests will encroach on the tundra, and the tundra on the ice desert (Figure 7.36).

Figure 7.36: *The tundra – a biome moving towards the poles*

Economic opportunities

Given the adverse impact and economic activities of settlements retreating from the coast, economic benefits are going to be few in number. Possibly these will occur mainly in agriculture. Climate change will allow farming to be pushed further towards the poles and to higher altitudes. New land will be opened up for food production in these two locations as well as in those parts of the world where change will mean a wetter climate (see Figure 7.31 on page 200). At the same time, however, change in the opposite direction to more arid conditions may well result in other farmland becoming much less productive.

The retreat of ice in high latitudes will 'uncover' resources such as oil, natural gas and minerals and allow them to be exploited (Figure 7.37).

Figure 7.37: *Oil exploration will push towards the North Pole*

Health

A warmer climate is expected to change the distributions of many diseases. For example, malaria will occur in higher latitudes and at higher altitudes. In those parts of the world that become drier, water will become a scarcer resource. Where this happens, and people are forced to use unclean water, outbreaks of water-borne diseases, such as cholera, typhoid and bilharzia, could become more frequent and widespread. Mortality rates would then be expected to rise.

Conflict

Global warming is expected to increase food insecurity and water insecurity. They could easily lead to conflict. Many people could be forced to migrate in search of food and water. It is even possible that people would be fighting over the remaining sources. The outlook is bleak.

Look at an atlas map of the Pacific Ocean and locate Tuvalu.

Case study: Tuvalu and Bangladesh are drowning

Tuvalu, formerly known as the Ellis Islands, is a Polynesian island state located in the Pacific Ocean midway between Hawaii and Australia. It is made up of four coral reef islands and five coral atolls (Figure 7.38). With a total land area of only 26 km² and a population of around 12 500 people, it can claim to be the world's fourth smallest country. The highest point of the island is 4.5 metres above sea level.

Figure 7.38: *Tuvalu – an island paradise*

The continuing existence of this country hangs in the balance. It may be the first to disappear beneath the waves. The Prime Minister of Tuvalu recently described the plight of his country and its people:

'We live in constant fear of the adverse impacts of climate change. For a coral atoll nation, sea-level rise and more severe weather events loom as a growing threat to our entire population. The threat is real and serious, and is no different to a slow and insidious form of terrorism against us.'

Tuvalu is one of the places on Earth that is most vulnerable to the affects of global warming. It could become one of the world's first 'ghost states'. In other words, it will become a nation of people that has no territory. The interesting questions are these:

- where should these people be resettled?

- can Tuvalu continue to be recognised as a state even though it is no more than a collection of coral reefs under the ocean?

Given how small Tuvalu is, it is unlikely that the rest of the world is going to worry too much what happens to it. What happens in Bangladesh may give rise to much more concern. Its combination of a huge population (154 million), high population density (1045 persons per km²) and its low-lying nature make it particularly vulnerable to global warming. Much of Bangladesh is one huge flood plain and delta formed by the confluence of the Ganges, Brahmaputra and Meghna Rivers. Nearly three-quarters of the country lies less than 10 metres above sea level.

For more information about Bangladesh, see:

- Chapter 1.5 (page 14)
- Chapter 1.8 (page 30)
- Chapter 2.5 (page 51)
- Chapter 4.3 (page 99).

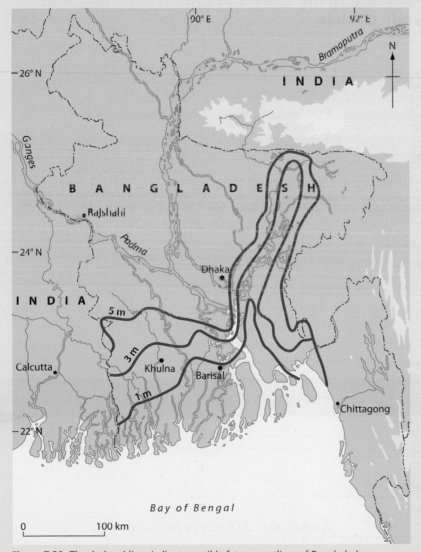

Figure 7.39: *The dark red lines indicate possible future coastlines of Bangladesh*

Figure 7.39 shows the predicted position of the Bangladesh coastline associated with three different rises in sea level. Even with a 1-metre rise, a large area of the delta will be lost and so too the homes and livelihoods of possibly up to 40 million people. What would happen to those people made homeless by the rising sea level? The problem is that it would not be easy to resettle them elsewhere in Bangladesh. Virtually all parts of the country are densely populated. Land that is not built on at present is in most cases badly needed for food production. Taking that land away to provide homes will only increase the likelihood of hunger and starvation.

Bangladesh is a multiple hazard zone (river and coastal floods, storm surges and typhoons). Climate change is likely to make these hazards both more frequent and severe. To add to Bangladesh's problems, health and well-being are likely to deteriorate.

7.9 Managing the causes of global warming and climate change

If we believe that today's global warming is simply part of natural climate change, then there is nothing we can do to stop it. All we can do is to adapt to the consequences that we looked at in Part **7.8**. However, if we believe that the increase in greenhouse gases is the main cause of global warming, then we can certainly do something. The most obvious actions would be:

- to cut down on the use of fossil fuels and so reduce carbon emissions and atmospheric pollution

- to find alternative sources of energy and so reduce the need to burn fossil fuels

- to reduce the rate of deforestation and encourage afforestation. This would ensure the world has a good stock of forests to absorb any surplus carbon dioxide

- to do more by way of **carbon capture** – that is releasing carbon dioxide into the ground rather than the atmosphere (Figure 7.40).

Global warming is something that is happening to the whole world. If greenhouses gases are responsible for it, then only global action on reducing carbon emissions holds out any hope for the future of the world. International cooperation is absolutely critical. All countries, especially the big polluters like China and the USA, need to be moving in the same direction of reducing emissions (Table 7.4).

Country	Carbon emissions (1000 million tonnes)	Country	Carbon emissions (1000 million tonnes)
1. USA	5762	**6.** Germany	837
2. China	3474	**7.** UK	558
3. Russia	1540	**8.** Canada	521
4. Japan	1225	**9.** Italy	447
5. India	1008	**10.** Mexico	385
Global total: 22,820,000 million tonnes			

Table 7.4: Carbon emissions from the major polluters (2009)

Study Table 7.4. What conclusions do you come to? Do you think that the population totals of these countries should have been taken into account?

Carbon going underground

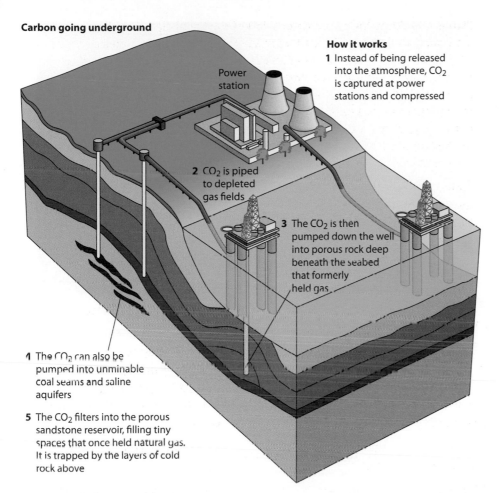

How it works

1 Instead of being released into the atmosphere, CO_2 is captured at power stations and compressed

Power station

2 CO_2 is piped to depleted gas fields

3 The CO_2 is then pumped down the well into porous rock deep beneath the seabed that formerly held gas

4 The CO_2 can also be pumped into unminable coal seams and saline aquifers

5 The CO_2 filters into the porous sandstone reservoir, filling tiny spaces that once held natural gas. It is trapped by the layers of cold rock above

Figure 7.40 Carbon capture

Many in the USA have been sceptical about the possible causes of global warming. They have therefore been reluctant to do anything. China has long refused to cut emissions as it continues to industrialise at a rapid pace. However, the melting and shrinking of the Tibetan glaciers that feed the Yangtze and Yellow Rivers may eventually lead to China re-assessing the threat of climate change. Russia claims that it is doing its bit. Its vast forests are a significant **carbon sink**. Along with China, countries such as India, Mexico and many other LICs see the ending of poverty as a more important challenge than global warming and climate change. HICs like Japan, Canada and most of the member countries of the EU have stated their willingness to cut carbon emissions.

Case study: The challenge of international cooperation over carbon emissions

The first step in international cooperation to cut greenhouse gases was taken in the Montreal Protocol of 1987. This recognised the particularly harmful effects of CFCs. They damage the ozone layer which protects us all from harmful ultra-violet radiation. Gradually CFCs have been replaced by less harmful substances (Figure 7.41). The Montreal Protocol raised hopes that further agreements on the emission of other greenhouses could be reached.

Figure 7.41: *CFC emissions have been greatly reduced*

Research the uses made of CFCs.

1992 saw the first **Earth Summit** meeting on the environment held in Rio de Janeiro in Brazil. It resulted in a range of global policies for the future use of resources and the protection of the environment. At the next summit, held in Kyoto (Japan) in 1997, a new treaty was set out to try to put into practice recommendations made by the United Nations Framework for Climate Change (UNFCC) (Figure 7.42). This required countries to cut their emissions of greenhouse gases by an average of 5 per cent by 2012 (based on 1990 figures). The Kyoto Protocol was seen as essential to reducing greenhouse gases and mitigating the effects of global warming.

Figure 7.42: *Delegates at the signing of the Kyoto Protocol in 1997*

For the treaty to be ratified it had to be signed by at least 55 countries responsible for most of the emissions at that time. Only 38 of those countries signed. They agreed to cut their carbon emissions by 5 to 8% by 2012. Very few of those countries now seem likely to reach their targets. One notable exception is Sweden which has already managed to cut its emissions by 10%.

However, action on carbon emissions and the reduction of global warming will only work if all the big industrialised countries agree to the treaty. However, the USA, China and India did not sign up. Between them, they account for nearly half of all global emissions (Table 7.4).

The Kyoto agreement also set up a Clean Development Mechanism (CDM). This is a sort of market in which 'carbon credits' can be bought and sold. Carbon-cutting measures, such as leaving forests standing and planting new ones allow countries to earn 'carbon credits' that can be offset against their emission reduction targets. Forests are often referred to as **carbon sinks** because they absorb and reduce the amount of carbon dioxide in the atmosphere (Figure 7.43). These credits can be sold by countries that reach their emissions target to polluting countries not meeting theirs.

Figure 7.43: Countries can offset their carbon emissions by planting forests

Despite initial agreement at Kyoto, the treaty has not yet been ratified by all the key countries. Emissions in many countries are still rising, rather than falling. The Kyoto Protocol runs out in 2012. It was hoped that a new protocol could be agreed at the Copenhagen Climate Conference held in December 2009. 190 countries, including the USA, China and India were represented, but there was much squabbling and indecision. No agreement could be reached on emission-cutting targets.

Whilst the USA, China and India showed some willingness to agree to the targets, it was the LICs that would not cooperate. Understandably, many of those countries are reluctant to cut emissions and risk missing out on development for the sake of future climate change. It may be that the HICs will need to support LIC living standards by funding low-carbon projects such as new renewable energy systems in those countries.

The UN continues to make efforts to achieve a binding treaty agreed to by all the nations of the world.

Check that you understand the following terms:

- carbon emissions
- carbon sinks
- carbon capture
- carbon credits.

Why is international agreement so important in the 'fight' against global warming?

Alternative energy sources

The key to lowering carbon emissions is for the countries of the world to become 'low-carbon' economies. This means moving away from the use of fossil fuels and fuelwood as sources of energy. Instead we should generate our electricity using renewable sources of energy (see Chapter **4.8** on page 110). These include wind farms, tidal barrages, hydroelectric power, giant solar panels, wave-power generators and, possibly, nuclear power. The problem with the first five sources is that the technology is expensive and the output of electricity is relatively small. Even if all those sources were to be used, it is unlikely that they could produce as much electricity as the burning of fossil fuel does. The situation is rather different if we were to make more use of nuclear power. However, this is the most controversial of all the so-called non-renewable sources of energy. There are major concerns about the security and safety of nuclear power stations (Figure 7.44), as well as about the disposal of used nuclear fuel.

A nuclear explosion occurred in 26 April, 1986 at the Chernobyl power station in the Ukraine. It sent a plume of radioactive fall-out into the atmosphere. This drifted across much of Europe to as far as the UK. Although only 50 deaths were directly due to the explosion, there haven been significant rises in cancer deaths in the area affected by the plume.

Figure 7.44: *The area affected by the nuclear explosion at Chernobyl in 1986*

It is also clear that the situation could be helped by using less energy (for example, making our homes more energy efficient). The motor vehicle poses a challenge. What do we use to power the different modes of transport? Electricity may be feasible for road transport. It is already used for rail transport, but what about air transport? Maybe this is where biofuel (a substitute for petrol) will have to be used. Perhaps the same applies for water transport, but maybe the sail will make a comeback!

Adapting to global warming and climate change

The main consequences of global warming were described in Part **7.8**. It is possible that the survival of the human race depends on major adjustments being made in terms of:

- where we live
- how we live.

The ways in which we need to adapt to the main consequences of global warming and climate change may be summarised as follows:

- **Rising sea levels** – invest heavily in coastal defences or retreat from the most vulnerable stretches of coast. Plan for the relocation of both displaced people and economic activities, and build new cities in inland locations.

- **More hazards** – improve our ability to predict them and invest in effective hazard preparation and adjustment.

- **Ecosystem changes and economic opportunities** – abandon those areas which are made too difficult to continue cultivating by climate change. Invest in the opening up of new lands for farming. Increase the search for resources in areas exposed by the melting ice.

- **Health and well-being** – improve the medical treatment of those diseases likely to spread as a result of climate change.

- **Conflict** – defuse food and water insecurity by international cooperation aimed at achieving a fairer distribution of both commodities.

More information on three of these bullet points may be found as follows:

- Rising sea levels – Chapter 2
- More hazards – Chapter 3
- Ecosystem changes – Chapter 5

End of chapter checkout

Checklists

Now you have read the chapter, you should know:

✓ how and why some environments are fragile

✓ the meaning of sustainability

✓ the causes of soil erosion and desertification

✓ the consequences and management of soil erosion

✓ the causes of deforestation

✓ the consequences of deforestation

✓ how rainforests might be managed in a sustainable way

✓ the causes of global warming and climate change

✓ the consequences of global warming and climate change

✓ how the causes of global warming and climate change might be managed

Make sure you understand these key terms:

Agro-forestry: the growing of trees for the benefit of agriculture, as windbreaks or as protection against soil erosion.

Alternative energy: renewable sources of energy, such as solar and wind power, that offer an alternative to the use of fossil fuels.

Chlorofluorocarbons (CFCs): chemicals once used in foams, refrigerators, aerosols and air-conditioning units. Their use in now banned because they were thought to be responsible for the destruction of the word's ozone layer and for part of the greenhouse effect.

Climate change: long-term changes in the global atmospheric conditions.

Deforestation: the deliberate clearing of forested land, often causing serious environmental problems such as soil erosion.

Desertification: the spread of desert conditions into what were semi-arid areas.

Famine: a chronic shortage of food resulting in many people dying from starvation.

Fossil fuel: carbon fuels such coal, oil and natural gas that cannot be 'remade' because it will take tens of millions of years for them to form again.

Fragile: a term used to described those natural environments that are sensitive to, and easily abused by human activities

Global warming: a process whereby global temperatures rise over time.

Malnutrition: a condition resulting when a person is unable to eat what is needed to maintain good health

Overgrazing: when pasture or grazing is unable to support the number of animals relying on it for food. The result is the vegetation cover declines and soil erosion sets in.

Population pressure: when the number of people in an area begins

Refugee: a person whose reasons for migrating are due to fear of persecution or death

Soil erosion: the washing or blowing away of topsoil so that the fertility of the remaining soil is greatly reduced.

Sustainable: a term used to describe actions that minimise negative impacts on the environment and promote human well-being.

Well-being: a condition experienced by people and greatly influenced by the standard of living and quality of life.

See the Glossary in the ActiveBook for more definitions.

Questions

Try testing yourself with these questions:

1   What are the threats most likely to disturb fragile environments?

2   a) What is the 'ecological footprint'?
    b) Explain what is meant by the term sustainability.

3   Describe the three main types of soil erosion.

4   Which of the following best describes the terms soil erosion and desertification? Put a cross (✘) in the correct box.

	soil erosion	desertification
desert like conditions covering a smaller area	☐	☐
little vegetation now covering an area	☐	☐
the washing away or blowing away of soil	☐	☐
the watering of land by people during dry weather	☐	☐
trees being cut down	☐	☐

5   Describe the human activities that cause soil erosion.

6   a) What is desertification?
    b) What are its main physical causes?

7   How have people contributed to the desertification of the Sahel?

8   Describe some of the worst consequences of soil erosion.

9   Describe methods used to combat or prevent soil erosion.

10 a) What are the 'goods and services' of the tropical rainforest?
    b) What is meant by the term deforestation
    c) Is it the exploitation of these goods and services that are the main causes of deforestation?

11 What are the other causes of the large-scale deforestation of the tropical rainforest biome?

12 Which land use most threatens the future of the tropical rainforest? Give your reasons.

13 What are the two main concerns about the deforestation of the tropical rainforest?

14 What is involved in the sustainable management of the tropical rainforest?

15 How is the sustainable management of the tropical rainforest most likely to be achieved?

16 a) Using Figure 7.26, describe how global temperatures changed between 1860 and 2000.
    b) Compare Figures 7.26 and 7.27. How similar are the graphs for global temperatures and carbon dioxide emissions?

17 a) What are the main greenhouse gases?
    b) Using Figure 7.29, describe the greenhouse effect.

18 Why is a rising sea level one of the consequences of global warming?

19 What is the link between global warming and more hazards?

20 How is human health likely to be affected by global warming?

21 Describe the challenges that Bangladesh is facing as a result of global warming.

22 a) Which countries are responsible for the greatest carbon dioxide emissions?
    b) What are the main sources of carbon dioxide?

23 a) Describe the main aims of the Kyoto Treaty.
    b) Why has the treaty not yet come into force?

24 What are the following:
    ● carbon sinks
    ● carbon quotas
    ● carbon capture?

25 Describe the main ways of reducing carbon dioxide emissions.

Chapter 8: Globalisation and migration

8.1 The rise of the global economy

The term **globalisation** was first used in the 1960s, but it is only since the 1990s that its use has become widespread. It is the process by which the countries of the world are being gradually drawn into a single **global economy** by a growing network of economic, communication and transport links. It is a process being driven by the more powerful nations and huge business empires. It is resulting in countries becoming increasingly dependent on each other. This means that economic decisions and economic activities in one part of the world can have important effects on what happens in other parts of the world.

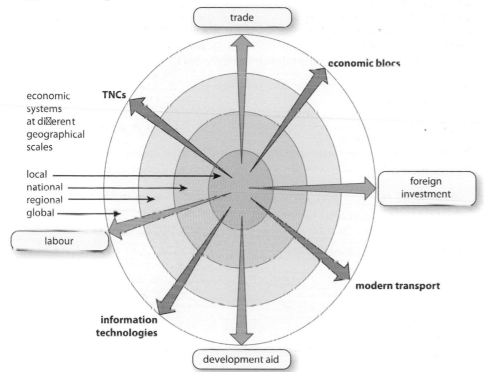

Figure 8.1: *The growth of a global economy*

Introduction

The first part of this chapter is about one of the most important processes affecting today's world – the growth of a global economy, otherwise known as globalisation. It looks at some of its specific changes, namely the shift in the location of manufacturing, the rise of global tourism and the increasing volume of migration between countries. All three changes certainly have their benefits. However they also have their costs and give rise to a range of issues.

It could be argued that globalisation is not a new process. For centuries, countries have been trading with each other, often over long distances. Perhaps the old European colonial empires of the 16th and 17th centuries were early expressions of globalisation. What has changed in recent decades is the scale of international trading and of the other economic links that are creating this **interdependence** (Figure 8.1). Four significant developments have helped this scaling up:

- the appearance of large **transnational corporations** (**TNCs**) with diverse business interests literally spread across the globe

Interdependence is when countries become more and more dependent on each other. This is a key feature of globalisation and the global economy.

- the growth of regional economic or trading blocs, such as the European Union (EU) and the North American Free Trade Agreement (NAFTA). By encouraging free trade between member countries, the barrier effects of national boundaries are broken down. In short, there is much more global trade

- the development of modern transport networks (air, land and sea) capable of moving people and commodities quickly and relatively cheaply. Due mainly to the aircraft, physical distances worldwide are much less important. We live in a 'shrinking world'

- advances in **information technology** and **communication technology** mean that important data and decisions can be whizzed around the globe in a matter of seconds. A TNC with its headquarters in London or another major city can closely monitor market trends around the world. It can easily check up on what is happening in its branch offices and factories scattered around the globe. Decisions can be quickly transmitted.

The outcome of these developments is today's **global economy**. There is scarcely a country in the world that is not participating in it is some way or another. The workings of the global economy involve five different forms of flow (Figure 8.1):

- **trade** – through the export or import of raw materials, food, finished goods or services

- **aid** – either as a donor or a receiving nation. Much aid is of an economic nature

- **foreign investment** – through investment, TNCs are able to exploit economic opportunities around the world, it might be oil in west Africa or sugar in Brazil

- **labour** – labour is vital to the workings of the global economy. Economic migration is commonplace these days as people move in search of work and a better life. Equally, TNCs are constantly on the look-out for cheap labour

- **information** – the fast transfer of data and decisions are crucial to the workings of the global economy.

> Be sure to remember these five flows that create interdependence.

> On an outline map of the world, plot the production chain shown in Figure 8.2.

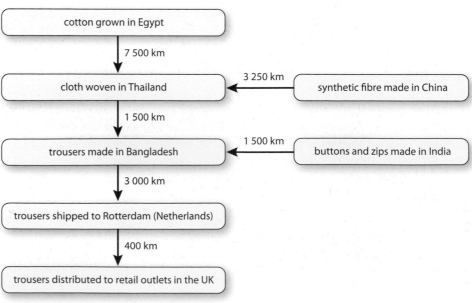

Figure 8.2: *The production chain of a pair of jeans*

Through the growing global economy and its flows we are all being drawn into a **global village** of interdependent nations. What is the material evidence of this? Most often mentioned are the production chains (also known as supply chains or **commodity chains**). A **production chain** consists of a number of stages involved in the making of a particular product. At each stage, value is added to the emerging product. Figure 8.2 shows the production chain involved in making a pair of jeans. The reasons for companies setting up these 'transnational' production chains are explained in the Part **8.2**.

Other evidence of the workings of the global economy include:

- the **call centres** for UK and USA companies located in India, Philippines and Thailand
- the **outsourcing** of food production and manufacturing in LICs
- the growing volumes of economic migration and international tourism.

Why are there so many call centres in India Philippines and Thailand?

8.2 The global shift in manufacturing

The global economy is not only expanding in size and extent, it is also changing. For example, new services are appearing within the tertiary and quaternary sectors. Advances in technology are creating new branches of manufacturing, most notably the high-tech industries. Modern communications are leading to new ways of working and new work locations. **Teleworking** and **outsourcing** are two such examples. However, no less significant is that established branches of manufacturing are shifting their locations, basically from HICs to MICs and LICs.

More information about the global shift in manufacturing can be found in Chapter 4.5 (page 105).

Figure 8.3: *A new cotton mill in India*

Look at Figure 4.4 (page 95) and Figure 9.2 (page 242) to see how the importance of the UK's secondary sector has declined.

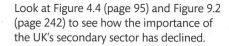

Perhaps the greatest impact that the TNCs have had is on the global distribution of manufacturing. As a result of their policy of looking for the cheapest locations at which to make their products, factories have been closed down in the HICs. They have been replaced by new factories (branch plants) set up in these cheaper locations. So the **global shift** in manufacturing is the outcome of **deindustrialisation** in the developed world matched by **industrialisation** in the developing world.

The UK was the world's first industrial nation. It led the Industrial Revolution. Today, however, manufacturing produces about 25% of the country's economic wealth (GDP). Fifty years ago, the equivalent figure was 40%. The UK has now lost most of its traditional industries, such as iron and steel, shipbuilding and textiles. The world is still producing those commodities, but in what the TNCs see as today's low-cost and more profitable locations. Basically, these are locations with some **comparative advantage**. It might be:

- nearness to some raw material source, such as iron ore or oil

- the availability of cheap land for building large new factories

- the presence of cheap labour or labour not regulated by trade unions. This would mean that a company could pay workers less and make them work longer hours – often in less safe working conditions

- the absence of tight anti-pollution regulations – this can be a strong attraction to those industries, such as the manufacturers of steel and chemicals, that are big polluters of air and water.

Because modern transport is so efficient and relatively cheap, it does not matter too much where these low-cost locations are situated. These factories can be thousands of kilometres from the main markets for their products, as illustrated by Figure 8.4. They can assemble parts made in different continents.

Who are the winners in this global shift in manufacturing? The main winners have been in Asia, particularly the so-called 'emerging economies' of China and India (Figure 8.3). In an amazingly short period of time, China has become one of the world's leading manufacturers. Look around your house and see how many things have a 'Made in China' label.

Do exactly that – look around your house for items with a 'Made in China' label. Make as list. What sorts of product are they?

The global motor industry

The manufacture of the motor vehicle is perhaps one of the most globalised of today's industries. A typical vehicle is assembled from thousands of parts made in locations scattered around the world. Those parts, in their turn, are made from a diversity of raw materials, again sourced from around the world. Fifty years ago, the motor vehicle industry was producing about 13 million vehicles a year. Fifty-four percent of those vehicles were made in North America and 40% in Western Europe. Today, annual output is in the order of 72 million. Figure 8.4 shows the distribution of motor vehicle production in 2007. Clearly, North America and Western Europe are still major producers. However, look how global the distribution of the industry has become. The credit crunch of 2007 to 2009 particularly hit vehicle output in the USA, the UK, France and Germany, thus pushing still further the global shift in this one branch of manufacturing. The motor vehicle industry is one of the most globalised branches of manufacturing.

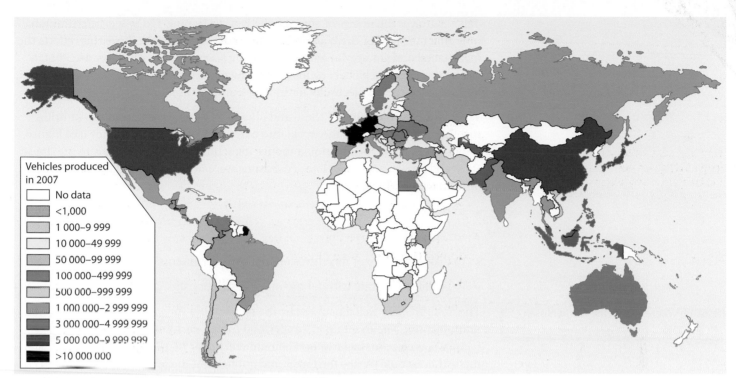

Figure 8.4: *The global distribution of motor vehicle production in 2007*

It would be wrong to think that the global shift in manufacturing has left the UK and other HICs without any industry. In fact, the UK still ranks sixth in the global league table of manufacturing nations. This is explained by the fact that many of the remaining industries are making relatively high value products. Good examples would be the high-tech industries, such as aerospace, telecommunications, biotechnology and nanotechnology.

8.3 Transnational corporations (TNCs)

The working of the global economy involves a number of major **players**, that is organisations that have great power and influence. They include the great business empires known as transnational corporations (TNCs) and global organisations such as the United Nations (UN), the World Bank, the International Monetary Fund (IMF) and the World Trade Organisation (WTO). Other powerful players are the USA, the European Union, Japan and OPEC.

Company	Main business	Location of head offices
Royal Dutch Shell	Oil and gas	The Hague, Netherlands
Exxon Mobile	Oil and gas	Irving, USA
Wal-Mart Stores	Retailing	Bentonville, USA
BP	Oil and gas	London, UK
Chevron	Oil and gas	San Ramon, USA
ConocoPhilipps	Oil and gas	Houston, USA
ING Group	Financial services	Amsterdam, Netherlands
Sinopec	Oil and chemicals	Beijing, China
Toyota	Motor vehicles	Toyota, Japan

Table 8.1: The world's top 10 TNCs in 2009

What conclusions do you draw from Figure 8.4 about the global distribution of motor vehicle production?

Try naming five more well-known TNCs, but companies which have their main business interests outside the oil industry.

Table 8.1 gives the names of some of the world's leading TNCs. It is interesting to note that over half of them are involved in the oil industry. Perhaps this reflects the fact that oil and gas are currently the leading sources of energy. They are vital to the workings of the global economy – as raw material sources, as fuel for transport, and as generators of electricity for industry and the home.

The **production chains** of these and other TNCs criss-cross the globe, knitting together the countries of the world into a network of interdependence (see Figure 8.2 on page 214). The overriding motive for setting up these chains is to maximise sales and profits. Four contributory reasons were noted on page 23. There are also other strong reasons:

- to be close to major markets

- to sell inside trade barriers

- to take advantage of incentives offered by governments

- to be able to operate without too many restrictions.

Research where else in the world Nissan has factories.

The first three are well illustrated by the factory that the Japanese car manufacturer Nissan set up in Sunderland (north-east England) in 1986. The factory was close to the large and affluent consumer markets within the EU. Cars made there would escape the tariffs and quotas that make it difficult for foreign companies to export directly to the EU. Even better, the EU and UK government were offering funds to help meet the costs of setting up the factory. They were doing this because they wanted to encourage the creation of news jobs in a part of England with a high rate of unemployment.

Figure 8.5: *A new Tesco store in China.*

Case study: Tesco – a transnational retailer

The supermarket chain Tesco is one of the few leading TNCs with its head offices in the UK. Currently it is ranked 50th in the global league table. The company started life as a single grocery stall in the East End of London. It did not set up its first self-service supermarket until 1956. It was during the 1970s, 1980s and 1990s that the company really took off to become the largest food retailer in the UK (Figure 8.6).

The key to the company's success has been:

- its strategy of diversification into new markets, such as toys, clothing, electrical goods, home products, financial services and telecommunications, in addition to its original business of food

- **outsourcing** its supplies of foodstuffs, clothing and other goods directly from producers both in the UK and in LICs such as Kenya , Sri Lanka and Bangladesh

- globalising its chain of supermarkets. This did not start until the 1990s with the opening of stores in Eastern Europe (Hungary, Poland, the Czech Republic and Slovakia). In 1998, it made its first move outside Europe, opening stores in Taiwan and Thailand and in South Korea the following year. Tesco's presence in Asia has subsequently spread to China (Figure 8.5), Japan and Malaysia. Today, 60% of the company's profits come from Asia.

Go into your local supermarket and look at the labels that tell you where a product has come from. Make a two-column list – one for the type of product and the other for the country of origin. Analyse you findings, perhaps presenting your findings on a outline world map.

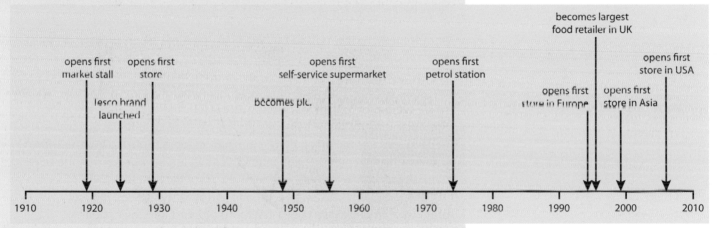

Figure 8.6 *A timeline of Tesco's globalisation*

From a single supermarket in 1956, Tesco now has over 4500 stores and employs around 750 000 people. Tesco has become a major TNC.

Case study: Rio Tinto in Namibia

Rio Tinto is a transnational mining and resources group, founded in 1873. At first, it concentrated its efforts on the mining of copper. As the company has prospered so it has turned its attentions to other minerals. Its network of mines is now global in extent.

Namibia is one of the world's major producers of uranium. Rio Tinto's Rossing mine is one of the world's five largest primary uranium mines (Figure 8.7). It is situated close to the seaside town of Swakopmund.

Figure 8.7: *Rio Tinto's Rossing mine*

At present there seems to something of a 'uranium rush'. It is based on the likelihood that nuclear power will play a leading role in filling the global energy gap. New mines are due to be opened. What has Namibia gained from the Rossing mine? The mine employs a few hundred Namibian workers and a small number of foreign technicians. These jobs mean tax income for the Namibian government. There are also the royalties paid to the government for the extraction of the uranium. The uranium oxide is exported in its raw form and enriched in countries with uranium converters such as France, the USA, Canada and China. So there is little or no 'secondary' employment other than in transporting the ore to the coast and shipping it overseas. Rio Tinto provides a limited range of services for its workers and their families.

There are however costs to be considered. Health is one of these. Exposure to even relatively low levels of radiation over a long period can be extremely harmful to the health of workers and communities living around uranium mines. Workers are exposed to dust and radon gas daily, and as a result develop diseases such as TB and lung cancer. Although mining companies usually deny any responsibility and refuse to compensate workers, there is increasing evidence of a link between uranium mining and workers' health problems.

Other aspects of the downside include the fact that uranium uses enormous amounts of water. Namibia is a water-deficient country. Mines produce huge amounts of waste and tailings. Once mining ceases huge holes remain. There are real environmental costs. These bring mining into direct conflict with tourism ventures that rely on Namibia's scenic beauty and wildlife as main attractions.

What do you think about the Rossing mine? Do its benefits outweigh its costs, or vice versa? Give your reasons.

The good and the bad

The growth of globalisation has given rise to a major debate about its real benefits. Its supporters point out that it is giving the poorest countries some opportunities for economic development. They say that even the poorest countries have something to offer to the global economy. Being involved in the global economy creates jobs, the opportunity for people to earn a steady wage and a chance to improve their quality of life (Table 8.2).

Benefits	Costs
Trade links with other countries set up	Profit-driven
Jobs created; regular wages	Profits 'leak' out of the country
Infrastructure developed	Investment moved to more profitable places
Foreign currency earned from exports	Exploitation of workers
Skills training of local labour	Often little regard for the environment
Investment in new technology	New technology may reduce workforce

Table 8.2: Benefits and costs to countries hosting TNCs

The trouble is that TNCs are businesses that are out to maximise their profits. They are inherently exploitive. They often ignore the environmental and social impacts of their investments. Few TNCs are answerable to the governments of the countries in which they invest. They are so powerful, they can do almost what they like. The profits that they make in any one country are most often 'exported' to open up new businesses elsewhere. Any investment can disappear as quickly as it came, if global or local economic conditions change.

The world's poorest countries have yet to see much benefit from globalisation. If anything, it has increased the so-called **development gap** between the rich and poor nations of the world. International trade only really benefits those who can afford to make, export and buy expensive imported goods, so many of the poorest people are penalised or excluded.

8.4 The growth of global tourism

Globalsisation is not just about manufacturing. As the Tesco case study (page 219) has illustrated, it is also about services. No service has grown and spread more spectacularly over the last 50 years than tourism. Today around 900 million people become international tourists each year – that is equivalent to more than one-tenth of the world's population.

Figure 8.8 shows that during the second half of the 20th century, the number of international tourists increased nearly 30 times. International tourism was born in Europe. It is still the leading continent – it both receives and supplies the most tourists. However, many other parts of the world are now sharing in the benefits of global tourism.

People have been taking foreign holidays for centuries. Up until the 20th century, however, it was something only wealthy people did, and often for months at a time. Today's international tourist does not have to be wealthy, and most overseas visits only last for a week or two. What has caused this change and the spectacular rise in the volume tourism? There are many reasons for the 'explosion' (Figure 8.9).

What conclusions do you draw from Figure 8.8 about tourist arrivals?

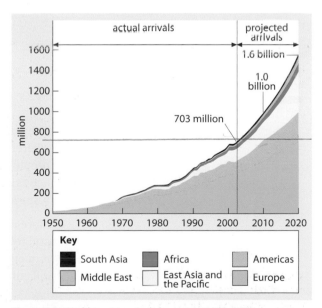

Figure 8.8: *World tourist arrivals by region, 1950–2020*

Most workers in HICs now work less than 40 hours a week and enjoy up to six weeks of paid annual leave (more in Europe than the USA). This combination of more leisure time and paid holidays has given a powerful boost to tourism. People are always on the lookout for new tourist destinations and new leisure experiences. Many people are taking early retirement and want to travel.

One of the benefits of living in an MIC or HIC is that regular work means that people have **disposable income**. There is money that can be spent on luxuries – including tourist activities such as a cruise or a safari holiday. Interestingly, whilst it is people in HICs who have the greatest amount of disposable income, an increasing amount of it is being spent in LICs on exotic holidays. As a result, the growth in tourism is helping economic development in those poorer countries.

Developments in transport have revolutionised travel. Journey times have been dramatically reduced. Long journeys are now more comfortable, and the relative costs of travel are lower. The introduction of modern forms of transport, such as wide-bodied jet aircraft, hotel cruise ships, cruiser coaches and high-speed rail networks, have all helped to make global travel a reality for increasing numbers of people. Even the world's most remote places are now accessible, for example the Antarctic and Amazon rainforest.

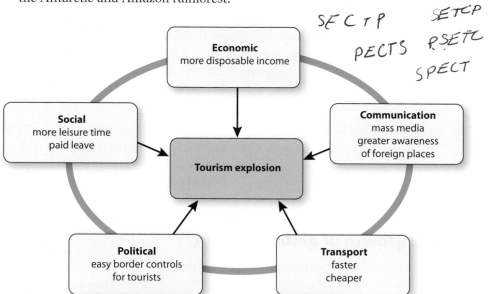

Figure 8.9: *Main causes of the tourism explosion*

Make sure that you understand each of the five causes of the tourism explosion shown in Figure 8.9.

The mass media, especially TV and the internet, have increased people's awareness of faraway places and possible tourist destinations. They have opened people's eyes not just to different destinations, but also to a diversity of holiday activities, from scuba diving and birdwatching to visiting cultural and historic sites.

More and more countries are realising the benefits of being a tourist destination, and relaxing their border controls. Governments stand to make large sums of money from tourist visas and departure taxes. Even the EU, which makes it difficult for workers to enter, warmly welcomes tourists.

- Tourism has become a 'commodity' which is marketed in much the same way as any new mobile phone or car. There is now a huge business sector made up of travel agents and tour operators set on promoting tourism. One particularly big promotion has been the **package holiday**. This consists of transport and accommodation advertised and sold together by a tour operator. Other services in the package might include a rental car, special activities and excursions.

Popular package tour destinations for UK tourists today include the holiday resorts on the Spanish 'costas' and islands (Majorca, Minorca, Ibiza and the Canaries), the Algarve (Portugal) and the Greek islands. The appeal of such holidays is that they are relatively cheap, everything is organised and there is plenty of entertainment and socialising.

There is one other factor that makes these destinations popular with UK tourists. Have you spotted it? Clue – it is to do with travel.

8.5 The impacts of mass tourism

The package holiday is the key part of what is known as **mass tourism**. This is a branch of tourism in which large multinational companies shape developments according to global demand. It is large-scale, highly commercial, focused on popular destinations and pays little regard to local communities. As with most developments in our modern world, mass tourism has brought both benefits and costs. These positive and negative impacts fall mainly under three headings – economic, socio-cultural and environmental

Economic impacts

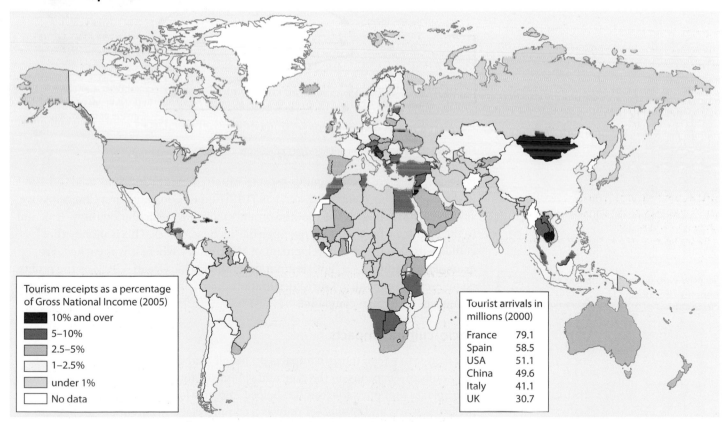

Tourism receipts as a percentage of Gross National Income (2005)

- 10% and over
- 5–10%
- 2.5–5%
- 1–2.5%
- under 1%
- No data

Tourist arrivals in millions (2000)

France	79.1
Spain	58.5
USA	51.1
China	49.6
Italy	41.1
UK	30.7

Figure 8.10: *The economic importance of tourism*

There is no doubt that tourism has positive impacts. Figure 8.10 shows that there are a growing number of countries which benefit from tourism. These are countries in Southern Europe, the Middle East, Africa, Southeast Asia and Central America. These countries benefit from tourism's multiplier effects, as shown in Figure 8.11. Tourism is labour-intensive, and it creates many jobs, not just in hotels and restaurants, but in other tourist services, such as transport. Whilst tourism is a service sector activity, it has indirect impacts on the other two sectors of agriculture and manufacturing. Tourists need food, so that is potentially good for agriculture. Tourists buy souvenirs and that can be good for manufacturing. The hotel staff, the ice-cream sellers and the souvenir shop owners then spend their money in the local shops. Tourism puts money into many people's pockets and, through the multiplier effect, the whole local economy can be lifted. Few would disagree that tourism can do much to help economic development in LICs.

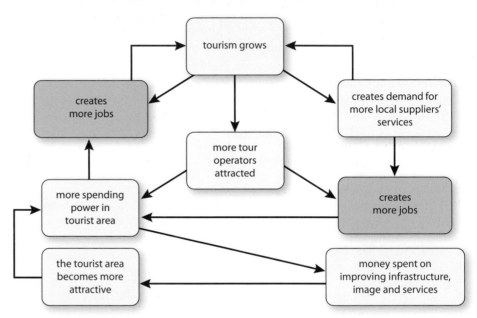

Figure 8.11: *The economic multiplier effect of tourism*

However, there are some negative aspects. Much of today's international tourism is in the hands of big companies, such as TUI, Thomas Cook and First Choice. As we saw in Part **8.3**, this means that the profits made in a particular country 'leak' out to the country where the tour operator has its head offices. This is money that could be used to help the development of the country where it was earned. For example, in Vanuatu – a 'hot' destination in the Pacific Ocean – 90% of the profits go to foreign companies. Tourist destinations, particularly in LICs, can become very dependent on foreign companies.

Socio-cultural impacts

The degree to which tourism impacts on people and their traditional ways of life – their culture – depends on the type and volume of tourism. It might be claimed in some places that mass tourism has helped to revive local handicrafts as well as the performing arts and rituals – if only as a commercial entertainment for visitors. However, generally speaking, the socio-cultural impacts of tourism are mostly negative. The greater the number of tourists converging on a location, the more

So how would you sum up the economic benefits of tourism?

likely there is to be tension with local people. Tourists can easily offend the traditional values of local people and their codes of behaviour in a number of ways:

- drinking too much alcohol and becoming loud and offensive
- ignoring local dress codes and revealing too much flesh
- encouraging prostitution and, unintentionally, crime
- eroding the local language by relying too much on English
- failing to behave in the proper way in churches, temples and mosques.

It would be good to think that international tourism provides the opportunity for people of different cultures to mix and learn about each other. However, that positive effect happens rarely. Indeed, in some parts of the world tourists are deliberately kept away from local people (or is it the other way round?). This happens, for example, in Cuba (for political reasons) and in the Maldives (for religious reasons).

Environmental impacts

It is also difficult to identify any positive environmental impacts. Again, it depends on the nature and the volume of tourism. Alternative **ecotourism** does provide some opportunities for people to learn about the environment and to become supporters of environmental conservation. However, it is easy to compile a long list of negative impacts:

For more information about ecotourism, see Part 8.6 (page 227).

- the clearance of important habitats, such as mangrove and rainforest, to provide building sites for hotels
- the overuse of water resources
- the pollution of the sea, lakes and rivers by rubbish and sewage
- the destruction of coral reefs by snorkelers and scuba divers
- the disturbance of wildlife by safari tourism, hunting and fishing
- traffic congestion, air and noise pollution.

For more information about:

- the value of mangroves, see Chapter 2.4 (page 44) and 2.5 (page 51)
- rainforests, see Chapter 7.4 (page 187) and 7.5 (page 190).

Case study: Spain's Costa Blanca – a premier package holiday destination

Spain's Costa Blanca is a 200 km stretch of Mediterranean coast running either side of Alicante (Figure 8.12). Arguably, it is the most famous stretch of coast in Spain. In the 1950s it was a fairly quiet coastal area, relying heavily on fishing. However, since the growth of cheap package holidays in the 1960s, the area has been completely transformed. Today it is an almost unbroken strip of high-rise hotels, holiday apartments, shops, cafes and restaurants. Millions of tourists are attracted here by the clear blue waters, the vast white sand beaches, the hot, dry, sunny weather and the wide range of leisure facilities, from water sports to golf courses.

This growth of mass tourism and the package holiday has brought many advantages to this part of Spain, especially in the form of jobs. More recently the infrastructure of the region has seen a number of improvements, benefiting visitors and local residents alike. This is part of the multiplier effect – more

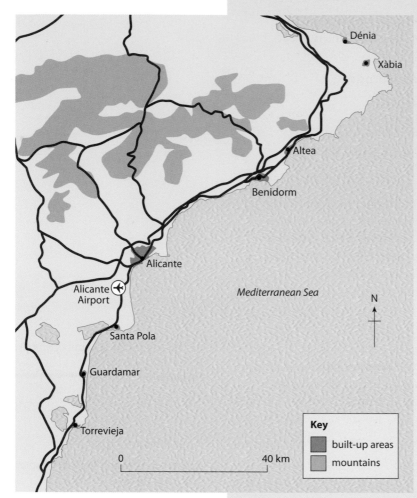

Figure 8.12: *The Costa Blanca*

tourists arrive, spending more money which creates jobs, not just in tourism but in the construction industry and for local suppliers, for example farmers.

However, such high numbers of visitors concentrated mainly from May to October, visiting a relatively small area around the Mediterranean coast, has increased pressure on what are often quite limited resources. This includes:

- high demand for water in areas where it is often a scarce resource. Tourists typically use almost twice as much water per day as local residents

- the production (and disposal) of over 50 million tons of waste each year

- increased urbanisation of coastal regions as more hotels and tourist facilities are built, damaging local ecosystems

- the increase in the number of second or holiday homes, which take up much more land than hotels but are usually only occupied for short periods

- high levels of pollution, particularly from cars, aircraft and boats.

Figure 8.13: *The beach in Benidorm*

Alicante is the capital and major city of Costa Blanca, but it is Benidorm that attracts the most visitors. Benidorm is one of the most famous modern Mediterranean holiday resorts (Figure 8.13). It has a permanent population of about 70 000, but during the peak summer season the population is more than half a million.

The development of Benidorm as a coastal resort started in 1954, when its young mayor drew up an ambitious plan of urban development. The whole project really took off in the 1960s when it became popular with British tourists on summer package holidays. Today, Benidorm's tourist season is all year round, and its attractions are now much more than sun, sea and sand. The nightlife – based on a central concentration of bars and clubs – is a strong pull, especially among younger people. Benidorm has been transformed from a small sleepy village into a modern pulsating urban area of skyscraper hotels and apartment blocks, theme parks, pubs, clubs and restaurants. It is a tourist hotspot in every sense of the word.

Protecting the coast

During the rapid expansion of the mass tourism industry, there was no overall strategy to guide the development of tourism along areas like the Costa Blanca. In 1975, however, the Mediterranean Action Plan (MAP) was set up, initially to protect the marine environment from pollution. In 1995, MAP was widened to promote the management of whole coastal regions not just the sea. Today it involves 21 countries bordering the Mediterranean. Its main objectives are:

- to bring about a massive reduction in pollution from land-based sources
- to protect marine and coastal habitats and threatened species
- to make maritime activities safer and its participants more aware of the marine environment
- to encourage integrated planning of coastal areas
- to limit and intervene promptly on oil pollution
- to promote sustainable development in the Mediterranean region.

Along the length of its coast, the Spanish government has brought in much stricter planning and building regulations. Some of the early substandard tourist developments have been demolished. Huge sums of money have been invested in improving sanitation and water supply.

Other examples of coastal management may be found in Chapter 2.5 and 2.7.

8.6 Making tourism more sustainable

Although there have been economic benefits, the rise of tourism has also, as illustrated by the Costa Blanca case study, put great pressure on popular tourist destinations. This had led to a general move to make this global industry more **sustainable** – to minimise its negative impacts. To ensure, as MAP aims, that future generations can enjoy the same amenities – clean seas and beaches, fine natural scenery and local cultures and their heritage.

Figure 8.14: *A tree canopy walkway*

An important part of this drive towards more sustainable forms of tourism has been the growth of **ecotourism**. This really lies at the opposite end of the tourism spectrum to mass tourism. It often involves small numbers of tourists visiting locations that are often relatively inaccessible (Figure 8.14).

The main features of ecotourism are:

- it is based on locations that are thought to be in some way 'special' or 'precious', because of their scenery, wildlife, remoteness or culture

- it aims to educate people and increase their understanding and appreciation of nature and local cultures

- it tries to minimise the consumption of non-renewable resources and environmental damage

- it is locally-oriented – controlled by local people, employing local people and using local produce

- its profits stay in the local community

- it is sustainable and it contributes to the conservation of biodiversity and culture.

It is definitely a much 'greener' form of tourism than mass tourism. However, both tourism extremes are challenged by the same issue, namely the burning of fossil fuels to fly and drive the often huge distances between the tourists' homes and the growing global network of tourist destinations. The issue is a particularly sensitive one in this day and age of concern about climate change and the need to reduce carbon dioxide emissions.

The issue of carbon emissions is discussed in Chapter 7.7 and 7.8, as well as in Chapter 4.7.

Case study: Bhutan – ecotourism on a national scale

There is a growing number of ecotourism ventures around the world pioneering this mode of tourism and demonstrating its benefits. Almost all of these projects are the outcome of private enterprise. To date, few governments have done much to promote ecotourism. Verbal support of the idea is often given, but little else. One notable exception is the remote Himalayan kingdom of Bhutan.

Figure 8.15: *Bhutan – an alternative tourist destination*

Bhutan's tourist attractions are spectacular mountain scenery and a rich Buddhist cultural heritage of ancient temples and shrines. These sorts of attractions are never likely to appeal to mass tourists. However, to alternative tourists, such as trekkers, birdwatchers and those with an interest in cultural history, Bhutan has a sort of utopian appeal (Figure 8.15).

Tourism began in Bhutan is 1974 when the King realised that the new hotels built to accommodate guests at his coronation could be used for tourism. Tourism, in turn, would generate foreign exchange and provide the means for the country's economic development. The decision to become involved in global tourism was a brave one. Bhutan had only just opened its doors to foreigners after 300 years of isolation. Initially, the number of foreign visits was limited to 2500 a year. That limited has since been more than doubled. All tourists must be part of an escorted group to specified locations. Tourists are required to pay a surcharge that currently stands at $240 a day per person. All tours must be organised by known, vetted companies. All developments, such as hotels, must use traditional architectural designs. The emphasis is on conservation of the natural environment and culture.

The country's attitude to tourism is ambivalent. On the one hand it is keen to reap the economic benefits, while on the other hand it views tourism as 'a serpent in paradise'. Hence a tourist strategy that tightly controls the volume and potential impacts of tourism has been developed. Bhutan's tourism ticks most of the ecotourism boxes.

Look at an atlas map of the Indian subcontinent and locate the Kingdom of Bhutan.

So far as ecotourism is concerned, 'small is beautiful'. So there is a tension between this fact and any attempt to expand ecotourism on a national scale.

8.7 Migration and population change

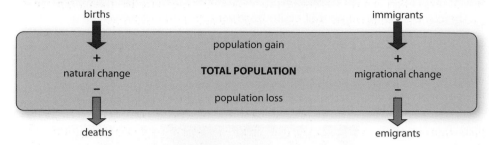

Figure 8.16: *Elements of population change*

Population change means an increase or decrease in the number of people living in an area. Population change is produced by two processes – **natural change** and **migration** (Figure 8.16). Natural change depends on the balance between **birth rates** and **death rates**. If there are more births than deaths, population will increase. If there are more deaths than births, population will decrease. **Migration** is the movement of people into and out of an area or country. If there are more immigrants (in-comers) than emigrants (out-goers), there will be **net in-migration** and a gain in population. If the situation is reversed (**net out-migration**), there will be a loss of population.

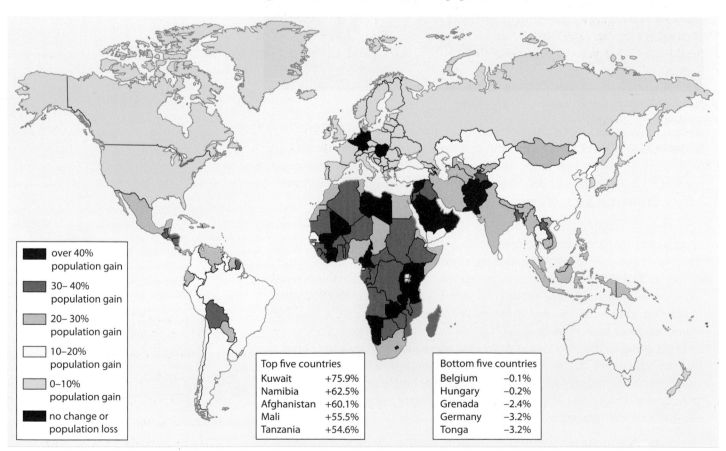

| over 40% population gain |
| 30– 40% population gain |
| 20– 30% population gain |
| 10–20% population gain |
| 0–10% population gain |
| no change or population loss |

Top five countries	
Kuwait	+75.9%
Namibia	+62.5%
Afghanistan	+60.1%
Mali	+55.5%
Tanzania	+54.6%

Bottom five countries	
Belgium	–0.1%
Hungary	–0.2%
Grenada	–2.4%
Germany	–3.2%
Tonga	–3.2%

Figure 8.17: *The global distribution of population change, 1990–2000*

The type (positive or minus) and rate of population change will depend on natural change combined with the change resulting from migration. If both are positive, then rates of population increase will be high. If both are negative, then there will be a high rate of population decrease. If one is positive and the other negative, then it is possible that they might cancel each other out – resulting in little or no change.

Figure 8.17 gives us a snapshot of global population change between 1990 and 2000. It shows some strong contrasts, as for example between the high rates of increase in Africa and the Middle East and the little or no gain in North America, Europe and Russia. In general, nearly all of the population change in Figure 8.17 is the outcome of **natural change**. The high rates of gain are produced by high birth rates and falling death rates. By comparison, the impact of net migration on the distribution of population change is very small. The only type of migration that would make an impact on Figure 8.17 would be **international migration** – migration from one country to another. **Internal migration** – the movement of people within a country – is only going to affect the distribution of population within that country.

Before going any further, we need to understand that migration is one of two different types of population movement (Figure 8.18). With **migration**, a change of address is involved. However, that change must last at least one year. Someone who works abroad for six months is not a migrant. **Circulation** is the word used to describe moves that are shorter in terms of time. The shift in location is only temporary, as with a foreign worker on a six month contract. Shopping, commuting and taking a holiday are three forms of circulation. These examples also show that we can distinguish between different types of circulation according to their purpose. We can also distinguish the different types, as in Figure 8.18, by the time involved:

- daily – shopping, commuting
- weekly – longer-distance commuting, holidaymaking
- seasonal – going away to university, UK pensioners spending the winter in Spain

Suggest reasons for the decline in the populations of the five countries listed in Figure 8.17.

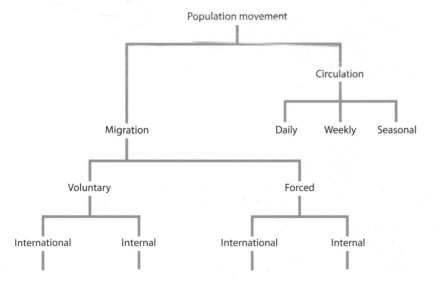

Figure 8.18: *Types of population movement*

Where on Figure 8.18 would you locate the following population movements:

- a daytrip to the seaside
- being deported
- a retirement move abroad
- counterurbanisation
- taking up an overseas work posting?

So circulation is really a vital part of everyday life. In contrast, for most people, migration means a serious change to everyday life.

8.8 Types of migration

Having made the distinction between circulation and migration, we can go further and say that there are many different types of migration. We have already made the distinction between international and internal migration. Another equally significant distinction is that between **voluntary** (by choice) and **forced** (compulsory) (Figure 8.18).

Voluntary migration

Voluntary migration is where people choose either to move inside their own country or to emigrate to another country. The normal reasons for this are economic (such as to find work or for higher wages) or for a better quality of life. In LICs, this usually means moving from rural areas into towns and cities. In HICs, there is an increasing volume of migration in the opposite direction as people move from crowded large cities into smaller urban settlements or even to the countryside. This is known as **counterurbanisation**.

Look at Figure 8.19. What comments would you make about the distribution of popular retirement areas in England and Wales?

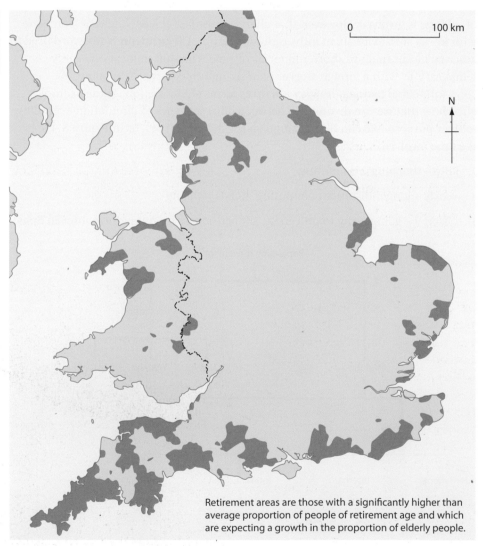

Retirement areas are those with a significantly higher than average proportion of people of retirement age and which are expecting a growth in the proportion of elderly people.

Figure 8.19: *Popular retirement areas in England and Wales*

There is no doubt that one of the outcomes of globalisation has been a huge increase in the volume of voluntary migration for largely economic reasons. One feature of much of this movement is that it is not migration in the strictest sense. Many of these so-called **economic migrants**, such as those arriving in the UK from Eastern Europe, stay for less than a year. However, some end up staying for a number of years. It would probably be best to refer to these short-stay workers and their families as temporary economic migrants.

Retirement migration

Another relatively new type of voluntary migration being experienced in the UK and other HICs is retirement migration. People are living longer. The average life expectancy for women in the UK is 81 years, and for men it is 76 years. Most people can expect to enjoy 10 or more years of retirement. With this prospect, more and more people are moving after they have retired from work. They are doing this for a number of reasons:

- it is no longer necessary to live close to what was their place of work
- to downsize into a smaller home
- to sell their home for something cheaper and use the difference in price as a pension
- to move into a quieter, calmer and more attractive environment.

Three main types of retirement migration may be recognised:

- **local** – where people stay in the same locality, but move house
- **regional** – where people stay within their country but move to what they think is a more attractive location (see Figure 8.19 for popular places in the UK)
- **international** – where people make the decision to move to another country, such as Spain, Portugal, France or even Australia.

Forced migration

Forced migration occurs when people are driven out from where they live – they have no choice. This is typically to another country, although in some instances they may only be displaced within their own country. There are many causes of forced migration. They are usually either because of a major physical disaster or for political or social reasons, including war and ethnic cleansing.

Natural hazards such as earthquakes, volcanic eruptions, violent storms, floods and droughts are all physical reasons for having to move. In most cases, the victims and survivors of such

Figure 8.20: *People forced out of Gisenyi, Rwanda, by ethnic cleansing*

disasters will move back home when it is safe to do so or when their homes and jobs are available again.

The biggest causes of forced migration result from the actions of people, especially war and persecution. Historically, this includes large-scale migrations such as that of the Jews as they fled from the Germans and Russians during the Second World War (1939–1945) or the Palestinian Arabs displaced by the creation of the Jewish state of Israel in 1948.

Many recent wars have in fact been civil wars – factions within a country fighting one another. In some cases, this has been in an effort to force out entire ethnic groups or communities – a process known as **ethnic cleansing**. This was the case when the member states of the former Yugoslavia erupted into civil war, and in Rwanda, where the Hutus attempted to remove the Tutsis, leading to 800 000 deaths and 2 million displaced people.

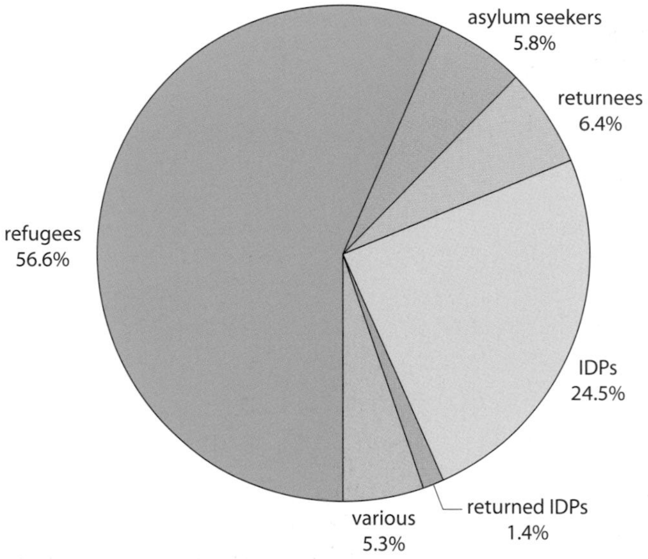

> Explain what is meant by 'ethnic cleansing' and give some other examples.

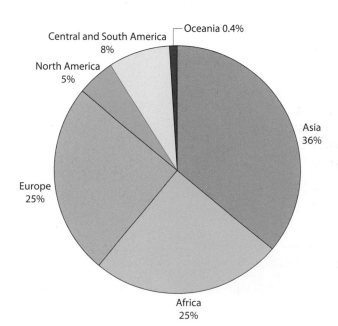

Figure 8.21: *Persons of concern, 2003*

Figure 8.22: *Persons of concern, by region, 2003*

Refugees

The United Nations High Commission for Refugees (UNHCR) has responsibility of all those people who are forced to migrate. These people are collectively referred to as 'persons of concern' to the UNHCR. Four different categories of person are recognised:

- **refugee** – a person who, owing to a well-founded fear of being persecuted (on account of their race, religion, political opinion or social group), lives outside their country of nationality. They are reluctant or refuse to return

- **asylum seeker** – a person who has left their country of origin, has applied for recognition as a refugee in another country, and is awaiting a decision on their application

- **internally-displaced person (IDP)** – a person forced to flee their home for the same reasons as a refugee or in order to escape natural disasters, but they do not cross an internationally recognised border

- **returnee** – a refugee or asylum seeker who has voluntarily returned to their own country or an IDP who has returned home.

In 2003, UNHCR recognised that there over 17 million persons of concern in the world. Figure 8.21 shows how that global figure was made up. Over half were refugees and one quarter were IDPs. There were around 1 million asylum seekers and almost the same number of returnees.

Figure 8.22 looks at the global distribution of persons of concern. Overall, one-third of them are in Asia, with a quarter in Africa and in Europe. The high value for Asia is the outcome of two things: i) the long-running troubles in Afghanistan, unrest in Pakistan and the conflict between rival groups in Iraq, and ii) Asia's huge population.

Push-pull factors

The decision to migrate is usually the outcome of two forces known as the **push-pull mechanism**. Figure 8.23 shows that the push force occurs in the potential migrant's home location. It is something that pushes the person to move away. In the case of forced migration, the push factor is paramount. The pull force is something that attracts that same person to a particular destination. Very often the pull factor is the mirror image of the push factor. For example, being out of work gets the person thinking that they must move to find a job. They hear that there is a labour shortage in a particular city or country. Thus the combination of the push and pull factors persuades the person to migrate. In the case of much voluntary migration, the pull factor is stronger in the sense that it often strongly influences the eventual migration destination.

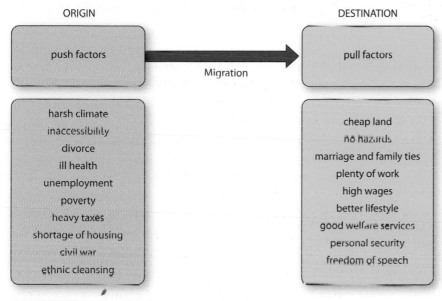

Figure 8.23: *The push-pull mechanism*

Are you able to add anything more to the lists of push and pull factors in Figure 8.23?

The growing volume of migration in today's world in not just a reaction to push and pull factors becoming stronger. There are three other factors that are important in the context of globalisation (see Part **8.1**).

- **Modern communications** – thanks to today's mass media, particularly the internet, would-be migrants are able to 'see' and 'feel' distant places without taking a step outside their home. The amount and reliability of information about places is much greater. With the risk of moving to an unknown and unwelcoming destination reduced, people are more willing to migrate.

- **Modern transport** – once the decision has been taken to move to a particular destination, the migrant is able to take advantage of modern transport. This can move them there quickly and cheaply.

- **Relaxing national boundaries** – many countries are willing to relax their boundaries, particularly if it is in their economic interests, for example, to admit skilled migrant workers.

8.9 Managing migration

One of the many responsibilities of any democratic government is monitoring and managing its population. A key issue is the rate of population change. Is is too fast or too slow? Whichever the answer, what needs to be done in terms of i) natural change and ii) net migration? Rates of natural change can be influenced by promoting birth control or encouraging parents to have more children. Governments are largely able to control the numbers of people crossing their borders. A government can encourage and discourage would-be migrants. The following case study illustrates how successive UK governments have managed migration in a way to meet its changing demographic and economic needs.

Case study: The UK's management of international migration since 1950

It was soon after the end of the Second World War that the UK opened its doors to immigrants mainly from the Caribbean and from what had been the Indian Empire (India, Pakistan and Bangladesh). The UK had a serious shortage of labour as a result of so many of its men being killed or badly injured in the war. The post-war reconstruction of the country to repair the massive amount of bomb damage also created a huge demand for labour.

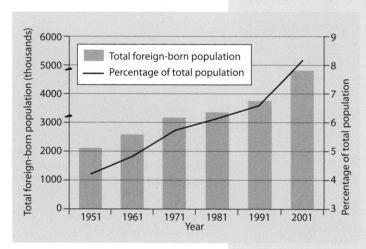

Figure 8.24: *UK residents born abroad, 1951–2001*

Immigration was encouraged by an Act of Parliament which gave all Commonwealth (ex-colonial) citizens free entry into the UK. By 1971 there were over one million immigrants from Commonwealth countries in the UK, and at this time the government decided that the country had more than enough labour. So controls were introduced to reduce the number of migrant arrivals.

Figure 8.24 shows the number of UK residents who were born abroad. Despite the controls on immigration, clearly the number has been steadily rising. So too has the percentage of the UK population that they represent.

In the 1990s, the UK once again found itself short of labour. This happened to coincide with the collapse of communism in Eastern Europe. This released huge numbers of people 'hungry' for work and a decent wage. The influx of workers into the UK was given a boost in 2004 when the East European states of the Czech Republic, Estonia, Hungary, Latvia, Lithuania, Poland, Slovakia and Slovenia joined the EU. Figure 8.25 shows the push-pull factors. In most cases, these economic migrants intended to stay only until they felt that they had made enough money to take home. Few intended to stay permanently. Figure 8.26 shows that well over half the migrants came from Poland, the largest of the new member states. The vast majority of migrants are young and single, with over 80% of them aged 18 to 34.

Some UK newspapers (and citizens) took and continue to take a very negative attitude towards these economic migrants. They are accused of depriving UK workers of jobs and taking advantage of the UK's benefits system. Figure 8.25 shows these accusations as two of a number of issues related to these

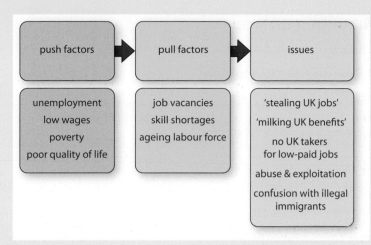

Figure 8.25: *East European workers – push-pull factors and issues*

economic migrants. However, the critics choose to ignore four facts:

- the migrants contribute to the UK's economy by the taxes they pay

- the jobs that many of them take up are mainly low-paid jobs in factories, hotels, farming and care homes. Such jobs are often avoided by UK workers

- the migrants have a strong work ethic, which can directly benefit employers. Unfortunately, there are employers who unfairly exploit these qualities

- less than 5% of them receive any sort of state benefit.

During the 2007–2009 recession, job opportunities dried up and increasing numbers of East European workers started to return home. For many of them the excitement of living in Western Europe had worn off.

As one migration issue recedes, so another one enters the frame. There is growing concern among some people about the overall ethnic mix in the UK. At present, the white component is 92 per cent, but that is declining. Looking for some sort of scapegoat, they direct attention to the level of immigration from Commonwealth countries and the growing volume of illegal immigration. In fact, legal immigration is quite tightly controlled by the UK Border Agency. The real cause of the slowly changing ethnic mix is that birth rates are significantly higher among the ethnic minorities. It is natural change that is shifting the ethnic balance – not immigration. Another responsibility of government could be to ensure that the public are properly informed about what is happening to the population.

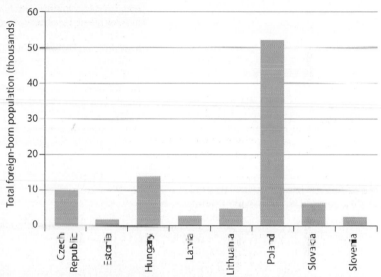

Figure 8.26: *The country of origin of UK's East European economic migrants*

The high figure for Poland simply reflects the fact that it has by far the largest total population. It would be of interest to express the migrant totals in Figure 8.26 as percentages of their total populations.

(handwritten) for increase of ethnic mix really. its down to high birth rates

End of chapter checkout

Checklists

Now you have read the chapter, you should know:

- ✓ what the global economy is
- ✓ the factors that have encouraged the growth of the global economy
- ✓ about the global shift in manufacturing
- ✓ the factors that have encouraged this shift
- ✓ the part that TNCs have played in this shift and the growth of the global economy
- ✓ about the growth of global tourism and the causes of that growth
- ✓ the impacts that mass tourism is having on the environment, economy and people of destination areas
- ✓ how tourism might be made more sustainable
- ✓ that migration is a component of population change
- ✓ there are different types of migration
- ✓ that most migrations are caused by push and pull factors
- ✓ why it is necessary to manage migration flows
- ✓ how these flows might controlled

Make sure you understand these key terms:

Asylum seeker: a person who tries to enter a country by claiming to be a victim of persecution or hardship.

Commodity chain: a sequence of stages in which companies to exploit resources, transform them into goods or commodities and, then, distribute them to consumers. It is pathway along which a good travels from producers to consumers.

Economic migrant: a person seeking work in another country.

Ecotourism: a form of tourism that tries to minimise its environmental impacts by using local resources and labour and by keeping profits within the local area.

Foreign direct investment: in which a company or government becomes involved in the economy of another country.

Economic globalisation: the increasing integration of national markets for goods and services into a single global market.

Global shift: the present movement of economic production to new and cheaper locations in the world.

Information technology: the use of computers and software to manage and process information.

Mass tourism: popular, large-scale tourism of the type pioneered in southern Europe, the Caribbean, and North America in the 1960s and 1970s.

Net migration: the balance between the number of people entering and the number leaving a country or region.

Package holiday: a holiday in which travel and accommodation are put together by a tour operator and sold as a relatively cheap package.

Push-pull factors: the things that encourage people to migrate from one area to another. The negatives in the area of departure (push) are balanced against the positives of the destination (pull).

Refugee: a person whose reasons for migrating are due to fear of persecution or death.

Tourism: any leisure time or recreational activity which involves at least one night's absence from the normal place of residence.

Transnational corporation (TNC): a large company operating in a number of countries and often involved in a variety of economic activities.

See the Glossary in the ActiveBook for more definitions.

Questions

Try testing yourself with these questions:

1 What is meant by:
   - globalisation
   - global economy
   - interdependence
   - global village?

2 Name the five flows involved in the growth of the global economy.

3 Use the words from the box to complete the paragraph below.

   | an export boom | factories | GNI | ICT services |
   | production | imports | rapidly |

   Many British companies now locate part of their _____ and _____ work abroad. The _____ of China and the offices of India threaten some British workers' jobs. These shifts are helping to cause _____ in China and India where GNIs are rising _____.

4 a) What is meant by 'deindustrialisation'?
   b) Describe the global shift in manufacturing.

5 Many TNCs have set up factories in LICs. State three advantages they gain from doing this.

6 a) State two characteristics of transnational companies (TNCs).
   b) Name three TNCs and describe their main business.

7 TNCs are said to operate globally. Give as many examples as you can to show how they operate in a global way.

8 Give reasons for the success of Tesco as a retailer.

9 Study Table 8.2. Which do you think is a) the greatest cost and b) the [   ]t benefit? Give your reasons.

   [   ] have tourist numbers in the world risen so quickly?

   [   ] is tourism such an important global activity?

11 a) What is ecotourism?
    b) Describe its main advantages.

12 a) What is a 'package holiday'?
    b) Why do you think it is such a popular form of tourism?

13 With reference to examples, describe the economic benefits of mass tourism.

14 Give some examples of the socio-cultural impacts of tourism.

15 Giving examples, describe the environmental impacts of tourism.

16 What is meant by 'making tourism more sustainable'?

17 Write an account of tourism in Bhutan pointing out its strengths and weaknesses.

18 What is the difference between:
    - migration change and natural change
    - migration and circulation
    - international migration and internal migration?

19 Explain why it is international and not internal migration that has an impact on Figure 8.17.

20 a) Give three examples of voluntary internal migration.
    b) Identify the push and pull factors in each of your three examples.

21 Using Figure 8.19, identify the popular retirement areas in England and Wales.

22 a) What is the difference between a refugee and an asylum seeker?
    b) Give some examples of the 'push' factors giving rise to internally-displaced people (IDPs)

23 Describe three factors that are increasing the volume of global migration.

24 Why do some governments try to manage international migration?

25 a) What is the strongest 'pull' factor attracting migrants to the UK?
    b) Why is there some opposition to the arrival of immigrants?

Chapter 9: Development and human welfare

9.1 The nature of development

Definitions

Development is a process of change that affects countries and their peoples. There are similarities between development and the growing-up of people. Both processes are about maturing and becoming stronger and more independent.

Development means making progress in a number of different fields. Let us call these fields the 'strands' of development. By far the most important strand is an economic one – **economic development**. This provides the power that drives progress in all the other development strands. Economic development comes from the exploitation of resources – minerals, energy, climate and soils. It also requires capital, technology and, above all else, enterprising people and good government. The other strands of development fall into five groups. Table 9.1 gives more details.

Group	Development strand
Economic	Employment – security and levels of pay
	Standard of living – raising the minimum
	Productivity – efficient use of capital and labour
Demographic	Life expectancy – rising with better health, hygiene and diet
	Birth control – right to choose family size
	Mobility – freedom to migrate
Social	Welfare – access to services
	Equal opportunities – no gender or age discrimination
	Leisure – restricted working hours
Cultural	Education – compulsory education for all
	Heritage – respect and conserve
	Ethnicity – mutual respect
Political	Right to vote
	Democratic government – regular fair elections
	Civil and religious liberties
Environmental	Pollution – effective controls
	Conservation – biodiversity and non-renewable resources

Table 9.1: Some strands of development

Advances in all or most of these strands add up to development. It might be a rising standard of living, greater life expectancy, more leisure and education, democratic government and more respect for the environment.

An improving **quality of life** might be thought of as yet another component of development. As you will see in Part **9.2**, when we explore what the term means, quality of life in fact takes into account a number of different development strands. For the moment, however, let us concentrate on the development process and economic development in particular.

Introduction

This chapter is about two important aspects of the modern world – development and the welfare of people. Development is certainly bringing change to virtually all parts of the world. However, its impact varies between countries and within countries. 'Gaps' exist between rich and poor, between successful and not-so-successful. They are especially reflected in the quality of life enjoyed by people. Can anything be done to reduce these 'gaps'? Part of the chapter also looks at an important issue in parts of the developing world – the rapid rate of population growth. This has a number of unwanted consequences.

Give one reason why economic development provides the power that drives development as a whole.

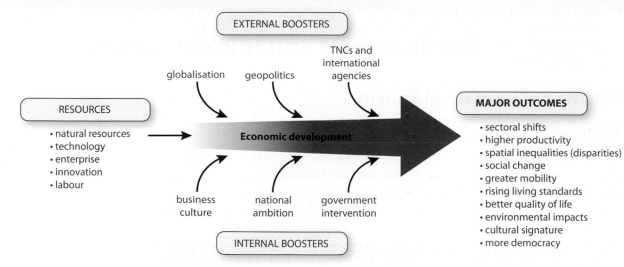

Figure 9.1: *Factors generating economic development*

Economic development

Figure 9.1 shows how the all-important process of economic development works. There are three main forces involved:

- **resources** – these get the process moving in the first place. There are natural resources (such as soils, climate and minerals) and human resources (such as enterprising business people, capital, labour and technology). The latter exploit the former and so provide the basic 'fuel' that drives economic development

- **internal boosters** – these come from within the individual country and include government intervention, national ambition, the growth of a business culture, etc

- **external boosters** – these come from outside the individual country and include the growth of the **global economy** (**globalisation**) that creates opportunities for countries to prosper. Others include key players in the global economy such as the transnational corporations (TNCs) and various international agencies of the United Nations.

Figure 9.1 shows also the outcomes of economic development. The list shows what are widely recognised as some of the signs of development.

For more information about the growth of the global economy and globalisation, see Chapter 8.1.

9.2 Development indicators

Since development is a very important global process, is it possible to measure it? Can we measure it in a way that will allow us to compare countries in terms of their level of development? Given what we now know, namely that development is a multi-strand process, it looks as if measuring it is not going to be easy. Do we have to measure all the strands separately or are some strands more important and better indicators than others? If so, which are they?

Given that it drives development as whole, our search for measures should start with economic development. There are two widely-used indicators of the strength of a country's economy:

- **gross domestic product (GDP)** – the total value of a country's economic production over the course of a year

- **gross national income (GNI)** – this differs from GDP in that it includes the total value of a country's economic production plus net income received from abroad. It too is calculated for a year. It used to be known as **gross national product (GNP)**.

These two indicators are not of much use because they do not take into account that countries vary enormously in size. As Table 9.2 shows, a large country is likely to have a large GDP. However, if we divide the GDP or GNI values by the number of people in a country, then we create an even playing-field. We arrive at two measures that allow us to compare countries in a sound way. These indicators are known as **per capita GDP** (or **GDP per head of population**) and **per capita GNI** (or **GNI per head of population**). Table 9.2 illustrates that two large countries can show very different per capita GDP values. The same also applies to small countries.

Country	Area (km²)	GDP ($US)	per capita GDP ($US)
China	9.6 million	7.9 trillion	6000
USA	9.8 million	14.4 trillion	47 500
Haiti	0.28 million	0.01 trillion	1300
UK	0.24 million	2.2 trillion	36 700

Table 9.2: Some international comparisons – area, GDP and per capita GDP

What conclusions do you draw from Table 9.2?

Per capita GNI is the most widely used indicator of economic development. The World Bank bases its classification of countries on it (see Part **9.4**). But there are other measures that we need to know about. There is one in particular – it is known as **sector shift**.

As the economy of a country develops not only do GDP and GNI become larger, but exactly how that economic wealth is produced changes. In the early stages of economic development, it is the primary sector that generates the most growth. Agriculture, fishing, forestry and mining are the mainstays of this economy. Gradually, however, the secondary sector becomes the main generator of economic growth. Raw materials are manufactured into goods that have a higher value than food, fish or minerals. However, as personal wealth increases, the tertiary or service sector takes over as the most important part of the economy. In most HICs, a new sector is beginning to appear. This is the quaternary sector which is based on information and communications technology (ICT) and research and development (R & D). Although growing, this sector is still greatly overshadowed by the tertiary sector as a source of economic growth.

For more information about sector shifts, see Chapter 4.1 and 4.2.

From this typical sector shift, it is possible to assess a country's level of economic development. It is done so by measuring the relative importance of the three or four sectors. Figure 9.2 illustrates this. Ethiopia is a country that has made little progress yet in terms of economic development – note that the primary sector is the largest. China is a country experiencing rapid economic development. Although the tertiary sector appears larger than the secondary sector, it is the secondary sector that manufactures the goods being sold across the world. These sales are the major source of China's economic growth. The UK is more economically advanced than China – the economy is dominated by the tertiary sector. Look how small the primary sector is.

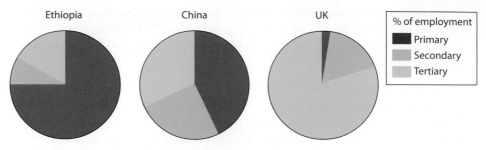

Figure 9.2: *The economic sectors of three countries (% of employment)*

Compare Figure 9.2 with Figure 4.4 (page 95). In the former, the piecharts have been drawn based on '% of employment'. In the latter, '% of GDP' has been used.

Calculating the relative importance of the economic sectors can be based on two different measures. It is based either on the number of people employed in each sector, or how much each sector contributes to GDP. In both cases, the sector values will be percentages. The pie charts in Figure 9.2 are based on the percentage of the total workforce employed in each sector (see Figure 4.4 on page 95).

Other possible indicators of development include:

- **energy consumption** – the greater the economic development of a country, the greater its consumption of energy for such things as manufacturing and transport. Energy consumption is also increased, for example, by the use of electricity in the home and to power many services (such as air conditioning in shops and offices, street lighting and telecommunications)

- **population rates** – with development, birth rates fall as a result of increased birth control. Death and infant mortality rates fall as a result of advances in medicine and healthcare, and of people living in better housing and having a better diet. As a consequence of this 'death control', life expectancy increases.

9.3 Quality of life and its indicators

Quality of life is a term that crops up frequently in studies of development. An improving quality of life is an important part of development. It is also a major element in **human welfare** – the general state or condition of a population or society as a whole. Indeed, just as economic development lies at the heart of development, so is quality of life a vital part of human welfare.

Quality of life is a term commonly used in everyday life. Often we might use alternatives, such as **well-being** and **standard of living**, assuming that they mean the same. Most of us have some sense of what these three terms mean. However, we would find it difficult to define the terms exactly and any differences between them.

In this chapter we will use the term quality of life. The difficulty with this particular term lies in the fact that it is not totally about material things, such as housing and income. It is also about how people feel about their lives. Are they satisfied with it? Do they feel secure and safe? Do they enjoy good health? Are they happy? These sorts of question mean that quality of life has a psychological aspect (Figure 9.3).

This psychological aspect is only one of four making up quality of life. All four are interrelated. For example, look at the 'Economic' box in Figure 9.3. Whether or not we feel secure will hinge on whether we have a secure job and a regular income. These in turn will affect our level of affluence and our standard of living. In the 'Physical' box, diet and housing can affect our state of health. In the 'Social' box a

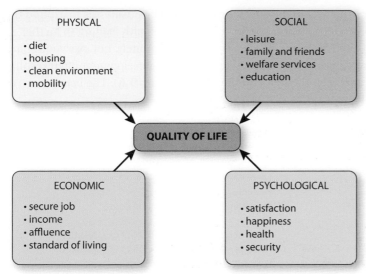

Figure 9.3: *Some components of quality of life*

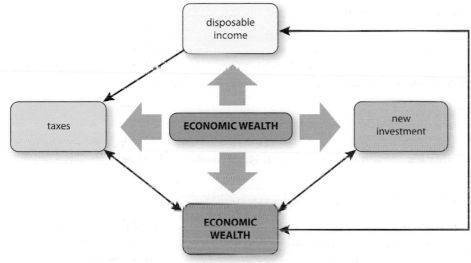

Figure 9.4: *The cycle of wealth*

What is the link between disposable income and taxes shown in Figure 9.4?

good education will play a considerable part in securing a secure job and enjoying a good standard of living.

You should have spotted that quality of life is made up of many of the same strands as development. Indeed, the two processes are closely connected. Compare Table 9.1 on page 239 with Figure 9.3. The link is a simple one. Economic development involves businesses of all sorts creating wealth. It creates a wealth cycle (Figure 9.4). Part of the wealth goes to the government in the form of taxes. If there is good governance, this money will be spent by the government on things like roads, defence, education and healthcare.

As with development, it is the economic aspect that it the most critical aspect of quality of life. Yes, we do live in a material world, and yes, money talks...

Another part of the wealth trickles down to people in the form of work and wages. This gives people **disposable income** that they can spend on a whole range of things, from shops to restaurants, holidays to hairdressers. Workers and their families should also benefit from the basic services funded by the government, such as schools and doctors. In these two ways, the quality of life improves for people. However, workers also pay taxes which help to pay from those services.

A third part of that wealth may well be reinvested by businesses to expand their operations (Figure 9.4). This starts a new cycle of wealth leading to further improvements in the general quality of life. Unfortunately, not everyone shares in the wealth and improving quality of life. Economic development often results in a widening gap between the rich and the poor (see Part **9.6**). The benefits are not shared equally.

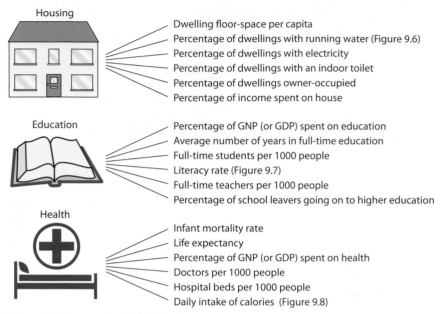

Figure 9.5: *Some quality of life indicators*

Look back at Figure 9.3 (page 243) and identify any other components of quality of life that you think can be measured fairly accurately.

Since quality of life, like development, is made up of many strands, we come up against the same questions as in Part **9.2**. How do we measure it? What indicators should we use? Figure 9.5 takes just three strands – housing, education and health. For each, it shows six indicators or possible measures. The three world maps (Figures 9.6, 9.7 and 9.8) are each based on one measure for each of those strands – dwellings with access to safe drinking water, literacy rate and daily food consumption.

Housing

Shelter is one of the very basic human needs. Housing conditions will directly affect quality of life, particular if all the basic services (clean or safe water, sewage disposal and electricity) are available and the density of occupation (i.e. the number of people per unit of housing space) is relatively low.

Figure 9.6 shows that over much of Africa and in scattered parts of South-east Asia less than 30% of the population have access to safe drinking water. It is also worth noting that there are some LICs where access is over 90%, as for example in Panama, Libya, Botswana and Iran.

Literacy

Education is thought to be the key to a better quality of life. It opens the door to regular employment. This means economic security as well as **disposable income** to buy those things that improve the quality of life. The percentage of a population able to read and write is a good indicator of the general level of education in a country.

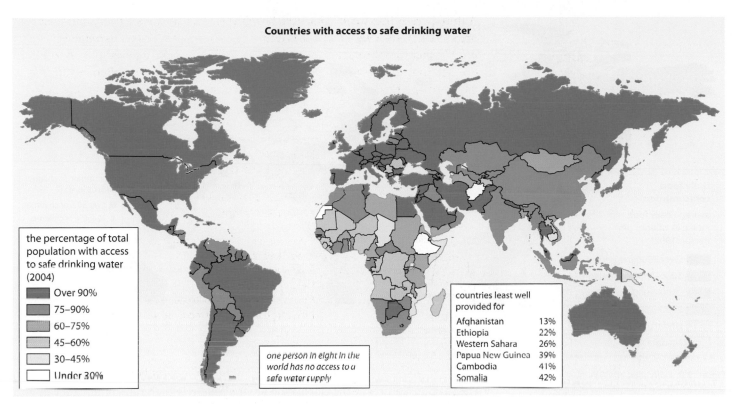

Figure 9.6: *Access to safe water*

Figure 9.7 looks at education from the negative viewpoint of illiteracy, i.e. the percentage of the adult population unable to read and write.

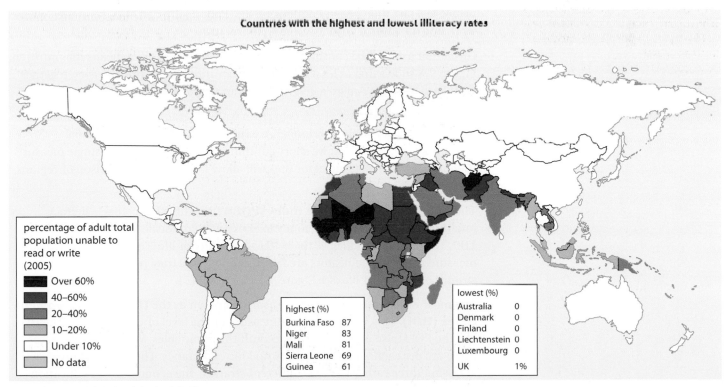

Figure 9.7: *The global distribution of illiteracy*

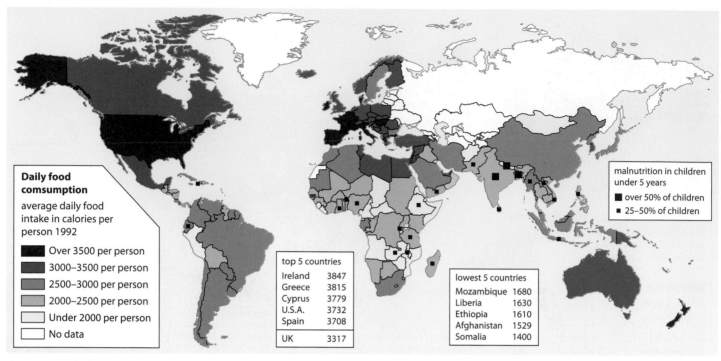

Figure 9.8: *Daily food consumption*

In which parts of the world is malnutrition a serious problem? Look at Figure 9.8 for the answer.

The striking features of the global map are the relatively high rates of illiteracy in Africa and South and South-east Asia. The middle of South America also stands out.

Daily food consumption

An adequate diet is important as far as health is concerned. Poor health, such as that resulting from not eating properly, can have a strong negative impact on how people feel and their general outlook on life. Poor health can also mean time off work and an adverse impact on economic security.

Given that a daily food consumption below 2000 calories often means malnutrition, Figure 9.8 shows that at least nine African countries fall in this category, together with Peru in South America and Afghanistan, Nepal and Mongolia in Asia.

Are these three indicators (access to clean water, literacy rates and daily food consumption) of equal importance? Are they all showing the same global distribution patterns? Can we short-cut things and come up with a single measure that provides a reliable indicator that will allow for a sound comparison of regions and countries?

The **Physical Quality of Life Index (PQLI)** uses three indicators – literacy, infant mortality and life expectancy to arrive at a final scale that runs from 0 to 100. The higher the index is, the better the quality of life. The limitation of this measure is that the indicators are few in number and they relate to only two strands of quality of life (see Figure 9.3 on page 243).

The most widely used aggregate measure is known as the **Human Development Index (HDI)**. This is also used as a measure of the level of development. The HDI, like the PQLI, also only takes into account three variables. With the HDI, these three are per capita income, literacy and life expectancy. Thus the HDI involves assessing three rather than two different strands: one economic, one education and one health. The calculation of the Index is a little complicated, but it assumes

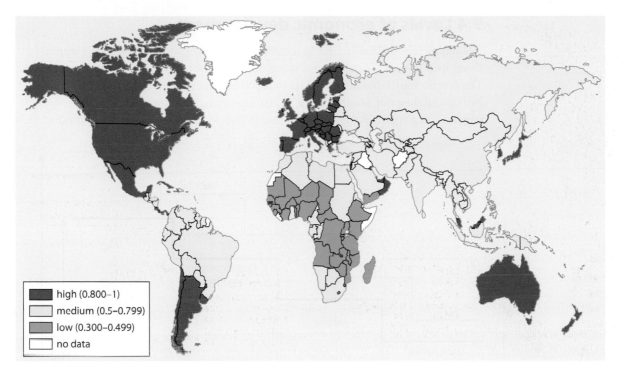

Figure 9.9: *The Human Development Index (HDI)*

key:
- high (0.800–1)
- medium (0.5–0.799)
- low (0.300–0.499)
- no data

that the three variables are of equal importance. The HDI is the average of the scores achieved by a country in those three fields. HDI scores range from 0 to 1. The higher the HDI is, the higher the level of development and the better the quality of life.

Figure 9.9 shows how HDI values vary at a global scale. The eye is drawn to the parts of the world where HDI values are high – North America, southern South America, Europe and Australasia. Can you identify and name the scattered countries in Asia? At the other end of the HDI scale, it is clear that Africa is the main focus of low and unsatisfactory values.

> Look at Figure 9.9. In which parts of the world are 'medium' HDI values encountered?

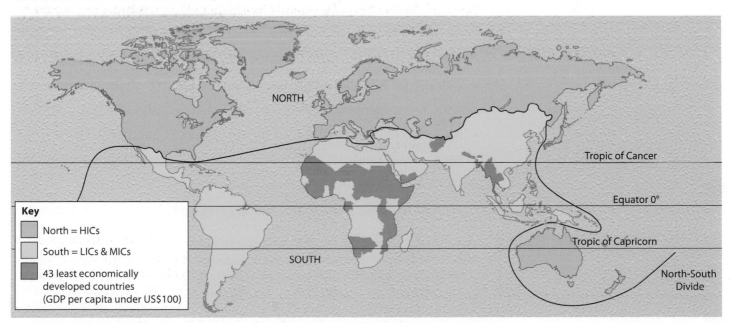

Key
- North = HICs
- South = LICs & MICs
- 43 least economically developed countries (GDP per capita under US$100)

NORTH

SOUTH

Tropic of Cancer

Equator 0°

Tropic of Capricorn

North-South Divide

Figure 9.10: *The North-South Divide*

9.4 Levels of economic development

It is often claimed that we live in a world of two halves – the Developing and the Developed Worlds. These two parts are also referred to as the North and the South. The North-South divide line is said to represent the boundary between the rich North and the poor South (Figure 9.10). However, is this simple two-fold subdivision a true reflection of the state of the development in today's world?

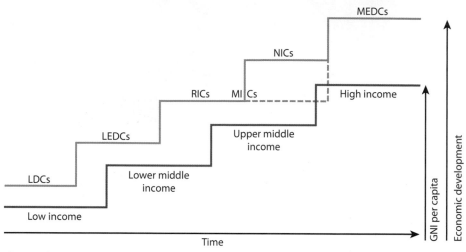

Figure 9.11: *Two versions of the economic development staircase.*

In Figure 9.11, two different versions of the development staircase are shown. They have simply been drawn one above the other to show how their steps compare.

Looking more closely at each of the two halves, it is clear that the countries within them vary in terms of their level of economic development. Altogether these different levels might be imagined as making up a flight of steps rising from the least developed to the most developed countries (Figure 9.11). As they develop, countries climb up that stairway but at very different speeds. At any one time, there are clusters of countries sharing the same step.

The World Bank recognises four development steps (low income, lower middle income, upper middle income and high income). The Edexcel Geography specification amalgamates the two middle-income groupings and so arrives at three-step stairway: low-income (LIC), middle-income (MIC) and high-income (HIC).

Other names often given to these steps or different levels of development are:

- **LDCs** – least developed countries (e.g. Ethiopia, Haiti, North Korea)

- **LEDCs** – less economically-developed countries (e.g. Cuba, Morocco, Vietnam)

- **RICs** – recently industrialising countries (e.g. Brazil, China, India, Mexico)

- **NICs** – newly industrialised countries (e.g. South Korea, Malaysia, Taiwan)

- **MEDCs** – more economically developed countries (Japan, UK, USA)

Figure 9.12 shows the global picture with different levels of economic development as defined by the World Bank. The four groupings are based on per capita GNI, one of the economic development indicators discussed in Part **9.1**. Looking closely at the map, the HICs are clearly located in North America, Western Europe and Australasia, plus Japan and South Korea. In contrast, the LICs are mainly concentrated in Africa and South Asia. Interestingly, despite its recent industrialisation, India is still

The World Bank's 4-step development staircase is more widely used these days than the 5-step one that is popular with some geographers and economists.

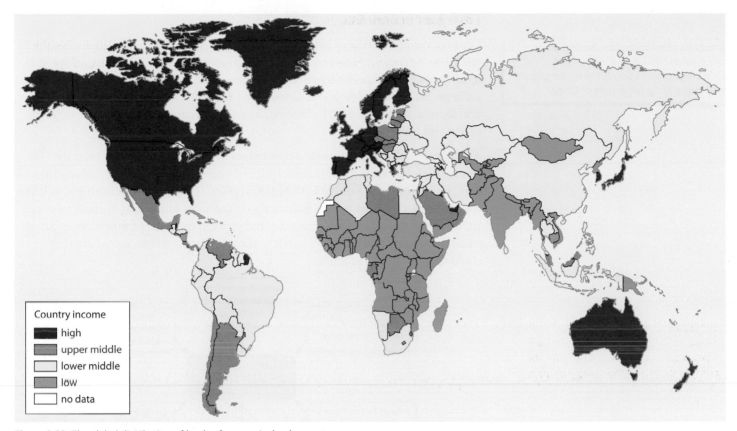

Figure 9.12: *The global distribution of levels of economic development*

classified by the World Bank as a LIC. South America, the Middle East and much of Asia are home to most of the MICs. It is perhaps more accurate to think of the world as divided into three thirds rather than two halves.

Most people would agree that the World Bank's map (Figure 9.12) gives the most accurate picture of economic development across the world. Equally, the map based on the Human Development Index (HDI) probably gives the most reliable picture of the worldwide state of quality of life (see Figure 9.9 on page 247).

What is encouraging about this three-level situation is that it suggests that the world is no longer divided into rich and poor countries. Some of these once poor countries are experiencing significant and relatively fast economic development. They are moving up the development staircase.

9.5 The changing patterns of global development

In part **9.4** the important point was made that today's world is a dynamic place when it comes to economic development. There are certainly some countries moving up the development stairway at quite a pace, namely some of the so-called MICs (see Figure 9.13). Let us take a closer look at this positive change in the global pattern of development.

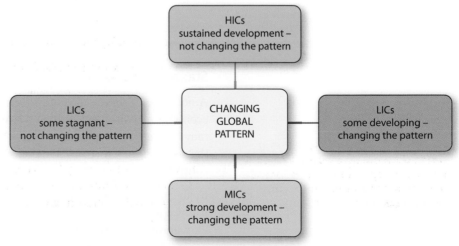

Figure 9.13: *The changing global pattern of development*

Emergent economies

In today's world, there are at least two different types of MIC. First, there are the NICs, like Taiwan and Malaysia, in which economic development took off some 30 to 40 years ago. Secondly, there are the RICs, which started moving up the staircase much later, say 10 to 20 years ago. Early RICs were Thailand, Indonesia and Mexico; more recent RICs include the so-called emergent economies – Brazil, China and India.

A major force driving economic development in these countries has been the so-called **global shift** in manufacturing (see pages 103 to 104). Manufacturing companies originally located in the UK and other HICs have been attracted to these countries by a number of pull factors. By far the most important of these has been the huge difference in labour costs. Labour costs in the emergent economies are a small fraction of what they are in HICs. Manufacturers will locate where they stand to make the most profit.

The NICs like Taiwan and Malaysia are often referred to as the 'Asian Tigers'. Other 'tigers' were South Korea, Singapore and Hong Kong (now part of China).

Figure 9.14: *Factors behind China's industrial explosion*

The outright winner so far in this global shift in manufacturing has been China. It is now ranked as the third most important manufacturing country in the world. Figure 9.14 gives the main reasons for its industrial explosion. Although China has a lot of heavy industry (e.g. iron and steel, chemicals), it is making a wide range of consumer goods that are now marketed worldwide. It is not surprising that the 'Made in China' label dominates world markets. India too is benefiting from the global shift in manufacturing. It also hosts call centres that provide well-paid jobs for well-educated, English-speaking workers.

It is important that you understand how each of the six factors in Figure 9.14 contributes to the Chinese industrial 'explosion'.

The rise of the emergent economies is just one feature of the changing global pattern of development. There are three other significant features.

Stagnant economies

Among the LICs there are countries missing out on the opportunities created by economic globalisation. Although it may not be immediately obvious, these countries may in a sense be contributing to the changing pattern of global development – i.e. to the widening of the so-called **development gap** (see Part **9.6**). Why are these countries not doing better?

In all cases, countries are being held back by some sort of obstacle. They become trapped in a cycle of economic stagnation. In Myanmar, North Korea and Zimbabwe the obstacle is misrule by undemocratic or corrupt government. In

Angola, Somalia and the Sudan it is civil war. The break-up of the former Soviet Union in the early 1990s put the brake, albeit temporarily, on development in former member countries like Romania, the Ukraine and Uzbekistan. In these three instances, the obstacles are political. In other countries, the obstacles are more economic. The obstacles include: a lack of natural resources or energy supplies, a lack of educated or trained labour, and a lack of capital, technology and enterprise. The obstacles are what is not there! Countries like Ethiopia and Malawi would fall in this category.

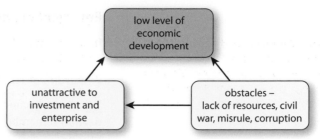

Figure 9.15: *The triangle of economic stagnation*

Awakening economies

Whilst there are many LICs in the 'stagnant' category, a few are just beginning to move slowly up the development staircase. In most cases, economic development is being triggered by the exploitation of resources such as oil (e.g. as in Nigeria), minerals (e.g. as in Botswana) and timber (e.g. as in Guyana).

The sad fact of the matter is that unless a country has a resource or resources that are in demand elsewhere, the chances of its economy be awakened are very small.

Advanced economies

You may be thinking that these HICs might not be doing too well, particularly as they have lost so much of their manufacturing. Despite this loss, the process of economic development continues based on new high-tech industries, an expanding range of services and a relatively new quaternary sector.

9.6 Development gaps

Given the various development indicators, such as per capita GNI and the HDI, it is clear that there is a huge difference between the highest and lowest values. This difference is referred to as the **development gap**. The question here is this – what have the changes that we noted in Part **9.5** in different countries done to this gap? Is it becoming wider or narrower?

Figure 9.16: *Two photos illustrating the global development gap*

Many claims are made that the development gap is widening. The poorer nations are believed to be falling further behind the rich ones. Unfortunately, it is extremely difficult to to prove or disprove this claim of a widening gap. The problem is that there is no way of accurately measuring change in the 'width' of the gap. On the one hand, in terms of per capita GNI, the difference between the richest nations and the poorest is increasing. On the other hand, the gap between the highest and lowest HDI values is decreasing.

If we look back at Figure 9.13 on page 249, the situation was one in which we have:

- a group of LICs that have made little or no progress at the bottom of the stairway

- a group of HICs that continue to enjoy economic development.

We can only conclude that the development gap is widening. However, what we need to remember is that this widening gap is being filled with an increasing number of countries which are beginning to enjoy economic growth.

Development gaps within countries

Not only do development levels vary between countries, they also vary within countries. Although development indicators are very useful to allow comparisons of development levels between countries, it is very important to remember that these are 'average' figures. Country data does not show the variations that occur within countries and between regions. Rarely is economic wealth shared equally between all the regions of a single country. Very often economic development and wealth are concentrated in just one favoured region of a country, which is referred to as the **core**. This concentration leaves other regions poor by comparison. These poorer regions are referred to as the **periphery**.

Case study: Italy

Italy is a country with a North–South divide (Figure 9.17). The north, especially the Po basin, is the core region and is wealthier and more developed than the south. The south of Italy is the periphery. Table 9.3 gives some indications of the difference between the two parts.

	North Italy	South Italy
Area (%)	60	40
Population (%)	63	37
Birth rate (per 1000)	11	17
Death rate (per 1000)	10	8
Income per person (million Euro)	>2500	<1600
Agricultural production (%)	65	35
Hospital beds (%)	74	26
Unemployed (%)	8	22

Table 9.3: The North-South divide in Italy

The following factors contribute to the South's lesser development

- mountainous relief makes communications and settlement difficult

- the climate of hot, dry summers and cold, wet winters is not ideal for agriculture

- the rocks are mostly limestone and form thin soils

- poor-quality grazing for sheep and goats

- poor transport links with the rest of country

- little employment outside agriculture – much emigration in search of work.

Italy is one of a large number of countries with a 'north-south divide'. The UK is another. Can you name any more?

Since 1950 the Italian government and the EU have invested money to try to improve the South. As a result:

- some new *autostradi* (motorways) have been built

- new irrigation schemes allow tomatoes, citrus fruits and vegetables to be grown

- some large-scale manufacturing, such as iron and steel and production of motor vehicles, has located in the South.

However, the North–South divide remains and the gap is widening. The reasons for the prosperity of the North include:

- good supplies of energy – natural gas in the Po basin and HEP from the Alps

- more jobs in manufacturing and services; a growing quaternary sector

- fertile lowland with irrigation water available

- large cities, for example Milan, Turin and Genoa (the so called Turin industrial triangle) are connected by an efficient transport system (Figure 9.17)

- close to large European markets

- better-quality housing and services, and a higher standard of living.

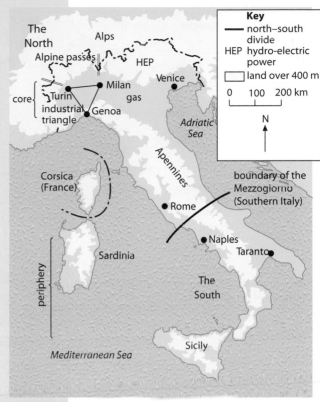

Figure 9.17: *Italy's North-South divide*

Case study: Multiple deprivation in London

London is a member of the elite club known as the **world cities**. Its plays a vital role in the workings of the global economy. As a consequence, it is not only one of the world's most influential cities; it is one of the richest. Many of its residents enjoy a high quality of life, but the city's wealth is far from evenly distributed. There are considerable areas of poverty and deprivation. These areas are revealed by a measure known as the **Multiple Deprivation Index (MDI)**. It takes into account a range of seven different indicators (Table 9.4). The beauty of the MDI is that it allows us to zoom in on any part of the UK.

Recall the names of five other world cities. If you are unable to do this, look at Figure 6.11 (page 151).

Indicator	Weighting in calculation of the MDI (%)
Income	22.5
Unemployment	22.5
Health and disability	13.5
Education, skills and training	13.5
Access to housing and services	9.3
Crime	9.3
Environmental quality	9.3

Table 9.4: *The Multiple Deprivation Index (MDI)*

At a borough level (Figure 9.18i), we can see that deprivation decreases towards the margins of London from a hard core of high deprivation located in the centre but to the north of the Thames. This pattern might suggest that

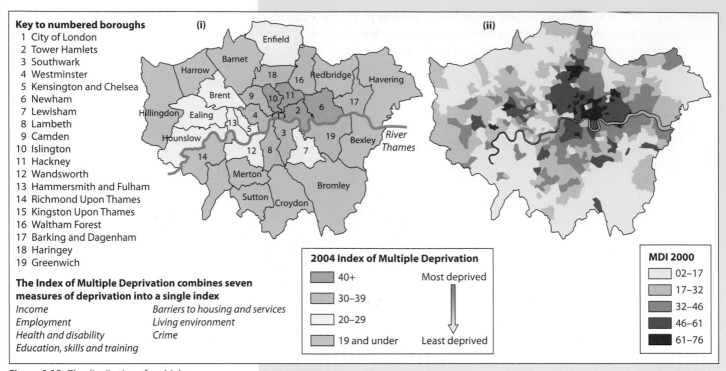

Key to numbered boroughs
1 City of London
2 Tower Hamlets
3 Southwark
4 Westminster
5 Kensington and Chelsea
6 Newham
7 Lewisham
8 Lambeth
9 Camden
10 Islington
11 Hackney
12 Wandsworth
13 Hammersmith and Fulham
14 Richmond Upon Thames
15 Kingston Upon Thames
16 Waltham Forest
17 Barking and Dagenham
18 Haringey
19 Greenwich

The Index of Multiple Deprivation combines seven measures of deprivation into a single index

Income
Employment
Health and disability
Education, skills and training
Barriers to housing and services
Living environment
Crime

2004 Index of Multiple Deprivation

40+	Most deprived
30–39	
20–29	
19 and under	Least deprived

MDI 2000

02–17
17–32
32–46
46–61
61–76

Figure 9.18: *The distribution of multiple deprivation in London i) by borough; ii) by civil parish*

See also the information about Birmingham in Chapter 6.7 (page 167).

high levels of deprivation are associated with the older parts of the built-up area. The deprivation decreases gently as one moves into west London, and more abruptly as one move east.

If we zoom in a little closer (Figure 9.18ii), the distribution of deprivation looks rather more complicated. The most deprived area now takes on a shape with axes running north-south and east-west. It is interesting to note the occurrence of some quite deprived areas close to the edge of the built-up area. These mainly coincide with large areas of social housing, many of which were constructed soon after 1945. The aim was to accommodate Londoners who were made homeless by wartime bomb damage and by large-scale slum clearance schemes in Inner London.

Rich and poor

Disparities within a country are not just spatial – that is between regions and within towns and cities. In all countries, there are differences in the distribution of personal wealth. In all populations, there are rich and poor people. How wide is the gap between them? Figure 9.19 is based on a statistical test known as the Gini coefficient. You need not worry about the calculations involved. In this instance, the test simply shows how equally the wealth of a country is shared by its population. The higher the Gini value is, the more unequal the distribution of wealth – in other words, the greater the gap between the rich and poor. Before looking at Figure 9.19, two important points should be made:

- many people in HICs live in poverty, as illustrated by the case study of London. In the UK as a whole it is estimated that 15% of the population live in poverty

- some people in LICs live in great wealth – perhaps the most publicised example is Zimbabwe where the wealth of President Mugabe and his close circle stands in stark contrast to the extreme and worsening poverty that surrounds them.

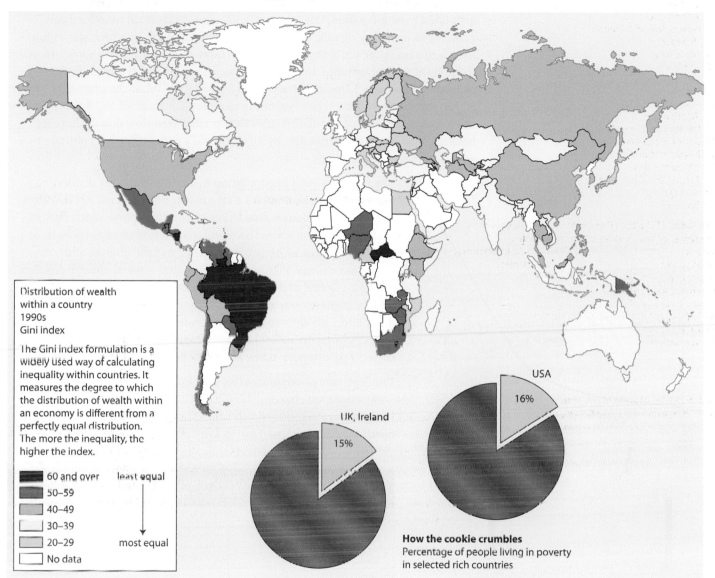

Figure 9.19: *The distribution of wealth within countries*

According to Figure 9.19, the most even distributions of wealth are found in some European countries and Japan, as well as in Egypt and Rwanda, both LICs. The greatest disparities in wealth occur in Brazil, Nicaragua and the Central African Republic. The first of these is currently one of the world's most rapidly developing economies; the last is one of the poorest countries in the world.

Two cautions need to be made when looking at Figure 9.19:

- the relationship between the level of development and the distribution of personal wealth is not a simple one (compare Figure 9.19 with Figure 9.12 on page 249)

- There are blank areas on the map where there is no data, particularly in Africa, the Middle East and Western Europe.

Can you think what might be the main causes of an unequal distribution of wealth among the inhabitants of a country? Start by thinking about the way a country is governed.

9.7 Rapid population growth

Population numbers and the rate at which they are growing are a major issue facing today's world. At the beginning of 2010 the global population was estimated to be 6.8 billion. Over the last 100 years, that global total has been growing at an alarming rate. This is illustrated by Figure 9.20 which shows how long it has taken for the global population to increase by 1 billion. It took 118 years from 1804 to double from 1 to 2 billion. Since then the length of time has shortened to a mere 12 years between 1987 and 1999. What the graph also shows is that the length of time is just beginning to increase – from 12 to 14 years. In other words, the rate of population growth is predicted to slow down. However, between now and some time after 2050, the world's population will continue to grow – but at an increasingly slower rate.

The recent growth in population has not been evenly distributed around the world. Much of that growth has occurred in LICs. Here the rate of population growth continues to be particularly fast. No matter where you are in the world, population change (growth or decline) is produced by two processes – natural change and migration change. Figure 9.21 shows that natural change depends on the birth rate and the death rate. If there are more births than deaths, population wil increase. If there are more deaths than births, population will decrease. With migration, a population will increase if immigrants (incomers) exceed emigrants (outgoers). If the situation is reversed, there will a loss of population.

The high rate of population growth in LICs is due to natural change – not migration change. The natural increase results from a high birth rate and a falling death rate. This is illustrated by the birth and death rates for Burkina Faso in West Africa (Table 9.5) over the last 50 years.

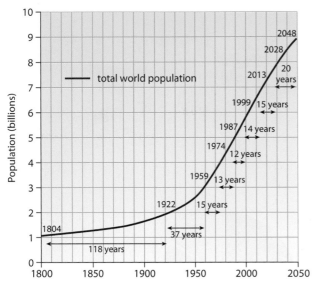

Figure 9.20: Global population growth, 1800–2050

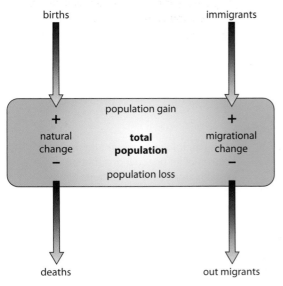

Figure 9.21: Elements of population change

Year	Birth rate per 1000	Death rate per 1000	Natural increase per 1000
1960	51	32	19
1970	51	29	22
1980	50	24	26
1990	47	20	27
2000	47	17	30
2010	44	13	31

Table 9.5: Rates of natural increase in Burkina Faso, 1960–2010

Why are birth rates so high in LICs like Burkina Faso? Part of the answer is that people see children as a financial asset. They can help with the work, especially on family farmland, and later look after their parents when they are old. Medical advances, improvements in public hygiene and sanitation, especially clean water supply, explain the drop in the death rate.

The major problem with this rapid population growth is that it is taking place in many countries that are already overpopulated. The number of people exceeds the resources needed to provide an adequate supply of food, water and shelter for everyone.

Overpopulation puts pressure on:

- housing – acute shortages mean homelessness and squatting, as well as poor quality and temporary dwellings
- jobs – too few jobs means there is much unemployment. This creates poverty and a low quality of life
- social services – many have no access to education or healthcare
- infrastructure – dwellings lack clean water and proper sanitation; roads and transport are poor.

All these factors contribute to a cycle of poverty in which many people find themselves trapped (Figure 9.22).

Unfortunately, poverty does not stop couples from having large families. If anything, it has the opposite effect. In turn, large families tend to make the poverty worse. It is agreed that one of the best ways of curbing the high birth rate is to ensure that all children should have access to schooling. Education should make them aware of the burden of large families, give them better expectations of life and educate them about the possible ways of reducing family size. Girls, in particular, should be encouraged to stay in school to upper secondary level. As a result, they are:

- more likely to know about contraception and family planning
- less likely to have children when in their teens
- more likely to want to have a career.

Education also increases the chances of finding a job and earning the money needed to break out of the cycle of poverty.

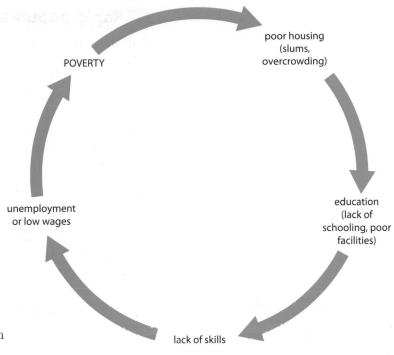

Figure 9.22: *Cycle of poverty*

Study Table 9.5 on page 256. What is happening to the rate of natural increase? How do you explain the change?

9.8 Government policies to manage population change

Overpopulation has been so great in some countries that it has been necessary for their governments to take action. What can a government do to lower the rate of population growth? The obvious target is the birth rate. If this can be lowered, then in time the rate of growth will decrease. The birth rate is usually lowered by encouraging birth control and making contraception either freely or cheaply available. It is important to understand, however, that there are some religions that are strongly against the use of contraceptives. In the case study that follows, rather than leaving Chinese couples to volunteer to limit their families, the policy forced all couples to do so.

Case study: China's one-child policy

In 1970, the Chinese government was faced by a high rate of natural increase (26 per 1000) in its already huge population (830 million). It decided to introduce various 'voluntary' schemes to cut the rate of population growth (Figure 9.23). Eventually, the birth rate started to fall – but not fast enough. So in 1979 it introduced its controversial 'one-child' policy. For nearly 20 years after that, no couple was supposed to have more than one child (Figure 9.24). Those who did were penalised in various ways. In some cases, they were sterilised and given forced abortions. Those who kept to the limit were rewarded with cash bonuses, better childcare and preferential access to housing. Free contraception and free abortions have helped couples to keep the required 'family of three'.

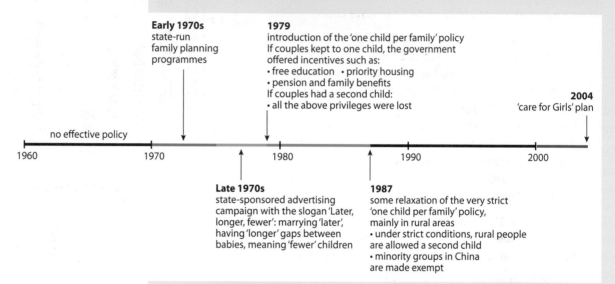

Early 1970s
state-run family planning programmes

1979
introduction of the 'one child per family' policy
If couples kept to one child, the government offered incentives such as:
• free education   • priority housing
• pension and family benefits
If couples had a second child:
• all the above privileges were lost

2004
'care for Girls' plan

no effective policy

1960   1970   1980   1990   2000

Late 1970s
state-sponsored advertising campaign with the slogan 'Later, longer, fewer': marrying 'later', having 'longer' gaps between babies, meaning 'fewer' children

1987
some relaxation of the very strict 'one child per family' policy, mainly in rural areas
• under strict conditions, rural people are allowed a second child
• minority groups in China are made exempt

Figure 9.23: *China's population policy timeline*

Figure 9.24: *Promoting the one-child policy in China*

Do you know of any countries that have had to introduce policies to increase their populations?

Since 1996 the policy has been relaxed a little, particularly in rural areas. Between 1970 and 2008 the birth rate fell from 34 per 1000 to 13 per 1000, and the growth rate from 24 per 1000 to 0.6 per 1000 (Figure 9.25). Even so, the total population has continued to grow from 830 million to 1320 million. The latter figure represents just over 20% of the world's population.

The policy has been much more effective in urban areas than in the countryside. In cities, finding enough living space for a family of three is difficult. Raising a child there is much more expensive. Urban couples have come to realise the benefits of having only one child. In rural areas, however, there is always the need for an extra pair of hands to help on the family farm. For these reasons, the policy was softened in 2001 and couples in rural areas were allowed to have a second child if the first was a girl. Further relaxation of population controls was announced in 2004 with the introduction of the 'Care for Girls' plan. The reasons behind it will be explained below. There are now two very different policies towards children – discouraging in urban areas; allowing in rural areas.

There is no denying that the one-child policy has been successful – it has put the brake of China's rapid population growth (Figure 9.25). Equally the policy has had a number of unwanted consequences. For example, the Chinese tradition is to prefer sons. Since couples have been limited to having one child, there has been widespread sex-selective abortion. If you look at the age bars in Figure 9.26, you see there are more males than females below the age of 50. There are now 120 males to every 100 females. This is having two consequences:

- parents 'spoil' their 'one-child boy' and as a result he tends to be obese, demanding and even delinquent. These young males are referred to as 'little emperors'

- because of the increasing shortage of women of marrying age, bartering for brides and 'bride kidnapping' have become common in rural areas. Young women commonly leave the countryside and set up home in towns and cities. Young men are preferred when it comes to farm work.

It is this imbalance between the sexes that lies behind the the 2004 'Care for Girls' plan. Girls now receive free schooling and families with girls have access to better housing and employment. However, it will take a long time to change Chinese traditional attitudes towards the gender of children.

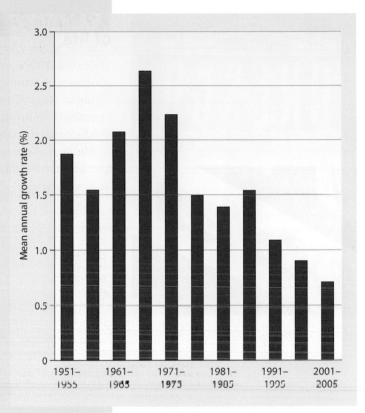

Figure 9.25: *China – population growth rates, 1970–2005*

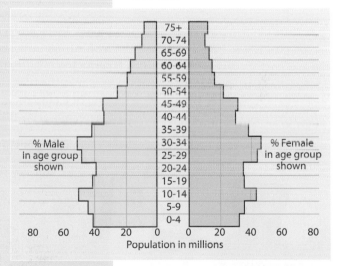

Figure 9.26: *China's population pyramid*

Can you see any relationship between what is shown in Figures 9.25 and 9.26? Clue – start by looking at the peak rate shown in former diagram.

Figure 9.27: *Two names associated with aid*

9.9 Managing disparities in development and quality of life

There is a wide development and welfare gap between the richest and poorest countries. A number of governmental and non-governmental organisations are trying to narrow this gap by helping the poorest countries. The governmental organisations include the United Nations and its various agencies such as the World Bank, the World Health Organisation and the UNESCO. Examples of non-governmental organisations include famous aid charities like Oxfam, the Red Cross and Save the Children (Figure 9.27).

The best way to help the poorest countries is to help them develop. Economic development is important here. Economic growth creates the money needed to pay for such things as education, housing and healthcare which are such important aspects of quality of life. However, what is the best form for this help to take? We shall consider two front-runners – aid and trade.

Aid

Aid is the transfer of money, goods and expertise to assist the development of LICs and improve the quality of life. Aid can come from two sources. The governments of MICs and HICs can be involved in two types of **official aid**. The first is **multilateral aid** where a government donates mainly money to large international organisations such as the World Bank or UNESCO. These organisations then allocate that aid to those countries believed to be most in need.

The second is **bilateral aid** where the government of a country gives the aid directly to the government of a receiving country. The aid may include grants of money, loans and technical help. An issue here is that governments tend to give aid with strings attached. The donor governments look for something in return, perhaps a military base, the purchase of weapons or a trade agreement. For example, the USA gave Peru large amounts of aid to search for oil. In return, Peru bought jet aircraft made in the USA and allowed fishing boats from the USA into Peruvian territorial waters.

Figure 9.28: *Photos of i) appropriate aid, a basic water pump ii) emergency aid being delivered*

As will be explained in the World Bank case study (page 262), aid in the form of loans is the least satisfactory for the receiving country. It would be much better if that aid was in the form of technical assistance. However, it is important that the technology being transferred should be right for the circumstances of the receiving country. It is no good installing very sophisticated machinery if there are no people with the skills necessary to run and maintain that machinery. It is also no good if spare parts are not easily available. The challenge is to match the technology to the needs and skills of the people in the receiving country. The answer is to be found in what is called **intermediate technology** (Figure 9.28). This is a lower level of technology that is more accessible to the people of an LIC. The technology needs to be easily understood. It should not require either a high level of training or the presence of foreign experts. In parts of the Sahel in North Africa intermediate technology used to combat the drought conditions has been in the form of wind pumps to bring water to the surface. Technical assistance with a much-needed project and involving intermediate technology would clearly qualify as **appropriate aid**.

Suggest some specific examples of appropriate aid.

Voluntary aid is a second major category of aid. This is the aid provided by non-governmental organisations (NGOs) such as Oxfam and the Red Cross. Often the aid delivered by these NGOs takes the form of emergency aid delivered in response to some natural disaster such as an earthquake or drought (Figure 9.28).

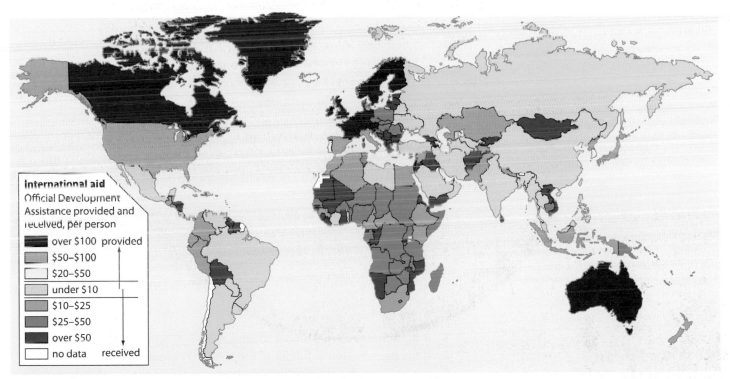

International aid
Official Development Assistance provided and received, per person

- over $100 provided
- $50–$100
- $20–$50
- under $10
- $10–$25
- $25–$50
- over $50
- no data received

Figure 9.29: *The global distribution of international aid (providers and receivers)*

Figure 9.29 shows the world divided into 'providers' and 'receivers' of aid. The division closely accords with the North-South divide (see Figure 9.10 on page 247), but with at least two interesting exceptions: 1) Russia and the countries of Eastern Europe are neither providers or receivers; 2) India and China are providers rather than receivers of aid (both countries have provided aid with strings attached in their quest for resources).

Trade

Trade is always thought to be a good way of stimulating economic development. In an era of **globalisation**, most countries want and need the chance to take part in international trade. Most countries have something which the rest of the world is prepared to buy. Those export sales allow a LIC to import what it needs to progress its economic development – machinery, vehicles, fertilisers and so on. Unfortunately, world trade does not take place on an even playing-field. There is much talk about free trade and ensuring that goods may be bought and sold across the world without duties, tariffs, quotas or import restrictions. The reality is that LIC goods often encounter various forms of **trade barrier**. The terms of global trade mostly favour the HICs at the expense of the LICs.

Figure 9.30: *Some Fairtrade products*

The Fairtrade Foundation is a non-governmental organisation set up in 1992 to promote international trade. It seeks to obtain a fair price for a wide variety of goods exported from LICs to the rest of the world (Figure 9.30). These goods include handicrafts, coffee, cocoa, sugar, tea, bananas, honey, wine and fresh fruit. The aim is to work with small-scale producers and help make them economically secure. This is an important step in encouraging economic development and eventually reducing the LIC–HIC disparity.

> Research how the World Bank obtains the money it uses to pay for its projects and development help.

Case study: The World Bank – a UN aid agency

The World Bank was set up in 1944 by the United Nations. Despite its name, it is not really a bank like a 'high street' one. It is an important source of financial and technical assistance to LICs. The 184 member countries of the World Bank are responsible for how money is raised and spent, but the main aim of the World Bank is to help reduce poverty. It has specific targets for education, infant mortality, maternal health, disease and access to water, set out in the Millennium Development Goals to be reached by 2015. Figure 9.31 confirms that the World Bank is the largest provider of development assistance in the world. Indeed, each year it lends between US$15 – 20 billion for a wide range of projects in over 100 countries. It employs more than 10 000 people in more than 100 offices worldwide.

The World Bank ...

1 is the largest external funder of education
2 is the largest external funder of the HIV/AIDS programme
3 is a leader in the anti-corruption effort
4 strongly supports debt relief
5 is one of the largest funders of biodiversity projects
6 works with partners
7 helps bring clean water, electricity and transport to the poor
8 involves civil society in every aspect of its work
9 helps countries emerging from conflict
10 is responsible to the voices of poor people.

Figure 9.31: *The World Bank's current 'top ten' functions*

The World Bank has been the target of criticism because much of its financial aid is the form of loans. The trouble with loans is that they have to be repaid over a specified period. Loans are also subject to percentage interest rates. This means paying back to the World Bank even more money. Over the years, a significant number of LICs have been unable to repay their loans. As a consequence, they have run deeply into debt. That debt burden makes it virtually impossible for the debtor country to make any sort of progress in terms of development and welfare. Under pressure, the World Bank is now involved in the Heavily Indebted Poor Countries Initiative (HIPCI). This is helping nearly 30 such countries by cancelling their debts, provided that the money is spent on welfare programmes – housing, education and healthcare for the poor. This is known as **debt relief**.

The World Bank is now supporting programmes with both money and technical help. No loans are involved. For example, it has taken a lead role in funding HIV/AIDS awareness programmes, especially in Sub-Saharan Africa. It is currently providing money and technical help to educate girls in Bangladesh and to improve healthcare in Mexico. It has promised to help rebuild Port au Prince (Haiti) after the devastating 2010 earthquake.

Not everyone thinks that debt relief is a good idea. Some see it like writing blank cheques to irresponsible governments. Others say that the benefits are unlikely to reach the people most in need of help. Still others think that it will encourage corrupt governments to take on new debts.

Case study: Oxfam – a non-governmental organisation

Oxfam is probably the UK's and one of the world's best known charities. It was set up in 1942 as the Oxford Committee for Famine Relief to help provide relief for the people of Greece under Nazi occupation. Today it operates in over 80 countries, employing 3500 full time staff and thousands of volunteers, many of whom help to run over 800 charity shops in the UK. It is a non-religious, non-governmental organisation.

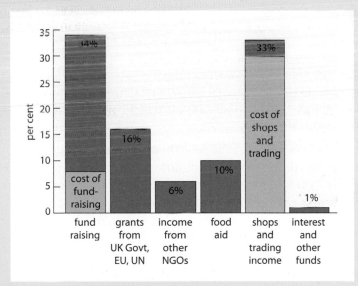

Figure 9.32: *Where Oxfam's money comes from*

Write a short account based on what you notice in Figure 9.32.

Oxfam's main purpose is to work with others 'to overcome poverty and suffering'. Most of its funding to achieve this goal comes from donations. However, it also receives grants from governmental sources (Figure 9.32).

Despite the growing number of Oxfam shops, they contribute relatively little to the overall funding because of the costs of running the shops. Whilst Oxfam often offers emergency support in response to disasters across the world, for example sending blankets and medicines in the aftermath of the 2010 Haiti earthquake, it also works 'in the field' to help improve the lives of some of the world's poorest people. This is often to help establish local water supplies by digging wells and boreholes and providing pumps.

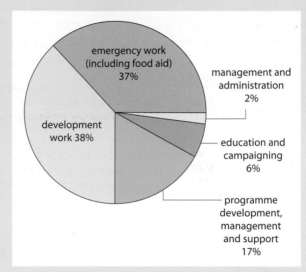

Figure 9.33: *How Oxfam spends its money*

Figure 9.33 shows that these two activities – emergency work and development work – account for roughly the same percentage of Oxfam's spending. Undoubtedly, it is Oxfam's emergency aid that hits the newspaper headlines. However, it is the development aid that is helping to reduce the disparities in development and quality of life that are characteristic of so many LICs.

Everyone knows about the emergency aid that is provided after a major natural disaster. But how might the aid organisations make us more aware of the development work they do?

There is no doubt that MICs and HICs have a strong moral duty to help the poorer countries of the world. It is important, however, that this help should be appropriate, have no strings attached and should not exploit the receiving countries. The aim is simply to trigger progress up the development staircase and to raise the general quality of life.

This principle of the rich helping the poor should also apply to the disparities or development gaps that exist within countries. Here, it is the responsibility of all governments to achieve a more even distribution of development and human welfare.

End of chapter checkout

Checklists

Now you have read the chapter, you should know:

✓ the meaning of development
✓ ways of measuring development
✓ the meaning of quality of life
✓ ways of measuring quality of life
✓ how countries are grouped according to their level of economic development
✓ how the global pattern of development is changing
✓ the meaning of development gap
✓ the symptoms of a development gap
✓ examples of development gaps at different spatial scales
✓ the consequences of rapid population growth
✓ some government policies aimed at reducing the rate of population growth
✓ possible ways of reducing differences in development and quality of life

Make sure you understand these key terms:

Affluence: wealth.
Core: the most important economic, political and social area of a country or global region – a centre of power.
Deprivation: when the standard of living and quality of life fall below a minimum level.
Development: economic and social progress that leads to an improvement in the standard of living and quality of life for an increasing proportion of the population.
Development gap: the difference in levels of development and standards of living between countries or regions.
Development indicators: measures that are used to measure the level of development, such as per capita GNI and the literacy rate.
Diet: the amount and kind of food consumed by a person or group of people.
Disparity: a great difference, as for example between parts of a country in terms of wealth.
Gross domestic product (GDP): the total value of goods and services produced by the economy of a country during a year.

Gross national income (GNI): The GDP of a country plus all the income earned by investments abroad.
Healthcare: the provision of a range of medical services, such as clinics, hospitals and homes for the elderly.
Intermediate technology: a technology that local people can use relatively easily and without much cost.
Literacy: the ability of a person to read and write.
Periphery: an area remote or isolated from its core and generally lagging in terms of development and influence.
Physical infrastructure: the services, such as transport, telecommunications, water and sewage disposal, that are vital to people and business.
Poverty: where people are seriously lacking in terms of income, food, housing, basic services (clean water and sewage disposal and access to education and healthcare). See also Deprivation.
Quality of life: the degree of well-being and satisfaction felt by a person or a group of people in a particular area.

See the Glossary in the ActiveBook for more definitions.

Questions

Try testing yourself with these questions:

1 a) What does GDP stand for? What does it measure?
   b) What are the advantages of using per capita GDP as a measure of development?
2 a) What are the three main forces behind economic development?
   b) Give an example of each.
3 With the aid of diagram, show how the relative importance of economic sectors changes with economic development.
4 Why is energy consumption a good indicator of economic development?
5 a) Name three indicators of quality of life.
   b) How would you rate your own quality of life on a scale of 1 (poor) to 8 (excellent). Try to justify your score.
6 a) What is meant by the term 'disposable income'?
   b) In your own words explain what is meant by the 'cycle of wealth'.
7 Describe the main features of the global pattern of access to clean water shown in Figure 9.6.
8 Compare the distribution patterns of Figures 9.6 and 9.7. To what extent are the patterns similar?
9 a) Write short definitions for: HIC, NIC, MIC and given examples of each.
   b) Describe what is meant by the 'development staircase'.
10 a) Why is Ethiopia classed as an LIC?
   b) State the term used to describe rapidly growing economies
   c) What are the main reasons for the poverty and low development levels within Ethiopia?
11 a) What is meant by the term 'an emergent economy'?
   b) Name three examples.
12 a) Name three countries that are classified as 'stagnant economies'.
   b) In each case, identify the main obstacle to the country's development.
13 a) Explain what is meant by the 'global development gap'.
   b) Suggest four reasons for the gap.
14 a) What do you understand by the core and periphery of a country?
   b) Draw a sketch map of a country and show its core and periphery.

15 a) What is the 'multiple deprivation index'?
   b) What indicators are involved in calculating the index?
16 a) Refer to Figure 9.19 and find out how equal the distribution of wealth is in your home country.
   b) Suggest reasons why the distribution is so unequal in Brazil.
17 a) Describe world population growth between 1800 and 2000.
   b) Describe how the world's population is projected to grow between 2000 and 2050.
18 a) What is meant by natural population increase?
   b) Give three reasons why birth rates are generally high in LICs.
19 Identify some of the symptoms of overpopulation.
20 Why is education so important in the fight against poverty?
21 a) Why is it necessary for governments to try to change population growth rates?
   b) Birth control is one way of slowing population increase. Give two other ways.
   c) How might a government try to increase the growth rate?
22 a) Write a brief report explaining China's population policies since 1970.
   b) Besides reducing the rate of population growth, describe some of the consequences of those policies.
23 a) What do we mean by the term aid?
   b) Why do so many LICs need aid?
24 a) Name the four main types of aid and write a sentence to describe what each one means.
   b) List the advantages and disadvantages of receiving aid.
   c) What is 'tied aid'? Why can it be a problem?
25 a) What is an NGO?
   b) Using Figure 9.33, describe how Oxfam spends the money it raises.
26 a) What is 'free trade'?
   b) Does it exist? Give reasons for your answer.

Index